GOLIATH
The Wilt Chamberlain Story

Wilt Chamberlain, basketball's answer to boxing's Muhammad Ali and football's Joe Namath, is clearly one of the most important and controversial athletes of modern times, a man whose image has endured as vividly in retirement as at the peak of his career. By now enough time has passed so that it is possible to take a look at this living legend and put in perspective the man and the myth.

It is a look Wilt could not take in his own book. We do not see ourselves as others see us. *Goliath* presents Wilt not only as he sees himself, but as his coaches, teammates, and opponents, as the writers, broadcasters, and fans see him.

Has he been, as he says he was, the greatest player of his time, or, as others say, did he run far behind the Bill Russells, Kareem Abdul-Jabbars, Elgin Baylors and Jerry Wests of his day? Has he been, as he has suggested, the greatest of lovers, or has he really been a lonely individual, this bachelor who built the most magnificent of mansions? Is he, as some say, a man who stands above other men, or, as others say, the littlest of giants?

Here, then, is Goliath in a world of Davids, a frank and full look at a man who is larger than life.

GOLIATH
The Wilt Chamberlain Story

BY BILL LIBBY
Illustrated with photographs

DODD, MEAD & COMPANY, NEW YORK

For Eddie Angel, who goes his own way, too

1 2 3 4 5 6 7 8 9 10

Library of Congress Cataloging in Publication Data

Libby, Bill.
    Goliath : the Wilt Chamberlain story.

    1. Chamberlain, Wilton Norman, 1936–   2. Basket-
ball players—United States—Biography. I. Title.
GV884.C5L5   796.32'3'0924 [B]   76–50104
ISBN 0–396–07392–1

ACKNOWLEDGMENTS

1950943

For their help the author wishes to thank Wilt Chamberlain for all past interviews, as well as Jack Kent Cooke, Franklin Mieuli, Eddie Gottlieb, Bill Sharman, Joe Mullaney, Frank McGuire, Fred Schaus, Pete Newell, Chick Hearn, Frank O'-Neill, Jim Brochu, Jeff Temkin, Tom Hawkins, Jerry West, Merv Harris, Rich Levin, Doug Krikorian, Doug Ives, Mal Florence, George Kiseda, Jack Kiser, Bucky Walter, John Simmons, Paul Silas, Dave Cowens, Phil Elderkin, Rick Barry, and several others who wish to be unnamed.

He is also grateful to Don Baker and the late Phog Allen of the University of Kansas, the late Abe Saperstein of the Harlem Globetrotters, the late Bob Feerick of the Golden State Warriors, the staff of the Los Angeles Lakers, Nick Curran of the NBA, all of the writers and broadcasters whose information contributed so much to the author's knowledge of the subject, and all of the photographers who contributed to the book, especially Jim Roark of the Los Angeles *Herald-Examiner* and Johnny Johnson and Wen Roberts of Photography, Inc., of Inglewood, California. The author wishes to thank especially William Whipple of Dodd, Mead for getting behind the project and others, including Philip James, who worked on it.

FOREWORD

With the exception of Muhammad Ali, the most commanding, colorful, and controversial athlete of recent times has been Wilt Chamberlain. Yet much less has been written about him and much remains to be said.

Curiously, many who know Wilt and have known him are reluctant to talk about him, as though afraid of him. In this way he is a sort of Frank Sinatra of sports, idolized and intimidating, a leader others dare not defy.

With David Shaw of the Los Angeles *Times,* Wilt did his own book a few years back, and it was interesting, but it was Wilt's world through Wilt's eyes, and perhaps it can be said that Wilt does not see himself as others see him, or his career as others see it.

So, perhaps, enough time has passed since his retirement to put him and his career in the proper perspective. Enough people have agreed to discuss him in depth for a book to be written as impartially as possible about this imposing player and personality.

It is a cliche, but Wilt really is a living legend. He looms somehow larger than life. But he is real, a hero to some, hated by others. The attempt here has been to put together a balanced portrait. The hope is that whatever Wilt is shows through in this work.

THE WORLD IS MADE UP OF DAVIDS.
I AM A GOLIATH.
AND NOBODY ROOTS FOR GOLIATH.

—*Wilt Chamberlain*

One melancholy moment, Wilt Chamberlain said, "Listen, dressing rooms all come to have the same stale smell about them after a while. Defeat and victory all smell the same after a while. You get so you don't feel elation, you just feel beat."

He was thirty-three years old, three years from retirement. He had been a basketball player almost twenty years. Basketball players are born old and die young. Their careers come to an end when their lives have just begun. An aging giant on arthritic knees, Wilt was near the end of this road.

He had played professionally for Philadelphia and San Francisco teams and now he was playing for the Los Angeles team. He was earning $200,000 a year, but twice he had been dealt off cheaply. He held almost all the scoring and rebounding records, but he had been labeled a loser.

In ten seasons of battling Bill Russell, Wilt's teams had won one championship, while Bill's Boston Celtics had taken nine. Now, Russell had retired, and the rookie Lew Alcindor, who had led UCLA to three collegiate championships, was about to confront Chamberlain for the first time.

This was the last Saturday of October, 1969, a few games into the new season. Alcindor, who had not yet renamed himself Kareem Abdul-Jabbar, was breaking into pro ranks as a member of the Milwaukee Bucks. He was supposed to be a winner who would do to Wilt what Russell had done.

Seven feet two inches tall, 230 pounds, goateed, with bushy black hair and eyes that glowed like bright coals, Alcindor was asked about Chamberlain. Sensitive, sullen, withdrawn, he said, "It feels funny to be facing him. He is a living legend.

"I will do what I can do. One thing I will not do is score a hundred points in one game or average fifty points a game this season or any other season. I have learned a lesson from him. That man made himself a monster. He did so much he could never do more.

"I will do what I can do," Alcindor repeated, withdrawing.

Seven feet one and one-sixteenth inches tall by his own measurement, 280 pounds, mustached and goateed, his black hair neatly trimmed, his eyes narrowed, Chamberlain was asked about Alcindor. Suspicious, independent, proud, he said, "I will be interested to see what he can do. He is highly touted.

"But it will not be me against him; it will be my team against his. This is not one-on-one; it is a team game. And it is just one game in a season of eighty games. I am not going to worry how I look in comparison to him. If I have to sacrifice myself for my team to win, I will do it. I am called a loser, but all I want is to win.

"I've had it up to here with ten years of man-to-man duels with Bill Russell, and I am not now going to start a new series with Lew Alcindor. I beat Bill Russell every way one basketball player can beat another, but no one saw that. He had the better teams behind him, and all people saw was that his teams beat my teams. Well, I am not going to worry about how I do against Alcindor because people will see what they want to see, anyway.

"My reputation precedes me from city to city. I am judged on what people have said I have done, not what I actually have done. I am judged on the past, not the present. It is unfair and

unfortunate, but I cannot control it, so I cannot concern myself
with it.

"I do know that if I dropped down from Mars today and
people knew nothing of me but what I put on the court, I would
be considered the greatest thing since sliced bread, and no one
would even be bothering about an Alcindor." He shook his
head, sighing, wistful with wonder.

He had come a long way from West Philadelphia, where he
was one of nine children raised on less than $100 a week by a
handyman and a domestic maid. Wilt was making $5,000 a
week in basketball and twice that outside of it. He owned
buildings in New York, Philadelphia, San Francisco, and Los
Angeles. He owned a travel agency, music and recording com-
panies, even race horses.

"I have lawyers and accountants and business managers, but
I make my own deals because I am the best businessman I know
and make the best deals for myself," Wilt pointed out.

He was living in a $350,000 mansion in Beverly Hills. It was
owned by Billy Rose's sister, Polly Gottlieb, and Wilt was
renting it. Filled with antiques, it was not the big guy's sort of
pad. He was building his own modernistic mansion in Bel-Air,
but it was not yet ready for him to move in. For the time being,
he moved warily among the antiques.

He had cavern-sized closets full of fine clothes. The garage
housed a Bentley and a Maserati, worth more than $25,000
each. He also owned a custom-made high-powered boat, worth
more than $35,000, with which he water-skied. He said, "I like
nice things and I live in style, but I am not wealthy. Taxes make
it difficult for a man to build a personal fortune today. I can't
have everything I want. For example, I would love to own a
yacht, but I can't afford it."

A few nights earlier in Baltimore, he had checked out of the
team's hotel because he found his room unsatisfactory and
moved into a plusher place. "The other fellows can do what
they want, but Wilt Chamberlain does not live like a skid-row
bum," he commented.

3

On the morning of the Milwaukee game, Wilt, who is a night person, slept late. When he got out of bed shortly before noon, he mixed himself some orange juice and orange sherbet in a blender, which would be his only nourishment until late in the afternoon.

He threw on some casual clothes, turned jazz music on the stereo, and prowled the place restlessly. He checked with his answering service and began to receive telephone calls. His number is unlisted, but not unknown. Friends kept calling all afternoon.

"I have a lot of friends," he said. "But I do not have as many as some of them think I have. A lot of people want to be friends with me because of what I am, not who I am. I am mistrustful of strangers. But I am the best of friends to my friends.

"I have friends all over the world. I travel to be with my friends. I like to get away from this country, where I am considered a freak. I am recognized wherever I go here. I am so tall I cannot hide. There are a few places I go where I am not hassled. Otherwise my home is my hideaway. When I go to other countries, I go to escape.

"I love many countries. I speak many languages. I am a man of the world," he said.

This day, his friends kept calling to wish him well with Alcindor. It annoyed Chamberlain because he wanted it to be considered just another game, and he considered himself above being tested.

Hanging up on a conversation with a young lady in San Diego, Wilt smiled with satisfaction and said, "She'll be coming in next game, not this one. She wants to see me, not Lew."

A bachelor who fancied himself a ladies' man, Wilt said, "I have a weakness for women, but I have not been hooked by one. I like variety. What do I like to do with them? What do men like to do with women?

"I take them out if there is a place to go where we will not be pestered by the public. Otherwise, I go to their pads or bring them to mine. I am a good cook and sometimes cook for them,

4

though I prefer to have them cook for me if they are capable.

"I would not marry a woman because she was a good cook or homemaker, however. I can hire a maid for that. I would marry a woman only if I wanted to be with her all the time. I like to move out where I want and when I want.

"I am not against marriage, but I am not sure it is for me," concluded Chamberlain, who had been linked with movie stars. Yet there are those who have played on his teams or covered him for years who say they never have seen him with a girl.

"It is not easy for me to slip through shadows, but I pursue privacy," observed the big man.

"When you are seven feet tall and black, it is hard to avoid attention. And when you are a great athlete, you are recognized everywhere," he commented. "But I would not change anything. I might like to see what it would be like to be six feet tall and white sometime, but I would not trade.

"I like looking down on the world. It is not everyone who gets to see things from my vantage point. And I have found I enjoy being outstanding in every way.

"I have been criticized by brothers for dating white women. I date black women, too. I date women of all colors. I am proud of my color, but I will not segregate myself from society.

"More than anything else, I am Wilt Chamberlain, an individual," he commented. "It is my individualism I treasure most. I go my own way and do my own things.

"Basketball is something I do very well, but if I did not enjoy it, I would not do it. I no longer need it and will not do it much longer. When I am done with it, there will be other things to do. There is more to my life than basketball," he concluded.

He dressed in maroon undershorts and undershirt, maroon socks, a maroon suit, shirt and tie, even shoes trimmed with maroon suede. Stuffing a fat roll of bills into his pocket, he went outside and got into a maroon Maserati. He drove south on the San Diego Freeway, and off and east on Manchester to the Romanesque-style Forum in suburban Inglewood.

Arriving a little after five, he went into the fancy dining room and had a dinner of sand dabs and iced tea, which is not the typical athlete's pregame meal.

"I have acquired some expensive tastes, which will make it hard for me to retire from my basketball salary. I use money very well," he admitted. "But I have found the things I enjoy most are simple and do not cost much: good music, good companions, playing volleyball at the beach. Often, I am content to dine on hot dogs," he insisted.

As he ate, he was watched by other diners, even here where he was well known. He was used to it and paid no attention to it. When he was done, he got up and walked downstairs through dim corridors in the belly of the building and into the Laker locker room.

He was the first player inside and he slowly stripped off his civvies and put on his purple and gold uniform, number 13. He defies superstition.

He has a strange build—long legs, high hips, a short upper torso. He appears awkward but is considered the most powerful player in the history of the sport, with weight-lifter strength in his arms and chest.

He says his height has not been measured since he was young. "Why bother?" he asks. "A person weighs himself because he can diet off fat. I do not measure myself because I can't cut off inches.

"It is not my height that matters, anyway. Height helps. And strength. But I am a player. People don't see this because they don't want to see it." Sighing, he sat down on a stool in front of his locker. He sort of collapsed onto the stool, seemingly all bony arms and legs.

An envelope of mail had been left in his locker. He dumped it in front of him and it spilled onto the rug. He went through the letters, reading return addresses, opening some, not others. There were business letters and fan letters, love letters and hate letters. There was a letter telling him how to shoot free throws, which he never has figured out.

There was a letter from a girl in Russia, and another from

a French girl in Long Beach. Her earlier letters had interested him and he had requested a photo from her, which she now sent. He looked at it and liked it. "I usually don't do it this way, but I will probably make a date with her," he said.

The other players had begun to drift in to dress. Most players being interviewed in a dressing room speak softly, privately. Wilt speaks up loudly, publicly. As he reconstructed his day and discussed his life, his voice boomed around the room.

"The locker room fraternity is groovy, but what I'll miss most when I go is the game itself. I get tired of the tough schedule, the traveling, the plane rides, the airline terminals and hotel rooms. But I think I know and love the game of basketball as few do," he said.

"I may be the only superstar who enjoys playing at off times in school gyms or deserted playgrounds. I've heard Alcindor does, but I don't believe Russell did. I don't think Elgin or Jerry or Oscar does. They pay me to play under pressure. I prefer playing for fun. I would do so if they didn't pay a dime. How many others would?" he asked challengingly.

West, who was there by then, looked up and smiled, but did not say anything. The other players were talking, kidding around among themselves. They did not say anything to Wilt, whose locker was way in a corner, and he did not say anything to them. They were his teammates, but he seemed set apart from them.

As he took off his civvies, Wilt took a ring off his finger, emptied his pockets and, as he always did, handed trainer Frank O'Neill the ring and a roll of bills. "Keep these in your pocket," he said.

Later, O'Neill said, "He wouldn't put them in the safe with the other players' valuables. I was always responsible for carrying about ten thousand dollars worth of rings and cash in my pocket and I was always afraid of getting rolled in the corridor."

The coach came in and this writer left. It was time for the team to talk about the game and almost time to play it. Down

7

by the dressing room you could barely hear the crowd noise swelling above. When the players came out of the room and through the corridor, out onto the arena floor, the noise suddenly slammed against them and they were swallowed up in it.

As big as basketball players are, they were dwarfed by the arena, rising two long levels, full of fans and writers and photographers and broadcasters. A regular-season local-record crowd of 17,489 paying customers had come out to witness the first confrontation of these fabled giants, and the press tables were packed with those who would record it.

Alcindor, number 33 in his yellow and green uniform, paced around nervously when not shooting in practice. Wilt stood calmly, one hand on his hip, when he was not otherwise occupied.

The lights dimmed and the highly polished hardwood floor was spotlit. Although Wilt was playing for the hometown team, it was Lew, for four years the star at UCLA here, who received the greater ovation when they were introduced.

Wilt turned away to the bench, spanning with one finger the rubber band he always wore on his wrist to remind himself of the days when he and his fellows could not afford new socks and kept spare rubber bands to support their socks when the elastic wore out.

He put on the gold terry wristbands and headband he wore to keep the sweat off his hands and out of his eyes. Sales of the sweatbands soared out of sight when he started to wear them. The management sold Wilt's sweatbands at the concession stands here.

He walked onto the court with his teammates and went to the center circle and shook hands with Lew. The referee threw up the ball and the game began. All was madness from that moment on with the crowd noise washing over the athletes as they performed their profession.

Early, the uniquely quick and agile Alcindor danced around his heavier adversary, hurling in hook shots with both hands. He blocked a jump shot by Wilt and, incredibly, an attempt at a stuff shot, and he pressured him into ball-handling errors.

On one play, Wilt blocked one of Lew's sweeping hook shots with such force he sent the ball spinning into the seats to the amusement of the crowd.

But the poker-faced Alcindor kept coming at Chamberlain. One time he went right with the ball in his right hand, fell back, shifted the ball to his left, and hooked it over Wilt's outstretched reach. Wilt stood there a second, as though startled by the balletlike move.

Another time, Lew shot and missed on one side, took the rebound on the other side, and stuffed it before Wilt reacted to it.

Wilt tried to overpower Lew, leaning his great bulk on the youngster, but Alcindor dug the points of his elbows into Chamberlain's back to keep him off. It was like a boxer outmaneuvering a puncher.

Both had help. Milwaukee had a young team with ordinary talent other than their rookie, but Alcindor seemed to inspire his teammates. With little Flynn Robinson flinging in shots from far out and Bob Dandridge banging in some from the corners to assist Alcindor, the Bucks began to pull away.

Nor was Wilt alone. The aging but still agile Elgin Baylor and skinny, sharpshooting Mel Counts up front, and the wonderful West and young Willie McCarter in the backcourt contributed to Chamberlain's cause, though the Lakers could not keep up.

But this game, more than most, seemed to rise and fall on the fortunes of the spotlighted centers. And for twenty-four minutes, the younger man had the upper hand. As the teams trotted off at intermission, the Bucks had built a 60–54 lead, and all were awed by Alcindor.

The second half was another story. Wilt worked on Lew and started to overpower him. He pushed Alcindor out of position, muscled past him, wrestled rebounds away from him, slammed dunks over him. It was as though he had reached in and turned on a tap, and now the plays streamed from him.

With the unheard crowd screaming around them, the adversaries remained expressionless, but they were soaked with sweat and starting to tire. However, Wilt kept pounding on, ponderously, while his younger rival, giving away fifty pounds, seemed to fade as they shoved each other around under the basket. Alcindor was gasping for breath now, his dancer's legs wobbly. Wilt moved in for the finishing punch.

Reaching up over Alcindor, Chamberlain rolled the ball off his fingertips into the basket. LA, which, after all, had the better team, caught and passed the Bucks.

With five minutes left, Wilt reached up with his large right hand, plucked a soft hook shot from Alcindor right out of the air, fed off to start a fast break, and set off a string of eight straight points which broke the backs of the Bucks.

At the finish, Wilt was dominant, and the Lakers had won, 123–112.

It was Wilt who was cheered as the weary warriors trotted off the court and through the corridors to their dressing rooms. The reporters poured into the rooms to surround the giants.

Wilt was stripped, wearing only two small, round Band-Aids on the nipple of each breast, to protect them from rubbing raw against his sweaty jersey. His dark skin was shiny with sweat. He smiled a little as the reporters came at him. He remained standing so they would have to tilt their heads and look up at him as they talked to him. Towering above his subjects, the king held court.

What, he was asked, did he think of Lew: "He's a very good boy," Wilt said. Were there any surprises? "He's quicker and more agile than I expected. He has better moves than I expected." Was he hard to play? "He could dig ditches with his elbows." Wilt smiled. And what did he think of Lew's future? "I'd like to have it," he said, his smile widening.

And how did he, Wilt, feel he played? "Ordinary," Wilt said. "I was tired. Not from the schedule. I can't get tired after five games with seventy-five to play. From you guys and all the rest of the people asking me about Alcindor." Was he satisfied with his performance? "Hey, my man, listen, I'm never satisfied. I'm a perfectionist, you know," Wilt said.

Had he been "up" for the game? "I'm always up for every game," Wilt said, putting it down. "No special preparations for this one. However, I didn't go around kissing any girls last night," he laughed. Had he learned anything from the encounter? "I always learn," Wilt said. "But I hope he learned more than I did. He has more to learn, you know."

Handed a sheet of statistics, Wilt crumpled it without looking at it and tossed it in his locker. Then he waved a hand, dismissing the press, and retreated to hide in the shower room awhile. The reporters scattered among the other players, almost forgotten, and then one by one left.

In the Milwaukee dressing room, Alcindor, dressed now in shades of brown, his eyes hidden behind tan-tinted sunglasses, endured his inquisition from members of the media who had been waiting for him. He sat, so the writers could look down on him. His smiles and his interview were shorter than Wilt's had been.

"I feel I did all right, but I know I have to do better," he said. "He is a great player, of course. I've barely met him, but I respect him for what he's accomplished. He didn't intimidate me and he doesn't scare me, but he did almost break me in half. He's very powerful. It was an educational experience."

Alcindor seemed exhausted, his face drawn. He confessed, "I am tired. In college ball, we play a couple of times a week. Here, in pro ball, we play night after night. I wish I could stop to draw a deep breath." He had finished his fifth game and had seventy-five left.

When Wilt returned from the showers, the Laker dressing room was almost deserted. He retrieved his valuables from the trainer. As he dressed, diamonds gleaming under the overhead light, Wilt said, "No one asked me about the game, about us winning, you know," and he shook his head with disgust.

The writer mentioned that Lew was beseiged by reporters in the other room. Wilt said, "I don't know Lew. I met him, but

I don't know if I like him or not. But I know I feel for him. The tensions he faces only I know."

He stood up. "People can't understand why I'm not worked up. I been here before is why," he said.

He stooped down and scooped up the crumpled ball of stats from his locker and stuffed it into his pocket swiftly so maybe no one would notice. Then he went outside to where the television crews begged him for a few minutes, which he gave them, in a brightly lit studio room, answering the same questions all over again.

As Wilt left, Alcindor was emerging from his dressing room. They nodded but did not speak. The TV crew grabbed Lew. He submitted to it, too, his hands wrestling as he answered the same questions.

Meanwhile, Wilt stood in the lobby surrounded by youngsters who thrust scraps of paper at him, asking for autographs. Sweat dripped from his face and beard as he leaned to his task. "C'mon, kids," he growled impatiently when they got in each other's way. "That's it," he said, finally, as he strode off to hide in the Forum Club. A few moments later, he sipped a glass of wine while his admirers watched him.

Lew left, ducking out a side door, running from the fans, speeding off into the dark night. It was nearly midnight when Wilt accordioned into his sports car in the deserted parking lot and drove to The Windjammer, a rocking spot.

Here, he was hailed like a conquering hero. Here, he sipped some more wine, rapped with pals, chatted with some chicks, relaxed, listening to the loud music.

After a few hours, he went home. He spent the last part of his big night alone in his house, sitting in his living room and watching an old Rod Cameron western on television. It was almost daybreak before he climbed into bed and lay there looking at the darkness and thinking about the challenge he had faced so well.

But the morning newspaper the next day headlined, "Wilt, Lew Draw." And Wilt was angry when he got to the arena and

12

spread out the wrinkled stat sheet and read what was there. Wilt had scored 25 points and collected 25 rebounds. Lew had scored 23 points and collected 20 rebounds. Wilt had blocked 3 shots, Lew 2. And Wilt's team had won.

He sat down, staring moodily into his palms. "What'd you expect?" he said. "I didn't get the credit I deserved when I faced Russell, I won't with Alcindor. It doesn't matter to me," he said. "It just doesn't matter. I don't care. I really don't care. I know the score, even if no one else does. You can't please the public. No way. The more you give them, the more they want.

"Nothing I do," he sighed, "ever seems to be enough."

The writer has watched Wilt for more than twenty years. My first vivid memory of Wilt stems from an incident after a game Chamberlain played in White Plains, New York, early in 1955. Wilt had just completed his senior season at Overbrook High School in Philadelphia and as the most touted scholastic basketball prospect of all time was taken on a tour of games in which Philadelphia all-stars faced all-star scholastic teams in various communities. Someone cashed in on Wilt's celebrity.

Wilt had almost reached his full height, but was far from his full weight. He was an extremely tall, extremely skinny young black at a time before the seven-footers and the blacks had taken over this sport in any real numbers. It is hard to remember much about the game except Wilt, who was outstanding. He stood out in every respect.

I was with the great professional and college coach Joe Lapchick and a great high-school coach, Joe Seidell from Yonkers, and we went down to the dressing room to visit with Wilt afterward. A short man no one knew and his small son had somehow sneaked into the room and went right to Wilt.

"Stand up," the man told Wilt.

Wilt, who was unbearded and boyish-looking at eighteen, was startled.

"Stand up," the man repeated, as if an officer addressing a private. "I want to take your picture with my son."

Wearily Wilt stood up. The man shoved his son to Wilt's side. The little lad was dwarfed by the young giant. "Wowee," the man said, raising his camera and backing up halfway across the room to get all of Wilt into the picture. The flashbulb popped. "You sure are something," the man said, shaking his head with disbelief. He took his son's hand and headed off without so much as a thank you.

Wilt sat down and looked at the floor at his feet. I remember how wistful he looked. The memory is as clear as if it had occurred today, though it happened many years of yesterdays. It was not the first time and certainly not the last time Wilt would be asked to pose for such a picture or be pushed this way or pulled that way, but it was not long before he would refuse such orders or rebel at such discourtesies.

Lapchick, who at six feet five had been in the 1920s one of the first big men in basketball, whispered that the poor kid had a hard road ahead of him. Moving to Wilt, Joe laid a hand on the youngster's bony knee, leaned over him, and said, "I'm Joe Lapchick, and it's been a pleasure to watch you perform."

Wilt looked up and said, "Thank you, Mr. Lapchick. Coming from you, that's very nice."

Lapchick, then coach of the New York Knicks, said, "If I was still at St. John's I'd be after you."

"That's all right," Wilt said. "Everyone else is anyway."

Wilt was the eighth of eleven children born to William and Olivia Chamberlain. The first two died in infancy. Wilt's father had been a welder in the shipyards. He was working as a handyman for Sears when Wilt was born. For most of Wilt's youth, his father worked as a handyman and a janitor for Curtis Publishing Company, which produced *The Saturday Evening Post,* As Wilt remembers it, his father did not make anything

15

near $100 a week at any time in his life. He helped make ends meet by doing odd jobs for neighbors, such as repairs and painting. Wilt's mother helped by hiring out as a domestic maid and cook until he retired her after he entered pro basketball.

All the children helped by working and pitching pennies into the pot. Wilt swears he was working at the age of five, delivering groceries and newspapers, washing windows, shoveling snow, and such. He used to scavenge nearby neighborhoods for old clothes, metal, and newspapers which he'd sell at a local junkyard for a few pennies. He even raided his own cellar for stuff to sell, sometimes upsetting his mother. But, then, his sister once sold the family piano to a passing junkman. Later, Wilt would go down to the local produce district, buy fruits and vegetables, and haul them on a wagon through the streets, selling them at a profit. In time, Wilt began helping his father, then formed his own painting and clean-up crews.

This was in the World War II days of the 1940s through the early 1950s. The Chamberlains did not have much, but they made do. Wilt once recalled, "My folks managed. They didn't deny us anything that mattered. We were a close family. Hell, we slept two, three, four to a room. But we always had room to squeeze in family or friend who needed a roof over their head. We always had a dollar for someone in need. We always had clothes on our backs and food on our table. I know what it is not to have money. I paid my dues. But my parents always had time for us. They taught us right from wrong. None of us went wrong, and we were raised in a neighborhood where a lot of kids went wrong."

That was in West Philadelphia, in the Haddington section, concrete and almost treeless, a black belt. It was a congested but tidy residential area. It was made up mostly of attached two-story structures called "row houses," which stretched repetitiously for blocks. The Chamberlains lived at 401 North Salford Street in a two-story, eight-room, gray-brick house that shared a common wall with an identical house next door. It was close to the trolley-car barn, and the trolleys used to awaken them early every morning as they rattled by to begin their runs for the day.

The Chamberlains did have a tree in their backyard. They had, as Wilt remembers it, a neat house. Although he grew up with six sisters and two brothers, the older ones started to move away, and he does not remember their four-bedroom home as being congested beyond reason. Although as an adult he has almost always lived alone, he remembers with affection the good feeling of having family around, and he has continued to be close to his family.

Although he does not like to admit losing at anything, he is fond of saying he lost every one of thousands of checker games he played with his father from boyhood on. However, he does say he got to the point where he often beat him in pinochle or other card games. I asked him a few years ago if there was anything he wished he could do in life that he could not do. He said, "Yes, play cards just once more with my father." Wilt's father died in 1968.

Wilt's father was only five feet eight, his mother an inch taller, but her grandfather was about a foot taller. Wilt's tallest brother, Wilbert, was six feet five, his tallest sister, Selina, five-eight. When Wilton Norman Chamberlain was born shortly before midnight, August 21, 1936, he was a big baby—twenty-nine inches long, seven pounds thirteen ounces heavy. As he grew up, he was always the tallest in his age group. He hit six feet at the age of ten. He was six-three at twelve when he graduated from grade school. He was six-seven at fourteen when he graduated from junior high school. He was six-eleven halfway through high school when he stopped measuring himself. He probably was past seven feet at eighteen when he finished high school. He may have added a fraction or so to top seven-one after that to attain his full height.

His street pals used to tease him about having to "dip" under doorways. Thus, his nickname, "The Big Dipper" or, to his friends, simply "Dip," stemmed from the streets, though it was reinforced when he began to rise above baskets to dip basketballs through them. He always preferred it to "Wilt the Stilt," which was given him by a Philadelphia sportswriter, Jack Ryan, and which Chamberlain felt made him seem like some monstrous artificial man. He has been asked "How's the weather up there?" since he was a teen-ager, and he has long since wearied of it. "People always have tried to make me feel like a freak," he sighs. "Some people are tall, some are short. Some are fat, some are skinny. Tall is my thing, but I'm just a person."

He once remembered that when he was a lad and closing in on seven feet in height, people in the streets could not help taking a second look at him though they tried not to embarrass him. He played a little game wherein he would walk past them three or four feet while they pretended not to notice him, and then try to turn around to look back at them just at the instant their heads turned to stare at him.

He was sensitive about his height. He says he sucked his thumb until his teens. He was skinny, sickly, and subject to colds as a boy. He had a hernia operation at two, and pneumonia, which set him back a year in school, at ten. When he went to an uncle's farm in the South summers he'd get insect bites which would fester. His bony shins ad knees were especially sensitive. They'd scab, and remain scarred. He took to wearing long socks and knee pads to protect his legs when he played basketball.

Wilt was not turned on by basketball at first. He liked to run. After he found out he was fast, he was always running. When he was in George Brooks Elementary School he was selected as the youngest member of a relay team that ran—and lost—in the 1946 Penn Relays. But it was a thrill he remembers. The races were televised that day, and it was Wilt's first public performance.

His original ambition was to be an Olympian. He was successful in track and field in high school and college, and still loves it. He says, "I gave up on it because there was no money in it." But after retirement, he sponsored a women's track team, and at the 1976 Olympic trials in Eugene, Oregon, and at the Montreal Olympics, Wilt was in the stands, stopwatch in hand.

But Philadelphia always has been a basketball town. Players like Paul Arizin, Tom Gola, Hal Lear, and Guy Rodgers came from Philadelphia and became basketball stars while Wilt was maturing. Wilt played against Arizin and Gola in summer leagues. The color barrier was broken in pro baseball by Jackie Robinson in 1947 and in pro basketball by Chuck Cooper in 1950, and this gave black youngsters hope for a future in professional sports other than boxing, which Wilt's father favored. Wilt entered high school in 1951 just as the barriers were dropping.

He did not get into basketball until in his teens he was taunted by others that anyone with his height should go into the game. His friends all were playing, so Wilt followed. The more he played, the more he liked it. "I was better than the others, even the older ones. I liked that," Wilt once observed.

He began in basketball at Shoemaker Junior High School, but his home court became the one at the Haddington Recreation Center, which was built in 1949 at 57th and Haverford, a few blocks from his home. Jackie Moore preceded Wilt and Wayne Hightower, and Walt Hazzard and Wally Jones followed him, as pro stars who prepped at Haddington and then at Overbrook High School. Wilt also played at the Christian Street YMCA and at a couple of churches in his area. A lot of youth organizations provided courts to keep the poor, rough kids off the street and out of trouble. In the process, they developed a few pros. And lost some to drugs and crime, jail and death.

As a player, Wilt was awkward at first, though less so than others of height. "Blinky" Brown, who coached him at Haddington, once recalled, "His legs were so skinny it didn't look like they could keep carrying him down the court. He was timid and let people push him around. They used to bet he'd never be strong enough or tough enough to become a star. But he just had to develop. He had that great height and unusual speed for a lad so tall. He never was mean, but he wanted to be the best. He worked at it. He had good competition on our courts and pretty soon he was coming into his own. Pretty soon everyone was coming to see him play."

Although he was a Baptist, Wilt was sought by the coach at West Catholic High School, a basketball powerhouse in his area. St. Thomas More School, which was out of his area, even offered him carfare and lunch money to come and compete for them. This was when Wilt first saw what his size and skill might be worth to him. But he went to Overbrook High, the public school where his friends were going. Sam Cozen, who coached him as a freshman there, said, "You could see Wilt was going to be great."

Any doubt about it was erased when Wilt and his YMCA team won the city title and a trip to High Point, North Carolina, where they won the national title tournament. Wilt and teammate Claude Gross were the only high school players selected to the YMCA All-America team. Claude, who later married Wilt's sister Selina, with Wilt as best man, went to Ben Franklin High, which dealt Wilt's Overbrook High team one of only two defeats it suffered in his sophomore season. The other was to West Catholic in the city championship contest after Overbrook had won the public school crown.

The West Catholic coach had his team prepare for the outsized sophomore by having his center stand on a table in front of the hoop. When the ball was thrown to him, the defenders swarmed all over him, leaping at him, waving their arms, trying to distract him. In the game, these tactics limited Wilt to "only" 29 points, but they worked to the extent that Overbrook was beaten, by 12 points.

Wilt blames defeat on the failure of his teammates to hit open shots while four defenders gathered around him at all times.

The following season Wilt was subjected to a series of swarming defenses and really rough tactics as awed foes figured they could beat him by beating on him. However, Wilt overpowered the opposition, and Overbrook coach Cecil Mosenson worked

Wilt's sidekicks on outside shooting that took advantage of openings presented. Overbrook did not lose a game, and Wilt was celebrated throughout the city as no Philadelphia school-boy had been previously.

After Overbrook defeated Northeast for a second straight Public League title, followers sought to lift Wilt to carry him off the court in triumph, but the gangling youngster was so big they could not get a grip on him. Halfway to their shoulders, he slipped off and fell in an inglorious heap.

Overbrook went on to win the city title as well that season. The following season it again swept both crowns, winning a third straight public school title and a second straight city title. In the latter, they thumped West Catholic by 41 points as Wilt tallied 35 and teammate Vince Miller 31 to atone for the earlier loss.

Wilt had grown up with Vince, Howard Johnson, Tommy Fitzhugh, and Marty Hughes, who were all starters as seniors. There was a togetherness about them that was not present on Wilt's later teams. However, it did bother Wilt that the most popular player on the team was not he, but Hughes, a flashy ball handler. It bothered him because he was more than seven feet tall, while Marty was less than six feet. "Everyone always likes the little guy," Wilt has sighed. Here was the birth of his Goliath theory.

Wilt's team went 20–2 his sophomore season, 20–0 his junior year, and 18–1 his senior year. They lost a one-pointer in a Christmas tournament that last year. Thus, they went 58–3 during his three seasons as a schoolboy star.

Mosenson, who coached Wilt during his junior and senior seasons, said, "Wilt had unusual coordination and stamina to go with his unusual size and strength. He had good coaching and competition as a kid and came to us strong on fundamentals. We worked on his moves in the pivot, his positioning on rebounds and stuff like that. As he got better, he just totally dominated his rivals. We had a good team without him. We were a great team with him.

"People compared him to Tom Gola because Tom was the most recent star to come from Philadelphia. But there was no comparison. Tom was a super player. He could do everything and he seemed to do it without effort, like Oscar Robertson. Tom contributed to his teams in a lot of ways that did not show in the box scores. It is no surprise he led LaSalle to the NCAA title and became a pro star. But Tom didn't have Wilt's size and strength. Tom never could dominate a game the way Wilt could."

Along with his height, Wilt had long arms. Standing under the basket, he could reach to within six inches of the twelve-foot-high rim. When he got the ball in close, schoolboy rivals could not handle him. He went up and dunked it with ease. But he also had a good jump shot from a little way outside.

He became a good ball handler. He could dribble and pass, sometimes behind his back, and he was a better free-throw shooter than he was to be a few years later.

Wilt scored 32 points in his first varsity game as a sophomore and went on from there. As a sophomore, he tied a state record by scoring 71 points against Roxborough High. Poor Roxborough. As a junior, Wilt broke the state record by scoring 74 points against them. As a senior he scored 90 against them, 64 in the second half. This was in the 32-minute games high schools play. It was the equivelant of 112 or so in a 40-minute college contest or 135 in a 48-minute pro game.

In the latter contest, Roxborough was ripped, 123–21. Wilt averaged 45 points a game through his senior season. Overbrook topped 100 points and won so many games by 50, 60, 70, or more points that Wilt often was taken out after playing less than half the games. Accordingly, his high school career total of 2,252 points and average of almost 37 points a game was a lot less than it might have been. But it broke Tom Gola's Pennsylvania schoolboy record.

Overbrook lost only three games in his three seasons, and there simply was not any need to embarrass the opposition any worse than it already was. Wilt not only scored almost at will and grabbed most of the rebounds at both ends of the court, but embarrassed rival shooters badly by blocking their shots regularly, usually swatting them into the stands. He had not learned to control these blocks. He was an undisciplined player with overpowering assets.

Not only college coaches but pro people were impressed by the youngster. NBA publicist Haskell Cohen arranged for Wilt to spend his summers as a part-time bellhop at thirteen dollars a week and part-time basketball player at Catskill Mountain resorts in upstate New York, where so many prize prodigies prepped. Red Auberbach, the Boston Celtic coach who spent part of his summer vacation coaching in the Catskills, coached him there and was awed by him. "The first time I saw him, I just stood and watched him walk. Just watched him walk," Red has recalled. "It was incredible how graceful he was for his size. He was comparable to the best college stars I had there, and it was obvious he was going to be great."

Red rode Wilt hard. The cigar-chewing Auerbach wasn't about to admit to Wilt what he thought of him. He pushed him in practices, harangued him at halftimes. He had Wilt hustling drinks for him and his cronies at card games. He did toss him ten-dollar tips. And he did try to talk him into attending a Boston-area college. This was when the NBA had a territorial rule in its draft which gave its members first-round rights to graduating collegians in their geographical area, and Auerbach anticipated drafting Chamberlain for his Celtics. What a team Chamberlain and Russell would have made on the Celtics!

Eddie Gottlieb beat him to the punch. Little, round Eddie, a sharpie, wasn't about to be outwitted. One of the original league leaders and a powerful force in NBA politics, Gottlieb pushed through a rule over the opposition of Ned Irish and the New York Knicks that permitted member teams to use their first-round territorial picks for any high school graduates in their area. Accordingly, Gottlieb in 1955 drafted Wilt as a "future" for his Philadelphia Warriors, and there was no doubt where Wilt was headed after that, no matter where he went to college.

"I had the rule changed. I just did," Gottlieb says now. "We were fighting for survival in those days. Hometown boys were big at the box office. I wasn't the only one to want it. Cincinnati got Jerry Lucas that way. It was smart, see." But Jerry Lucas wasn't Wilt Chamberlain.

Everyone wanted Wilt. He went to New York and scored more than 50 points to pace a Philadelphia all-star team over a collection of outstanding local schoolboys. Ned Irish reported, "This boy is ready for the big leagues right now." *Sport* magazine headlined a story, "The High School Kid Who Could Play Pro Ball Now." Every major magazine in the country that dealt with sports, including *Time* and *Newsweek, Look* and *Life,* featured stories on the youngster.

Unlike today when Moses Malone and others have been selected from the synthetic "hardship" draft right out of high school, players in those days were ineligible for professional play until their college classes graduated. But Gottlieb and others were ready to revise the rule for Wilt. Gottlieb says today, "Wilt was one of the few who could have played with the pros right out of high school. Gola was another. I don't know about Malone. He was successful in the ABA. But that wasn't the NBA.

"There haven't been many who could have made it in the NBA out of high school. Some make it into the league but aren't ready to play. Wilt was ready. You didn't have many good big men in those days. Not like today. When Wilt got out of high school, George Mikan was the best big man in big league basketball. He dominated the game. No one could compete with him. But Wilt was going to be better. Wilt made mincemeat out of All-Pro centers like Neil Johnston in the Catskills.

"We had Johnston, but Wilt would have started for me. If the rules had permitted it, I'd have taken him and put him right on my first team. But the other guys didn't want to change the

24

rule. They didn't want to wreck their relationship with the colleges. The colleges were their minor leagues. They polished the prospects for us, and it didn't cost the pro teams a dime. But I'd have taken Wilt. Wilt was special.

"It was a waste of time for Wilt to go to college," the old pro concludes.

It was, indeed, as it turned out.

By Wilt's sworn count, more than two hundred colleges tried to recruit him. This probably is a record for a scholastic sports prospect, though Kareem Abdul-Jabbar came close later at a time when more schools were concerned about increased investigations by the NCAA.

It started when Wilt was a sophomore and didn't stop even when he announced a month before his graduation in his senior year that had chosen Kansas. Indiana recruiters continued to pursue him until he played his first game for Kansas, trying to talk him into transferring.

Wilt has complained, "A lot of people said I was lucky to be in my position, but the pressure recruiters put on me was just terrible. I couldn't walk into my house without finding someone waiting for me. The telephone and doorbell never stopped ringing. Coaches were coming through the windows to get at me. Every mail brought more offers. I was hounded."

He has said he asked his coach to screen the offers and block out visitors to free himself, but Wilt started to visit schools in his sophomore season in high school, and Mosenson usually went with him. There were rumors that Mosenson was selling his services as a coach along with Wilt's as a player as a package deal. When such a deal did not develop when Wilt went to Kansas, Mosenson retired from the sport, though he later returned to it.

Wilt took almost all the free rides offered him and admits he had fun. He visited the campuses at Kansas, Indiana, Dayton, Denver, Iowa, Illinois, Cincinnati, Michigan, Michigan State, and Northwestern. Some he visited two times. Kansas he visited three times. He laughs and admits he got to be well known at the Philadelphia airport.

He also got a laugh out of it when Jim Enright, a Chicago sportswriter who doubled as a basketball referee, figured him for a fan. "I saw him in the stands at four different campuses four different weekends and figured he was following me around," Enright said with a straight face.

Wilt simply ran out of time to visit the campuses of other schools which also went after him hard, including San Francisco, UCLA, Notre Dame, Ohio State, Oklahoma, Missouri, Purdue, North Carolina, North Carolina State, Holy Cross, and the Philadelphia-area powerhouses of Penn, Villanova, St. Joseph's, Temple, and LaSalle.

LaSalle hoped it had the inside track because of the glamour of outgoing grad Tom Gola and because another graduate, who tried to sell the school, Jackie Moore, had befriended and coached Wilt at Haddington. But Wilt said he wanted to get away from the East in general and Philadelphia in particular, which did not endear him to his hometown followers.

Wilt said he did not want to go to the Far West because he did not believe they played topflight basketball on the Pacific Coast. He says he made a mistake where John Wooden's UCLA teams were concerned, but they were not winning much at that time. This ignores the fact that Bill Russell's San Francisco teams were on their way to two straight national titles. Actually, Chamberlain did not want to follow Russell's act. He thought he could win his own championships. And the seeds of his rivalry with Russell were sown at this time.

Wilt said he did not want to go south because he did not want

27

to cross with the Ku Klux Klan. He still says he believes some southern schools who wrote him did not even know he was black. However, there probably was not a basketball coach in the South who did not have scouts or contacts in Philadelphia or did not know that blacks went to Overbrook. Wilt used to tell a story about an alumnus of Missouri who asked him if he wouldn't like to be the first black basketball player at his school. Wilt told him he'd rather be the second. Years later Wilt admitted the "alum" actually was Wilbur Stallcup, the coach at Missouri. He intercepted Wilt at the airport in Kansas City, trying to sidetrack him from Kansas U.

Wilt has said he wanted to go to a midwestern school because he had heard the best basketball was played there, but no one in Philadelphia or the East ever would admit to that. He says he ruled out Ohio State, Michigan State, Michigan, and Notre Dame because basketball wasn't the big game there, football was. He certainly did not want to be overshadowed at a football factory.

Wilt narrowed his choices down to Dayton, Indiana, and Kansas. He has said he eliminated Dayton after he discovered that he received room service at his hotel there not because, as he believed, he was being given the best, but because he would not be served in the dining room. He has said he eliminated Indiana after he discovered the coach, Branch McCracken, was henpecked, and after he heard McCracken "did not like Negroes."

Yet, Indiana was one of the first midwestern schools to recruit black athletes. George Taliaferro had been a football star there while Wilt was growing up, and Bill Garrett was McCracken's starting center there, the first black basketball player in the Big Ten, while Wilt was in high school. And Wilt was recruited by two black friends from the East who were playing there, basketball star Wally Choice and track and football star Milt Campbell, and they told him he'd be treated well there.

The fact is that restaurants and other establishments in the college towns of Bloomington, Indiana, and Lawrence, Kansas, were equally segregated, and there were quota systems at both schools. When Wilt, who said he did not want to be a trailblazer, went to Kansas, there were few blacks in the school, much less on the sports teams, though another black, Maurice King, was brought onto the basketball team.

Wilt was not blind to bigotry. He saw right through it when on his visits to Kansas such prominent black citizens as newspaperman Dowdall Davis, industrialist Lloyd Kerford, and singer Etta Moten were brought to court him. They told him they wanted him to break racial barriers there.

He was refused service at a restaurant in Kansas even before he enrolled there. When he went to his "sponsors" in anger about this, they told him to fight back. But they left it up to him.

He went everywhere and waited until he was served. He was served. Other blacks got behind him, but, as Wilt sees it, he singlehandedly broke the color barriers in the college town of Lawrence and around the state of Kansas.

Yet, this was just what he had said he did not want to do. He admits he never was happy in Lawrence. Blacks had little social life there. Wilt found friends there and in Kansas City and he kept taking off for the Negro sections of Kansas City to party.

His grades were about average at the C level in Kansas. He started with a major in business administration, but then switched to a straight bachelor of science course of study. His grades got worse as he went along. He lost interest in the education being offered him, and blamed it on basketball.

He wanted desperately for Kansas to take with him two of his Overbrook teammates, Vince Miller and Marty Hughes, but they were black, and the school took instead a third, Doug Leamon, who was white and who did not last long. Wilt is still bitter about this. He believes Leamon was not nearly as good a player as the others and that Miller in particular might have become a star, but he did not.

Yet, in spite of such insults, Wilt went to Kansas. And the question asked then—why a black basketball star from Philadelphia would travel halfway across the country to attend school in Kansas—remains as valid now and is not adequately answered by Wilt's comments in the *Sports Illustrated* or *Look* magazine stories he by-lined for fat fees, in the 1973 Macmillan book, *Wilt,* or in other interviews.

He speaks of the great basketball tradition at Kansas, where the coach, Forrest "Phog" Allen, had been tutored by the sport's inventor, Dr. James Naismith. But Kansas had won only one national collegiate title, while Indiana had won two, and Indiana had defeated Kansas in the title game in 1953, while Wilt was being recruited.

Coach Branch McCracken of Indiana and Allen of Kansas were bitter rivals, although they did not often meet because they refused to schedule each other. They simply disliked each other. McCracken later told this writer, "We thought we had Wilt. He was announced for here. Phog stole him away from us. I didn't mind losing him so much as I minded losing him to Allen."

He later publicly charged he had been offered Chamberlain for $5,000 up front and said Wilt was too rich for his blood. This sparked a new investigation of the recruiting of Wilt, but NCAA and IRS investigators had been grilling the youngster about money he had made or been offered and other offerings since long before he got out of high school.

With the wisdom of the streets, Wilt denied everything. He gave them nothing to hang on him with which to hang him. Following a four-hour interrogation, one investigator said Wilt told a nice story, but he didn't believe a word of it. Wilt says he thinks this was a terrible thing to say to a high school lad.

Yet, as a matter of fact, Wilt was offered everything from soft jobs to soft ladies, from fast cars to outright cash to play for different colleges. The coaches often tried to steer clear of trouble by having outsiders do their dirty work for them, but one coach confessed in confidence to me, "We offered him $5,000 a year for phony jobs, a free car, free round-trip plane rides home every vacation. But others offered more." Wilt has said Indiana offered to double anything Kansas offered.

30

Allen admitted to me in a hotel room one night, "The people in Kansas wanted another Jackie Robinson. And they wanted to win. Wilt was a way to kill two birds with one stone. I wanted to win. I didn't care about another Jackie Robinson. I played every angle I could think of to get him. One way was to have the Negro talk to the Negro. I brought in colored leaders from our community to pitch to him. I didn't dwell on racial segregation in our state."

Called "the champion recruiter of mamas," Allen followed Wilt and his family to a YMCA banquet in Philadelphia one night. He recalled, "I talked to the boy's mother more than I did to the boy himself. I talked to her about the education her son could get at our school more than about basketball. Mamas like to believe they are thinking more about education than about basketball."

Allen admitted, "I rolled out the red carpet every time Wilt came to town. I shot every barrel. I not only landed my prey, but had the pleasure of seeing some of the fall-out wound good old IU and my good friend, Branch McCracken," the coach chuckled. He considered his success a "classic textbook case in the history of recruiting," and commented he was sorry, "the world will never know the entire story."

Allen visited Wilt repeatedly and got Wilt to come to the campus three times. One time a Negro fraternity leader even turned over his girl friend to Wilt for a date. Allen was the first coach to get Wilt to his campus, and he was still there firing away at the finish.

Wilt admitted, "I really liked old Phog. He could charm you. He turned the charm on Mama and won her over. She loved him and probably played a part in my decision. Phog was no phony like most of those other cats, sneaking around and hinting I could have this or that. Allen laid it on the line."

At a time Celtic Bob Cousy was the highest paid pro in basketball at $22,000 a season, Boston boss Walter Brown said, "It's a matter of fact no pro team can afford to pay Chamberlain what he gets at Kansas. Leonard Lewin of the New York *Daily*

Mirror said, "I feel sorry for the Stilt when he enters the NBA four years from now. He'll have to take a cut in salary."

Max Kase, sports editor of the New York *Journal-American,* asked, "Isn't the NCAA investigating reports of a special trust fund due to mature on Wilt the Stilt's graduation?" The NCAA was, but could not crack Chamberlain.

Wilt insisted that Kansas offered him only the allowable room, board, tuition, laundry money, and job. He insisted it and insisted it for years and years. He said he was paid fifteen dollars a month laundry money and fifteen dollars a month to sell programs at football games. In fact, he did sell programs at football games.

He says he was offered phony jobs at other schools, such as one requiring him to keep seaweed out of the stadium. At Kansas, he was given a job selling cars. He admits he would check in, take off, return, and check out. His boss confesses, "His sales weren't tremendous." The first eight customers he brought in were turned down by the company's credit department. He was paid up to a hundred dollars just to visit and attract attendance at a nightclub.

For a year or so Wilt kept a low profile by driving a three-year-old car he said was purchased with his savings from summer jobs. He since has admitted he was told that when he wanted anything he had only to go to any one of several rich supporters of the school's basketball program and ask for it. When he wanted a car, he did, and he got it. Shortly, he fell in love with a Cadillac. He got that, too. Two years after he left school, the NCAA put the school on probation for the $1,500 paid for his Caddy. But that was all they could hang on the school.

He always has loved fast, fancy cars. He survived a couple of celebrated smashups while still in high school and was nailed for speeding several times in college. He used to brag of driving the Kansas Turnpike at speeds above 125 miles per hour. But he brags also of having built the turnpike itself with the tax money he created at Kansas basketball games.

He now has admitted he received from $15,000 to $20,000 in ten- and hundred-dollar bills handed him by fans following Kansas games. Confronted with charges that a slush fund of $30,000 was established for his future, Wilt has said, "No way." Smiling, he added, "It didn't come close to that."

Of course, he didn't play his senior season, either. Nor did he play in the Olympics. When an Olympic official was outraged that Wilt did not try out for the 1956 Games, Wilt said he wasn't interested, although that had been his boyhood dream. Allen attacked the official verbally for meddling.

However, J. Suter Kegg, sports editor of the Cumberland, Maryland, *Evening Times,* had reported that Wilt had played in an exhibition game there under an assumed name, and Harry Grayson of NEA news service spread the story nationally. Wilt said he never was there. But he was.

He since has admitted he played there and elsewhere in the East under an assumed name for small sums. And he was warned away from the Olympics so that he would not create the scandal the Jim Thorpe case did when it was discovered he had played for pay under assumed names as a semipro prior to his Olympic victories; Thorpe was stripped of his medals.

Many of Wilt's dreams developed into nightmares. His college roommate, sprinter Charlie Tidwell, said, "I'd read about him in newspapers and magazines and I'd look across the room and see him studying and it wouldn't seem like the Wilt they were writing about and the one I knew were the same person. He just wanted to be another student and he was a good guy. We played practical jokes on him and he played practical jokes on us."

However, another who knew him then says, "The recruiting hassle hardened him and made him cynical. You can't be told constantly from the time you're twelve years old that you're the greatest thing since the wheel and not begin to believe it. You can't sell yourself and not feel like a prostitute. The more money he made, the more he wanted. The simple life no longer was enough for him. I can't blame him. But it hurt him. He changed."

And another says, "The same people who had been writing raves about him started to rap him. He began to get a bad press and was put down by statements that he was good only because he was big. And that he was greedy. But when you wave a bunch of dollar bills in front of a poor boy, is he supposed to refuse them? And should he have wasted his size and ability? He felt he was treated unfairly. He was."

A third says, "The guys and gals were coming at him, wanting a piece of him. He got so he couldn't figure out who his friends were and who weren't. He felt like there wasn't a lady he could trust who wasn't after his fortune. That's why he's kept so many of his old friends, who were with him before he was a star. And made so few in basketball who wanted to get in on his glory."

They did not want to be identified because, one said, "Wilt figures his friends shouldn't talk about him. He'll drop anyone who does."

Wilt says, "I'm a good friend and a bad enemy. I'll do anything for anyone who is for me, but anyone who turns on me better beware." Asked once if any had, he answered "You better believe it." Asked how he had been hurt in his life, he said "By people. People are the only ones who can bring you real hurt. Happenings don't matter to me. But people can get to me."

Asked about his college career, he says, "It wasn't what I expected it to be." He insists, "I never regretted going to Kansas." But with another breath he admits, "I was disappointed by developments there."

The first disappointing development came when Phog Allen fell victim to the university's mandatory retirement age at seventy before Wilt's first varsity contest at Kansas. Allen admitted to the writer, later, "One reason I went after Wilt so hard was I was sure they would not retire me if I got them Wilt. I told that to Wilt.

"I was wrong. It was unfair and I can't forgive them for it. I had done the school a service and was deserving of an exception. Basketball was my life. And Wilt was championships. I'd have won with Wilt, I assure you, even if others could not."

His assistant and his successor, Dick Harp, could not. When Harp first took over Wilt and the team, he insisted, "Wilt does whatever I ask of him." After Wilt left, Harp admitted, "Wilt just lost interest."

Wilt praised him at the time, but later said, "He wasn't much of a coach." 1950943

Wilt insists he always liked Harp, but complains Harp later never once wrote him to encourage or congratulate him. However, Wilt admits he never wrote Harp, either.

Actually, they never got along. Wilt says sadly that one reason he went to Kansas was to play for Phog Allen, and regrets that the opportunity was taken from him. Perhaps Phog could have been more candid about the possibility he would be forcibly retired, but Wilt retained a feeling of fondness for Phog right up to Allen's death.

Wilt is convinced his reputation as a "loser" started with his failures at Kansas under Dick Harp. Wilt was, of course, a winner at Kansas. His teams won most of their games. But, his sophomore season his team lost the ultimate title, which is the one that matters most. And his junior year, his team did not win enough to even get into the title tournament.

He was sensational, yet not as dominating as anticipated in advance. Harp put him in the pivot with instructions to stay there, almost immobilizing him. But he was a power in there.

In an exhibition, he led his freshman teammates to a victory over the varsity. A record crowd of 14,000 fans and coaches turned out to watch Wilt, who scored 42 points despite double-teaming defensive tactics.

On one play, Wilt soared toward the hoop, twisted to turn his back to the basket, held the ball in one hand, helicptered it around his head, and dunked it backhanded.

Nebraska coach Jerry Bush, who had come to see what he had ahead of him, admitted to a seatmate, "I feel sick."

Phog Allen applied a lot of pressure to Wilt by predicting, "With Wilt, we'll never lose a game. We could win the national championship with Wilt, two sorority girls, and two Phi Beta Kappas."

That was what people expected of Wilt and it disappointed them when it developed that he was no guarantee of titles. More was expected of Wilt than he could deliver.

A *Saturday Evening Post* story one week before his first varsity game, asked in headlines, "Can Basketball Survive Chamberlain?"

Officials legislated against him in an effort to insure this. Teammates would shoot toward the basket and Wilt would jump and steer the shot in. This was outlawed so no offensive player could touch a teammate's shot until after it hit the basket area. Wilt would leap forward as he launched a free throw, rebound it and stuff it in. This was outlawed so no foul shooter could leave the free-throw line until after the ball hit the basket area.

In his collegiate debut, Wilt drew 17,000 fans to the fieldhouse at Lawrence, and led an 18-point rout of Northwestern, breaking Kansas school records with 52 points and 31 rebounds.

Legislation over the years limited Wilt, but did not destroy his ability. However, he could be beaten by good basketball and tough tactics. He was not always at his best. Even at his best, he had to have help. He had a good but not great supporting cast at Kansas.

With Wilt, Kansas won its first twelve games before being beaten. Iowa State coach Bill Strannigan went a step farther than those who double-teamed Wilt. In Strannigan's strategy, a big center fronted Wilt in an attempt to stop passes to him, while both forwards sagged between him and the basket to block him when he did get the ball. The guards chased the other shooters.

Wilt did not hit a basket from the field in the first half and only five the second half. He averaged just under 30 points a game that season, but scored only 17 in this game. He hit two free throws to tie the game near the end, but a basket at the final buzzer beat Kansas, 39–37, in a slow, cautious contest.

A myth of invincibility was shaken.

After five more victories, Kansas was beaten again. Wilt tallied 32, but the master of slowdown basketball, Henry Iba, had his Oklahoma State team controlling the ball at a slow tempo, taking only good shots and in a position to prevail, 56–54, on another basket at the buzzer.

Kansas came on to win its final four and close out its best campaign in twenty years at 21-2, second-ranked nationally to undefeated North Carolina.

Kansas had cancelled contests with Texas teams prior to the season, but when it went into the NCAA tournament as Big Seven champion, it had to go to Dallas for the western regionals. Wilt took a lot of racial abuse from fans during the opener and, despite scoring 36 points, was emotionally upset, and his side was carried into overtime before SMU could be put away, 73–65.

In the final, a foe kept up the taunts of "Nigger" and such, but Wilt tallied 30 points, 14 of them on fouls, and Oklahoma City was overcome, 81–61.

Referee Al Lightner charged that Oklahoma City players deliberately roughed up Chamberlain and King because they were "dark-skinned."

Wilt later admitted that after growing up in a largely black and somewhat mixed neighborhood, it toughened him to go to Kansas and beyond and find out what life was like in much of this country for those of a minority color. This, too, hurt him, put him on the defensive, made him sensitive to slights, suspicious of others, wary, resentful.

In the first game of the final round the following weekend at Kansas City, Kansas took care of defending champion San Francisco easily, with Russell graduated, 80–56. In the other game, undefeated North Carolina was carried into a triple overtime before it could defeat Michigan State, 74–70. If Johnny Green had not missed two free throws near the end of regulation time, the Spartans would have won.

"I always figured we were fated to win after that," North Carolina coach Frank McGuire later said.

Weary, North Carolina could have been a soft touch for fresh Kansas in the title contest, but the Tarheels, 31-0, were tough. And their mentor, McGuire, was a master strategist and psychologist. Ironically, he later would coach Chamberlain in pro ball and Wilt would come to call him the smartest coach he ever had.

When Wilt first went to Kansas, McGuire asked Allen if he was "trying to kill basketball." He said, "There might be somebody in the pen who can handle Wilt, but there is nobody in college." He never meant a word he said.

"I was upset because we weren't taking blacks then and I couldn't recruit him," the coach commented to me later, laughing. "There never has been a player who couldn't be defensed. But it was tougher with Wilt than anyone else."

Frank didn't have an outstanding player, although Lenny Rosenbluth was an All-American forward in college ranks before he flopped as a pro. McGuire's center, Joe Quigg, was only six-eight, and ordinary. But McGuire had good players who played disciplined ball. He had recruited all his starters from his home New York and they played together well.

And he didn't think Kansas had extraordinary players other than Chamberlain. "I was awed watching Chamberlain against San Francisco, but I figured we could concentrate on him and have a chance. In talking to my team, I talked only about Chamberlain, not the rest of their players," he recalls.

"I said he was so good, maybe we better not show up. I said he might stuff some of them through the basket with the ball. I said we didn't have a chance unless our entire team defensed him at all times, and he'd still probably beat us so bad it would be embarrassing to go home.

"Of course, I was kidding them, and they knew it, but it was psyching them up and loosening them up at the same time. Like, hey, let's not take this seriously, it's only a game. But they were gung-ho.

38

"I said I was going to have Tommy Kearns jump center against them and they thought that was funny. He was our smallest player, only five-ten. I told him if he jumped high enough, he might reach Wilt's stomach. Later, he told me he jumped as high as he could, and only hit Wilt's kneecap.

"Oh, yes, he did jump against him. I mean, you know, you're not going to get the tap, anyway, so why waste a big man? Wilt looked freakish standing there so far above our man, and I guess it got to him a little bit. Did Wilt win the tip? Oh, God, yes. But our guys were laughing and loose."

McGuire plotted defensive strategy in which his center, Quigg, would front Wilt and try to keep him from receiving passes. Any time the ball was thrown or shot in his direction, the other forwards would fall in behind him to prevent him from turning in to the basket or following shots. This would free other Kansas players for outside shots, but the coach was willing to take that chance.

He plotted a slowdown offense in which Quigg would shoot from outside in hopes of drawing Wilt out to guard him, while Rosenbluth would swing inside for shots. McGuire says, "If we'd run with them, they'd have blown us out of the building, but we figured if we could neutralize Wilt, we could outshoot them."

Wilt has recalled, "My teammates had trouble getting the ball in to me past their center. When I did get the ball, they seemed to have everyone on their damn team alongside me or behind me. I couldn't get many shots. My teammates had shots, but couldn't hit them. I should have stayed inside on defense, but they were hitting every damn thing they threw up from outside."

With 10,500 fans in Kansas Municipal Auditorium setting up a tremendous din, and millions more listening to the national radiocast, that fourth Saturday in March, 1957, North Carolina spurted to a 9–2 lead with Quigg, a poor scorer, tossing in two from outside. Almost five minutes elapsed before Wilt hit his first basket, but Quigg and forward Pete Brennan brought North Carolina a 19–7 lead.

Harp called a time-out and switched from a zone defense to a man-to-man, which brought Wilt out to guard Quigg. Rosenbluth started to slip inside for open shots. He missed only two shots in the first half, scored 14 points, and helped North Carolina to a 29–22 lead at the intermission. North Carolina had shot almost 65 percent in the first half, compared to less than 28 percent for Kansas.

But Carolina could not keep it up and Wilt could not be contained entirely. Kansas caught up early in the second half, Carolina pulled away again, Kansas caught up again in the late stages. With less than two minutes left, Rosenbluth fouled out. He had 20 points, but Kansas led, 46–43, with 1:43 to play and the tide apparently turned.

Wilt admits he was thinking of the celebration to follow.

However, Gene Elstun missed the free throw that might have iced it. The ball bounced into North Carolina hands and Quigg connected to pull Carolina within one point. Kansas tried to freeze the ball, but lost it when Ron Loneski threw the ball away on an inbound play. Kearns was fouled and hit the free throw to tie it, 46–46, and send an NCAA championship contest into overtime for the first time.

All was madness in that barnlike building then.

In the first overtime, the teams stalled cautiously. Rosenbluth's replacement, little-used Bob Young, sneaked in for a layup to put Carolina in front, but Wilt hit a jumper from the post to tie it at 48–48.

Carolina played for the last shot, but Loneski tied up Brennan and won the jump, but missed the last shot.

By the second overtime, the pressure was so heavy the players felt as if their skulls might cave in. Neither team could score, and when Chamberlain and Brennan wrestled for a loose ball and had to be pulled apart, players from both benches erupted onto the court. There was shoving and pushing before order could be restored.

Cool Kearns opened the third overtime with a set shot from the side. Kansas shot and missed, Kearns got the ball, was fouled and hit two free throws to make it 52–48 as Carolina supporters screamed. The ball reached Wilt underneath, who went up for a shot, made it, was fouled, and made his free throw to make it 52–51.

With 2:30 left, King of Kansas was fouled and hit one free throw to tie the game, but missed the second. Carolina controlled the ball and played for a last shot. But John Parker stole the ball from Quigg and fed it to Elstun. Kearns clobbered him and referee Gene Conway called a deliberate foul. Elstun missed the first free throw but hit the second for a 53–52 lead.

Kearns went up for a shot, but Chamberlain swatted it away. Quigg grabbed it and was fouled with six seconds left. After a time-out, he went to the line and hit his first, then his second. Carolina led, 54–53, and its rooters roared from the stands. The crowd had to be cleared from the court so Kansas could use the last seconds. Elstun arched a high pass toward Wilt under the basket, but Quigg went up in front of him and batted the ball to Kearns, who heaved it into the rafters.

Carolina coach McGuire and his players embraced in joy as their fans swallowed them up in celebration on court, while Kansas, with Wilt, walked off in defeat and disappointment. The giant Chamberlain sat on a stool in his tomblike dressing room later, his head hung between his long legs, and when the reporters reached him and asked him about it later, he said only, "We lost, that's all, we just lost."

Later, he blamed his teammates in general for failing to hit open shots and Loneski in particular for throwing the ball away on the inbound play when Kansas led near the end of regulation time. He has admitted he is more bitter about this defeat than any other in his career because he considers it the first of several that caused him to be labeled "a loser."

"That started it," he has said. "A triple-overtime loss to an undefeated team started it."

At the time, McGuire said, "Jack chopped down the beanstalk and the giant came tumbling down." Today, McGuire says, "I feel bad about it because he got a bad deal out of it. We did a job on him even though he got twenty-three points. Eleven came on free throws. We held him to fifteen shots and six baskets in fifty-five minutes.

"But he didn't have much help. We had the better team. He put pressure on us all the way. Our club had a lot of character. You couldn't defense him that way in pro ball because the other players are too good and would do you in. We played him, not Kansas. We beat Kansas, not him.

"I watched Wilt walk off. I knew how he felt because when I coached St. John's we lost to Kansas in the finals in 'fifty-two out on the coast. There were twelve ballplayers, myself and a priest, and we were all alone when we walked off the court. Clyde Lovellette was the star of Kansas then and everyone was all around him and we were the loneliest team on earth.

"Wilt and I have talked about it many times. There's just no place but first place. Second place isn't anywhere. You're better than all the other teams in the country and you're not good enough. You work and you win and you go so far and you lose and you're nowhere. And it was a waste.

"Now I know there is more to it than that, but the athlete doesn't. Wilt is a proud person and his pride was hurt. He thought he could do it all by himself. When he found out he couldn't, it took something out of him.

"He knows now there's more to it than winning. He knows there is the playing the best you can. He knows it's a team game and the individual sometimes has to lose. But no one else seems to know it. And when he says it, he's accused of copping out.

"He has been, I think, the loneliest man on earth at times."

Wilt says, "No one is as lonely as the loser."

Wilt played well that night. He came through in the clutch several times. But he didn't dominate the game as he had been expected to and as, perhaps, he should have. And that game, twenty years ago, was maybe the most important game he ever played, because it has haunted him.

The myth of Wilt's invincibility was shattered for good.

Although Wilt had played well enough to be voted tourney

42

MVP, he was deeply depressed by the defeat and disenchanted by basketball.

He returned reluctantly for a second season of varsity ball.

Collapsing defenses, dirty tactics, and racial and other abuse depressed him. After one big game, his opposing center asked Wilt if he wasn't ashamed of himself. When Wilt wondered why, the fellow said, "For picking on little guys."

Although Wilt averaged a little more than 30 points a game, he did not show the same intensity as a junior he had as a sophomore. Something seemed to have gotten away from him he could not get back. And his team, with three starters gone from the year before, was not as strong.

After ten straight victories, they lost two-pointers to Oklahoma and Oklahoma State when Wilt was sidelined with an injury he suffered when he was kneed in the groin. He returned, but his third game back Kansas was beaten by Kansas State by four points. Wilt tallied 35, but said he was still below par physically.

Other injuries struck and Kansas lost twice more. Although it was healthy for the finale, when it put Kansas State to rout, Kansas State had clinched the conference crown and tournament berth. With an 18-5 record Kansas was through for the season. And with 42 victories in 50 contests in his two-season collegiate career, Wilt was through, too.

Rumors had spread since his sophomore season that he was thinking of quitting Kansas. He denied them. They continued through his junior year. He continued to deny them. "Iggy" McVay, a representative of *Look* magazine, offered to buy his "retirement" story. Wilt sold it. While it was being written, Wilt continued to deny his departure.

In an early June, 1958, article entitled "Why I Am Quitting College," Wilt said he wanted to play "real basketball" rather than the game he had been playing and was going to arrange an all-star tour because he wanted money to retire his fifty-seven-year-old father from handyman labors and his fifty-six-year-old mother from hiring herself out as a domestic.

43

Although he said then he wasn't sure he would join the NBA, he agreed to sell the story of his first NBA season to the magazine at that time, too.

The tour, which Wilt planned as a confrontation between ten blacks and ten whites, might have been a bloody battle which could have done disservice to the sport, but it never developed.

Abe Saperstein got to him. Roly-poly little Abe owned the Harlem Globetrotters. Secretly, he also owned a piece of the Philadelphia Warriors. Another round little man, Eddie Gottlieb, had the big hunk, and Abe and Eddie were buddies.

Saperstein had offered Wilt a $12,000 contract to come right out of high school to join his black band of comics, but his buddy Gottlieb, worried that Wilt would develop bad habits and be tempted to continue with the clowns, talked him into retracting the offer.

Now, however, with Wilt quitting college with a year to wait before he would be eligible to enter the NBA, Gottlieb did not want Wilt wandering the world on any risky tour of his own. He agreed to back Saperstein in a new bid.

Goose Tatum, who with Marques Haynes had left the Globetrotters to form the Harlem Magicians, and who had hosted and befriended Wilt in Kansas City, wanted Wilt on his team, but Wilt wanted to stay with the NBA bunch, and went with the Trotters.

Wilt toured with them a year, big towns and small, this country and others. He says he enjoyed it immensely, especially the sexual encounters with women around the world, which he describes in detail in his book.

As a gimmick, he played guard with the Globetrotters. Although he has said he does not consider his sport a joke and is a proud person, he participated in many of the team's standard comedy routines, though not in the more extreme ones which many consider Uncle Tomfoolery and demeaning to blacks. Observed Wilt, "The highest-paid performer in the world is Bob Hope. He's a clown. Is that bad?"

He brought the ball downcourt, dribbling behind his back.

He shot two-handed sets from far out. And one play that always wowed the fans was when he'd glide in from his guard position, leap high above the basket, and bat a teammate's shot in with his elbow.

At a time when blacks were just beginning to fill up the NBA, the Globetrotters still had a strong team. Playing their own setup opposing team of white losers or pickup teams, the Globetrotters rarely lost, of course. Wilt insisted, "I learned more traveling with them in one year than I did in three at Kansas."

With Wilt as the star attraction, attendance soared. So much so that Saperstein made a substantial bid for Wilt to continue with his team. Gottlieb was furious. The long friendship of the pair was severed.

Wilt returned to the Trotters for eleven straight summers through 1968, but he wanted to prove himself the supreme player as a pro. He went with Gottlieb's Warriors back in his hometown of Philadelphia.

After three years in Kansas and a year out in the world, Wilt was quite a different person from the lad who had left. Gottlieb says, "He was tougher. He was hungry. He was ready."

Saperstein sneered years later: "Gottlieb goaded him into it. Eddie said Wilt was a star and belonged in the big time. Russell said Wilt was too tall, which challenged him. He didn't really want to go. He told me in Paris he liked being with us and we might get him back. He comes back every summer. My door is always open to him.

"We didn't play him in the pivot where he gets punished. We played him out on the court where he could reach his potential. We didn't put pressure on him. We didn't expect him to score a hundred points a night. We played a fun game. He didn't get his teeth knocked out.

"They call him a loser in the NBA, but he never lost a game with us. We played a fun game. The NBA is no fun for Wilt."

Arriving at the top with the announcement, "I am the greatest all-around athlete in the world," Wilt Chamberlain seemed determined to prove he was far from a "goon," which basketball's first big men, slow and clumsy, were called. An immodest man, but maybe merely more honest about his inner feelings than most, Wilt claimed, "I can run faster and jump higher than any other man in this sport. I also am stronger than any other man in this sport. In fact, I could star in any sport."

Possibly he could have succeeded in several. At a little more than seven feet one inch in height, and 240 pounds in weight when he entered pro basketball, and as much as 300 pounds at times in his NBA career, Chamberlain was massive yet slender and, until his last seasons, seldom showed any fat. He could not move like a little man, but he really could run and jump.

Sportswriter George Kiseda recalls landing in the hospital with Wilt, who was in for a checkup: "This cardiologist came in, checked Wilt's heartbeat, and compared it to a marathon runner's, it was so slow and steady. He said it was a pleasure to listen to."

Chamberlain admits his long-legged, high-waisted, short-tor-soed build helped make him appear awkward. And because he was a poor free-throw shooter, an art that requires rhythm and coordination, not size, he seldom was considered an athlete but, rather, a freak, which understandably infuriated him.

However, he repeatedly pointed to some arresting athletic credentials. In the Police Athletic League, he ran the 440-yard dash in 48.8 seconds, an excellent time for an early teen-ager. In high school, he ran the 440 in 48.6 and the 880 in 1:58.6, also excellent.

He high-jumped six feet six inches, and put the shot more than 47 feet, which were good enough to win Philadelphia Public School League titles his senior year.

In college, he ran the 100 in 10 seconds flat, the 220 in 20.9, and the 440 in 48.9. He surpassed 50 feet in the triple jump. He put the shot 56 feet, farther than any freshman in the nation his first year in college. He high-jumped 6 feet 6¾ inches to tie for first place in the conference meet his third year.

Coaches sought him as a candidate for the Olympics in the triple jump or decathlon, as well as basketball, in 1956 and 1960. He passed up the opportunity in the summer of 1956 when he worked as a bellhop and basketball player in the Catskills. He said he could not wait until the summer of 1960 since he could turn pro in basketball in 1959.

He always claimed he could have been the greatest decathlon performer ever, but he never once competed in the tough two-day, ten-event test of all-around track-and-field excellence. After his rookie season as a pro in the NBA he threatened to retire and tour with a troupe of pros in the decathlon, but abandoned the thought when he became convinced not many people would pay to see it.

Tom Hawkins, who was a high jumper at Notre Dame and competed with and against Wilt in college and pro ranks, says, "He really was a great all-around athlete and track man. He had great strength, surprising speed, and good coordination. He

47

had super potential, especially in the high jump. And in the long jump and triple jump, too. He had a nine-foot stride. He was something else."

Wilt says, "I have great powers of concentration and I've always been willing to work hard. Of course, God gifted me with size. But I built up my strength with weight-lifting. I always could run, but I mastered the technique of shot-putting and high-jumping by working at it. I spent a lot of lonely hours sweating away in the pit to improve.

"People don't realize what I had to put into it to get good. It didn't come easy to me, no more than it does to anyone else.

"I always wanted to be the best at anything I did. I just didn't have the time to do everything right, but if I had taken the time I could have been the best at anything athletic. I could go beyond that. I would like to be the best businessman, too, for example. Now, if I said I wanted to be the best singer or something like that, I am realistic enough to know that would be beyond me. Although I could be a good musician, I am sure. But anything athletic was well within my reach. I have a long reach, my man."

He used to say he could spring from a standing position to take a dime off the top of the backboard, but I couldn't find anyone who ever saw him do it. It is possible, however, as I have seen Spencer Haywood, who is shorter but springier, do it. Paul Silas, who battled Wilt under the backboards many times, says, "Wilt didn't have the spring of some cats like little Calvin Murphy or big Bill Russell, but when he gathered himself, crouched and sprang, he could go to the top of the board. His head often was above the basket when he dunked a shot."

Wilt really could run and loved running almost as much as he loved making bets. He regularly made bets that he could beat this person or that one in running races. Because he seldom extended himself on court, his basketball rivals found this hard to believe.

Elgin Baylor used to tease Wilt that he was slow. Once in New York, when Wilt was still in college, Wilt, Elg, and Oscar

48

Robertson were walking in midtown Manhattan when Wilt challenged the two to a race to the end of the block. They accepted, but when they took off, Elg just stood there, laughing. Wilt whipped Oscar, coattails flying, to the finish, however.

He remembers racing and defeating Chet Walker, a Philadelphia teammate, on the streets of Rome. Wilt remembers beating little Hal Greer and Larry Costello in Philly. Chet backs this up. Wilt also remembers whipping Jerry West on a practice court in LA. West, however, says he doesn't remember any such thing. Wilt says he accepted a challenge from football immortal Jim Brown at a party in LA in the early 1960s and defeated him three straight times.

One reason Chamberlain loved to run was it was one-on-one. He wasn't too much for relay races. He has said he didn't like being dragged down or held back by teammates, as he was in basketball, and he always liked the idea of a straight race between two men to see without argument who was best.

He admits to losing races only to track stars, such as his Kansas teammate Wes Santee, who held the record in the mile run, and roommate Charles Tidwell. "Charlie whipped my ass, but he could have been the best in the world," Wilt has said. "He just wouldn't work at it. He didn't want it enough. He didn't know what he wanted. I tried to help him, but he was a mixed-up young man."

Tidwell committed suicide a few years later.

At the suggestions of his track teammates, Wilt started to lift weights in college. He couldn't wait to get home to challenge the burliest of his buddies and beat them. He got to where he could clean and shoulder 375 to 425 pounds. He developed tremendous strength in his legs, his arms, and his upper body. He claims, and it has been confirmed, that he never lost an arm-wrestling match to powerful shot-putter Bill Nieder or discus champion Al Oerter, both from Kansas. They always claimed his long arms gave him an awesome advantage in leverage.

He turned down offers to turn pro wrestler, even in the

off-seasons. Promoters could see he would have been a great gate attraction, but Wilt could see how phony this sport was and he didn't want to ruin his reputation. He did consider serious offers to box professionally, one as early as 1957 from Jack Hurley, a boxing hustler, who wanted to train Wilt to take on Floyd Patterson, the heavyweight champion.

Ike Richman, Wilt's friend and a part-owner of the Philadelphia franchise, once confirmed, "I sat in on a conference when Wilt was offered three times his basketball salary, money up front, not to box, but to go to camp and learn to box, just to see whether he could do it. He secretly trained at the Harlem YMCA to see for himself, but he didn't take the money. He seldom hit back on the basketball court and it was a chance to take out his frustrations."

Wilt said at the time, "They say I'm not mean enough, but I'd like to see how mean I'd be after I was punched in the nose. Cassius Clay is the greatest fighter in the history of the world. I'd like to fight him because that would be the biggest challenge I could take on. And I like a challenge, whether it would be in basketball or dominoes. I worry about his speed, but I'd have size, strength and reach on him, and the element of surprise. He wouldn't know what to expect from me, but I'd have top trainers teaching me what to expect from him."

Chris Dundee contacted Wilt from Miami late in 1970 with an offer for Wilt to fight Clay, who had become Muhammad Ali by then, as a side show to the Super Bowl in the Orange Bowl. He offered $250,000 or 20 percent of a gate he figured would be about $5 million. But that would have been in two months and Wilt figured that too short a time to get ready.

Long before that, in 1967, a proposal was put to Wilt for him to meet Ali for the title. Jim Brown would have managed him and ex-champ Floyd Patterson's manager, Cus D'Amato, would have trained him for six months with the sole purpose of preparing him to defeat one man, Ali, in one fight. Wilt says he talked to Sugar Ray Robinson's former trainer, George Gainford, and was told it might work.

The fight was to have been in June of 1968 at the Houston Astrodome. Mike Malitz wanted closed-circuit television rights. Wilt claims Ali's camp was concerned about their champion meeting such a bigger man and that Ali's mentor, Herbert Muhammad, vetoed it at the last minute.

Wilt says that in 1971 when Ali was looking for big-money matches, his mentor relented. Wilt says he signed in February for a match in June in the Astrodome for a minimum of half-a-million dollars on condition that Ali defeat Joe Frazier, but that in March Frazier finished that by beating Ali.

Wilt says they still wanted it as an exhibition in July in the Astrodome and made their offer $500,000 *tax-free,* plus a percentage of TV and other income. Supposedly Jack Kent Cooke was against it on the grounds that boxing wasn't the sort of sport Wilt should get into, although Jack was in it as a promoter. Wilt says he waited only until season's end to proceed, however.

He says he and his accountant, Alan Levitt, flew into Houston to sign at a press conference, but pulled out after discovering the tax-free clause was not in the contract. Ali, who was to get a flat million, offered to split the two fees so each would get $750,000. But Alan was against it and argued and convinced Wilt he might be embarrassed and destroy the image he had worked so hard to build up.

Wilt has since said, "I wouldn't have gone into something like this unless I went all the way, so I would have had to give up basketball, which I wasn't at those times ready to do. I was like a groom who was unsure of his step the night before his wedding. At the last minute, I decided not to do it. But I boxed in the gym with boxers like Charlie Powell, who boxed Ali, and I believe I could have beaten Ali. We became friends, but we will neither of us ever know."

There is a picture of Wilt and Ali posed with left jabs extended that makes it look like Ali could not even have reached Wilt. Chamberlain looks so much bigger than Ali it appears it might have been a mismatch. However, there is a boxing saying that has been demonstrated again and again: "The bigger they are, the harder they fall." Ali simply smiled when asked about fighting Wilt and said, "Timberrrr . . ."

Haskell Cohen, the former NBA publicist, once observed, "Wilt doesn't believe anyone can beat him at anything, from boxing to cards. He is a marvelous athlete and a magnificent competitor, and I wouldn't have put anything past him, but him boxing Ali might have been like Ali playing basketball against him. Wilt wouldn't even have considered it except for his vanity. They got to him through his vanity. They almost got him."

Wilt proudly points out he was offered contracts in pro baseball and football, even pro soccer. He says he was a good first-baseman and end on the sandlots, but never tried soccer. He admits he was flattered when he was drafted by an Atlanta team in a new soccer league and made a six-figure offer to learn to play goal for a New York team. He says he was interested in making it in a sport his European friends loved, but didn't want to give up his summers of freedom.

He figured he had too big a strike zone to make it in baseball, but gave serious consideration to football when Hank Stram, the coach of the Kansas City Chiefs, approached him when both were working youth camps. He actually worked out with Stram, who says, "I tried one entire afternoon to overthrow him, but couldn't. In my estimation, Wilt would have been one of the greatest pass receivers in history." Wilt says he would have made too much noise when he was tackled down.

Wilt has averaged as high as 205 in bowling leagues, but has had a hard time breaking par in golf. "That game's just too frustrating for me," says the big guy who stands a long way above the little ball. He has not played a lot of tennis, but his long stride, long reach, and power give him top potential for the game. He is a strong swimmer, though one summer in Hawaii he got caught in an undertow, gashed his leg on coral reefs, and almost drowned before struggling back to the beach.

Obviously, he could be a candidate for the popular, lucrative television "Superstars" competition, but may consider himself past his peak at this point. He would hate to lose, too.

Assigned by *Sport* Magazine to cover the 1976 Olympics along with little Lynda Huey, a sprinter, he was talked into trying racquetball on a Montreal court. She reported, "In the six years I've known Wilt, I had never found anything at which I could beat him. From dominoes to volleyball, backgammon to backward running, he managed to dominate. I knew I could outspell him, but he wouldn't admit that. Here, once and for all, I had my chance to thrash him."

He had never played the game, while she was good at it. He grew intense as she sought to shut him out. At 19–0, he refused to move out of the way so she could get to his shot. "I felt as though he had sprouted roots. I pushed twice, but couldn't budge him. But I hit the ball, anyway." She won the point, and the next one, crashing right into him, to finish him off, 21–0.

"Just a week later, on the USC racquetball courts, Wilt was beating me," she sighs.

Even in retirement, the big guy remains active, especially in volleyball, which he got into when he went to southern California and to which he became addicted when he used it as therapy while recovering from his knee injury in 1969. He was coached by an international star, Gene Selznick. Wilt has played volleyball on the beaches and in the gyms and has toured with his own "Big Dippers."

He says, "It's more fun than basketball, and I could have been better at it than I was in basketball, but I got into it too late."

Going up to bat a winner, called "spiking," Wilt is imposing. Selznick has said, "His hitting has improved. He blocks very well. His defense is strong, too." Teammate Larry Rundle says, "His spiking is super. Blocking, he's a brick wall. But volleyball places a premium on quickness and agility, on diving and changing direction, which are not his strong suits." Pro basketball's Keith Erickson, another volleyball addict, says, "He's a good player, not a great one." Top collegian Tim Hill says, "In volleyball, he's just another player."

Wilt, in retirement, says, "For me this is fun, a great game and a great way to stay in shape. I will be an athlete of sorts to the day I die. I am an old man, close to forty, but I still run and I can still beat some of the girls on my 'Wilt's Wonder Women' track team, though not all. It comes as a shock to some of my young ladies when this old man with his three hundred pounds and size fourteen-D shoes outsprints them. Patty Johnson, the fastest woman hurdler in America, says, 'I'll race you,' and she does, but she doesn't beat me, and she is amazed.

"When I got into volleyball I spent seven or eight hours a day at the beach working hard at mastering it. There is not anything that is beyond me or anything in athletics I could not have conquered if I had started early and dedicated myself to it. The biggest regret I have is that I never had the time or took the opportunity to win the Olympic decathlon title or the world heavyweight boxing title.

"But basketball was my game and I set records in this sport no one will ever equal."

Wilt Chamberlain played in the National Basketball Association for fourteen seasons, and if his records remain for the most part out of reach, his stature as a player remains curiously in controversy. Taller players have come along, though none who were heavier or stronger, and certainly none who combined these physical assets as well.

Wilt was taller, heavier and stronger than George Mikan, who was the dominant center of the NBA's first ten or eleven years, and led the Lakers when they were in Minneapolis to five playoff titles. Mikan, a master of the elbow, pushed around his rivals, but they were not as outstanding as the centers of Wilt's day. Hook-shooting Mikan and Neil Johnston of Philadelphia may have been sharper shooters than Wilt, but they could not get baskets the way Wilt could.

Bill Russell, who reached the NBA three seasons ahead of Wilt and popularized defense, was quicker and defter, but smaller, not as strong, and nowhere near Wilt as a shooter or point-maker. However, he won eleven titles in thirteen seasons.

Kareem Abdul-Jabbar, who arrived after Russell retired and near the end of Wilt's career, was taller and quicker, more agile and a superior shooter, but lighter, nowhere near as strong and not as dominating.

No other center can be compared with Chamberlain.

Dave Cowens, who has come to prominence in recent seasons by leading Boston to titles, is a different sort of center, smaller and quicker, a hustling hard-worker, effective in an unselfish sense in the way Russell was. But he is not the scorer, rebounder, ball handler, shot blocker, or dominating center that Wilt was.

As a collegian who led UCLA to titles, Bill Walton was a lot like Russell, an absolutely unselfish team player, though a superior shooter. But he is a rebellious youngster who does not seem dedicated to his sport, has suffered from injuries, and is far from having proven himself as a pro.

Kent Benson, who led Indiana to the NCAA crown in 1976, plays like Walton, but with greater dedication. However, he has years ahead of him before he can claim a place in the ranks of the super centers. Many marvelous prospects have fallen far short of expectations.

In one sense, Wilt Chamberlain more than lived up to his physical assets and the public expectations of him. As a scorer, rebounder, defender, and playmaker he was spectacular. In another sense he was a disappointment because his teams did not win what was expected of them. Whether this was his fault, whether it was to be blamed on his play or personality, is a point in dispute.

However, Jerry West speaks for many when he says, "When I think of pro basketball, I think of Wilt Chamberlain. He just stood out." Even Wilt's bitterest rival, Russell, says, "He did more to attract attention to basketball, to popularize ours as a big league, than I or Bob Cousy or anyone else." The spectacular Cousy says, "He played every minute of every game, scored more points and grabbed more rebounds than any player ever. I don't know what more anyone could have wanted of him."

Eddie Gottlieb, who has been with the NBA since its beginning, said, "Wilt was the Babe Ruth of pro basketball. George

Wilt Chamberlain in his last season in NBA. *(L.A. Lakers)*

Above: Wilt (5) at Overbrook High School in Philadelphia in 1955 at the age of eighteen. *(Philadelphia Bulletin)*

Opposite: Wilt towers above immortal jockey Eddie Arcaro at awards fete.

Wilt at the University of Kansas, now wearing his famed number 13, in 1956 at twenty. *(U. of Kansas)*

Above: Wilt holds ball away from All-American Lenny Rosenbluth in Kansas' triple-overtime defeat to North Carolina in NCAA final in 1957. *(U. of Kansas)*

Top right: Welcome to pro basketball: Wilt Chamberlain clamps a head-lock on Boston's Don Nelson while Boston's Bill Russell, left, and Bailey Howell, right, and Philadelphia's Luke Jackson (54) look on. *(NBA)*

Right: Wilt loosens up in one of those practice routines he always hated to miss. *(Photography, Inc.)*

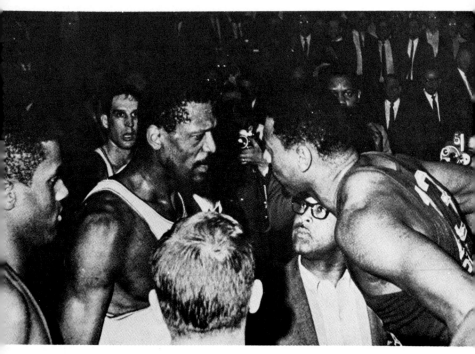

Wilt and Bill Russell, left, the bitter rivals, argue during 1966 playoffs at Philadelphia. *(UPI)*

Right: Abe Saperstein, owner of the Harlem Globetrotters, measures his new star. *(UPI)*

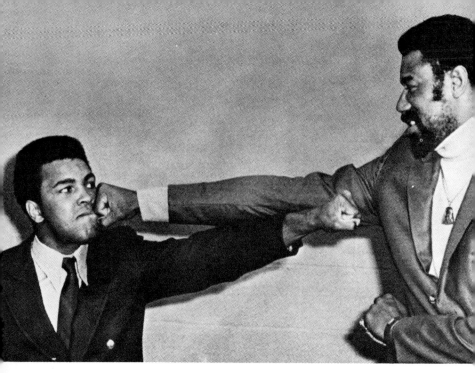

Maybe the two most controversial athletes of our time: Muhammad Ali, left, and Wilt Chamberlain square off during period in which Wilt was considering boxing bid. *(UPI)*

Now in San Francisco, Wilt shoots over Boston's Bill Russell in NBA finals in 1964. *(UPI)*

Wilt Chamberlain, who returned to Philadelphia in 1965. *(Malcolm Emmons, Philadelphia 76ers)*

Right: Wilt with 76ers finger-rolls one in over Darrall Imhoff and other Lakers in 1966. *(Photography, Inc.)*

Right: On a happy day, when Wilt was introduced to the media as the newest Los Angeles Laker, coach Bill van Breda Kolff, left, and Elgin Baylor and owner Jack Kent Cooke, right, flank the big guy. The coach and star were not so happy with Wilt later. *(Photography, Inc.)*

After winning first NBA championship, Wilt and other 76ers celebrate with champagne in 1967. Wilt is drinking from Luke Jackson's bottle. Above him are Dave Gambee, Wally Jones and Hal Greer. To the right are coach Alex Hannum and Larry Costello. *(UPI, Philadelphia 76ers)*

A pleased-as-punch Jack Kent Cooke. *(James Roark, L.A. Herald-Examiner)*

Chamberlain has rebounded and fed off to Elgin Baylor to start a fast break as Boston players begin to get back on defense in 1969 game. *(Wen Roberts, Photography, Inc.)*

The assists man, ball-handling and setting picks in the pivot, Wilt joins with Jerry West to squeeze off a foe as Zelmo Beaty of Atlanta waits in 1972. *(Wen Roberts, Photography, Inc.)*

Wilt falls back to shoot over outstretched reach of leaping Bill Russell in 1972 confrontation. *(Wen Roberts, Photography, Inc.)*

Mikan did much to make it a big league in our early days, but it was still struggling until Chamberlain came along. Russell won more, but he didn't mean nearly as much at the box office. Wilt was box office. He was big on the court and at the gate. He may have been controversial, but controversy sells tickets.

"Wilt was just outstanding. Physically, he was superior to any athlete who has yet come along. There may have been bigger football players, but none had Wilt's trim build. Imagine a three-hundred-pounder with a thirty-two-inch waistline! He was the first seven-footer who was not a freak. Maybe he wasn't a ballet dancer, but who buys tickets to ballet? For a big guy, Wilt could get around."

Fred Schaus, who coached against Wilt and managed him, says, "Wilt had height and muscular weight. Some football players are bigger, but most have excess weight. Wilt always was astonishingly trim. He had long, powerful arms and awesome strength. He just scared hell out of you, frankly. Other big men might beat you, but Wilt intimidated you."

Elgin Baylor, Jerry West, and Guy Rodgers played with and against Wilt. Elg says, "I could do things Wilt could never do, but I could never dominate a game the way Wilt could. No player ever could." Jerry says, "No small man can dominate a game the way a big man can, and Wilt was the most dominating big man ever. Smaller men may have been quicker and more agile, but Jabbar is the only man his height who has been, and Jabbar is not as heavy or strong or aggressive and dominating as Wilt was." Rodgers says, "Wilt had more moves than any big man ever. He was a big man who could play with little men."

However, Dolph Schayes, who coached him, once said, "If it wasn't for Wilt's size he wouldn't make this league." And Paul Seymour, who coached against him, said, "All Wilt has going for him is his height. That's why I always hated to lose to him." Another coach comments, "Take six inches and sixty pounds off Wilt and you would have taken him right out of the league. He was a goon, not a player. He was a monster so he was hard to handle. You can't compare him with a Jabbar, who is much more of a complete player."

Sportswriter Jim Murray wrote, "He is the Eiffel Tower in shorts, and about as maneuverable." Columnist Dick Young commented, "He is not a great player, he is not even a good player, he is just a big basketball player."

Rick Barry says, "Wilt worked on you with his size, but comparing him with players is ridiculous. Basketball is a badly constructed game. The court is too small, the basket too low, and a big man has too much of an advantage. Wilt was better than most big men, but he still didn't have the skills of hundreds of smaller men. Real basketball skills often are wasted in this game."

Rod Hundley says, "This is a game of hands and Wilt had the worst hands of any player I ever saw. He had strong hands. I've heard of him palming a bowling ball. But he had hard hands, stiff hands. Guys like Guy Rodgers learned to loop those soft, high passes in to him, because he couldn't catch a hard pass. So you couldn't make the fast, sharp pass to him. If he played with Pete Maravich his hands would have been broken. If he played with me, he'd have been killed. He was as agile as an elephant."

Frank McGuire says, "I think when Wilt went into weight-lifting he sacrificed finesse for strength. I think as he stayed with it and built himself up he lost a little of his shooting touch and gained a little in power."

Joe Mullaney says, "The stronger he got, the worse he shot. He tried to drill the ball through the hoop, and he never got a soft roll on the hoop. I think this more than anything hurt his free-throw shooting."

Fred Schaus says, "He never had a soft touch, but he seemed to be trying to overpower the basket more and more as he went along. However, I think he decided strength was more important in pro play and he used his size and strength to tremendous advantage."

Comments Jerry West, "The thing with Wilt was he was

always there, looming up like a mountain between you and the basket. You couldn't move him. Did you ever try to move a mountain? And when he wanted to get by you, it was like a mountain falling on you."

Wilt's endurance was incomparable. With the exception of the one season when he had knee surgery, he missed only nine games his other thirteen seasons. He played every game eleven of his seasons, including his last three when he was supposed to be an old man. And while he fouled out of a couple of games as a collegian, he never fouled out of even one game in his complete pro career. Russell fouled out of twenty-four in thirteen seasons. Jabbar fouled out of eight his first season alone.

Wilt insists, "I didn't foul out because I didn't foul. I played as aggressively when I had four or five fouls on me as when I had none, but I always played clean." Others dispute this. Former Philadelphia sportswriter Jack Kiseda says, "He developed the fadeaway to avoid fouling. You could see Wilt's game change when he got in foul trouble. He held back. The streak became bigger than the game. And no official seemed willing to dare break it."

Wilt played almost 48,000 minutes in his 1,045 regular-season games, a record. Plus more than 7,500 minutes in playoffs.

Aside from not fouling out of games, Wilt did not want to sit out any part of his games. The NBA plays 48-minute games and Wilt averaged almost 46 minutes a game for his full 14 seasons. He averaged 46 minutes a game his first season and 43 his last. He averaged 48½ minutes his third season. Impossible? Not with overtimes. It will remain a record forever.

He suffered most of his career from arthritic legs and a stomach ailment which eventually was treated as pancreatitis, but he convinced coaches he would stiffen up if he received a rest.

Wilt once said, "It was the only way I could play. I got in a rhythm and lost it if I stopped. And I did stiffen up. It wasn't as if there was someone better behind me." Halftimes? "They were hard on me," admitted Wilt, who sweat so much he was

59

the only player who changed into a new jersey every intermission. Bill van Breda Kolff, who coached Wilt a couple of stormy seasons, once said, "Wilt was insulted if you suggested a sub might take his place for even a few minutes. Taking him out was like taking your own life."

Frank McGuire recalls a game in New York when he was coaching Philadelphia with Wilt. "Eddie Gottlieb got me over to the press table and asked me to put in the sub center so he could see him. A hook shooter from Northwestern. I said it wasn't safe. I didn't know what the guy could do in a game. I hadn't seen him outside of practice all season.

"Eddie blew up. He said, 'Jeez, Frank, we're twenty-seven points ahead with four minutes to play. If you can't use the guy now, let's sell him so we can get something out of him.'

"Then I blew up. I said, 'Eddie, you promised never to interfere in my coaching.' But the fact is I felt guilty. Wilt was so sensitive I didn't want to upset him by taking him out. And he was so consistent game after game there never was a need to take him out. He didn't need a sub.

"I wish I could remember the sub's name. Poor guy. When you were Wilt's sub, you became a forgotten man. It must have been the worst job in the history of sports. Even Lou Gehrig's sub must have gotten in more innings during Gehrig's iron-man streak in baseball."

Of course, Wilt paced himself. He seldom used his speed. He seemed to proceed at half-speed. At first, when he was offensively oriented, he was slow getting back on defense and sometimes didn't get back. When he stressed defense later, he was sometimes not in on the offense at all.

Rod Hundley cracks, "Wilt was the greatest half-court player in history. When they talked about him coming back at forty, I said the way he played he could play until he was fifty." A former teammate admits, "It's discouraging to hustle hard up and down and have Wilt trailing the play or watching from the other end."

However, Wilt has asked, "Who does go a hundred percent?

60

John Havlicek hustles hard all the time. I can't play with the enthusiasm of a Havlicek. That's not my style. Oscar Robertson was the laziest-looking player ever, but he got the job done. That was his style. He didn't get criticized for it the way Wilt did. No one ever did. Dave Cowens? A lot of guys waste motion.

"Look, my man, Wilt could see if a ball was an inch out of his reach and wouldn't go for it. I'm not going to give it the grandstand try. I'm not going to waste myself. In college you go full blast because you can rest tomorrow. In pro ball, you've got a game tomorrow. Instead of forty minutes, you've got forty-eight. Instead of thirty games, you've got eighty.

"Hey, my man, if I lead the league in scoring and rebounding and I'm supposed to be saving myself, I take that as a compliment to my ability. All that matters is if a man does more than anyone else, and Wilt always did. I placed myself so I could put it on the court when it counted. I used my head as well as my body. I paced myself, but I'm not the only player who picked his spots."

Of course, he was not. Russell lagged behind a lot, too. So does Jabbar. Bill Sharman, who played with Russell and has coached Jabbar and Chamberlain, says, "All big men let the play go to the other end at times. They just can't sprint up and down the way a little man can. A coach has to accept it." Fred Schaus says, "You knew he was saving something for the fourth quarter when games were won and lost."

But another coach says, "Chamberlain won fewer games in the fourth quarter than any important player ever. Maybe Wilt would have been better if he'd taken his rests and gone all-out all the time he was out there. It's true that the Jabbars do it, too, but they're stealing from their teammates, cheating those who use all their ability, and destroying team spirit. The Wilts and Jabbars don't win many titles, you notice."

Red Auerbach has said of his title-taking center Cowens, "Dave doesn't have what a Wilt had, but he makes more of what he has."

61

Cowens comments, "Wilt didn't always work hard, and you could take advantage of that. It really bugged him when I came in running around like crazy. He wasn't used to chasing centers. He was the strongest player I faced by far, but you could neutralize his strength with speed. He might have been a fast straightaway runner, but he didn't have quick moves and couldn't go laterally. You knew he wasn't going to roll off you.

"He was a lot taller than me, but I was successful by going at his knees. A smaller man can cut down a big man by knocking him in the knees. Of course you took a beating around the head. But he didn't have the temperament to be brutal, so you could rough him up without fear of retaliation. He had this thing about not fouling out, you know."

Former Laker manager Pete Newell says, "Wilt's biggest weakness was you could foul him and he wouldn't foul you back. But back in college ball clubs were fouling out their centers and Wilt was sinking free throws and his side was winning. They were really roughing him up, but I took a different tack: Let sleeping dogs lie, you know.

"When I was coaching Cal we played Kansas at Lawrence and I told my center and other players to play it clean, to defense Wilt as well as you can, but every time he makes a basket you say 'nice play' and things like that to him. Well, we lulled him. He didn't go to the free-throw line but three or four times and only scored fourteen points or so.

"I don't think he ever enjoyed a game more.

"But the worse he got shooting free throws, the more his foes fouled him. And he got worse and worse, so he was butchered after a while as a pro."

Chick Hearn, a Laker official and broadcaster, says, "When he first came into the league, the way they beat on that poor youngster was absolutely awful. He talked about quitting, but he took it and came back for more. They never really stopped pounding on him.

"One of the amazing things about his stamina was that he always had giants leaning on him. Of course, he was a giant leaning back, but you only have to watch centers shove each other in the pivot for a few minutes to imagine how tiring it must be to do it for forty-eight minutes."

George Kiseda and Jack Kiser, who covered Wilt in Philadelphia, speak unkindly about the officiating. Kiseda says, "I feel the officials definitely changed the unwritten rules in regard to what was and was not permissible on the court with Wilt. If players did to people on the street what they did to Wilt on the court, they'd have been arrested for assault.

"The worst was Wayne Embry, who was an enormous man and leaned on Wilt like he was trying to break down a door. Others followed suit once they found out they could get away with it. Wilt complained to the refs, but they didn't listen. He really didn't complain a lot.

"When they had to get the ball back, they'd foul the worst free-throw shooter, Wilt. I've seen players literally chase Wilt all over the court, even out of bounds, to foul him. It got to be a joke."

Kiser says, "The refs were all five-seven or five-nine or five-eleven, and they enjoyed seeing this seven-one guy get beat up. When Jabbar came into the league he screamed bloody murder that there was a double standard of officiating, one for him and one for the others, but actually it started with Wilt, and now it applies to every outstanding big man."

Jerry West says, "Wilt could have stopped it, but he didn't. While it isn't his fault, it changed the game. If he had retaliated, the refs would have cracked down. But he didn't, and the practice of physical defense became commonplace and spread. Now everyone hand-guards everyone else, and even the little guard gets pushed and pulled and cut down.

"It's a shame because we're all cheated of seeing the skilled players perform the way they were meant to. Now it's a brawl, not basketball."

Kiseda adds, "Russell played basketball against Wilt at first, but as he slowed down, he got physical, too. One reason Wilt's teams didn't win as much as they might have was because he

63

let his opponents pound on him. Both Neil Johnston and Alex Hannum pleaded with Wilt to retaliate, but he wouldn't."

At the time, Johnston said, "They're getting away with murder. It would help if he would bop a few." McGuire says, "I didn't tell him to hit anyone, but we talked about elbows, you know what I mean?"

Wilt said, "I've never thrown an elbow in my life. You know with my size my elbows are weapons and I could kill someone."

Schayes sneered, "He knew his way with elbows."

Wilt smiled and said, "I was a lover, not a fighter." The smile fading, he said, "The officials did discriminate against me and it hurt me and it hurt the game, but it's not in my nature to hurt people. It was hard, but I had to learn to live with it.

"Ike Richman used to complain I lacked the killer instinct, and I guess I did, but I didn't let it affect my play. It was a tribute to me. It was the only way they thought they could stop me. But they couldn't stop me, anyway. I never felt punching anyone would help."

Kiseda says, "The rough play infuriated his teammates more than it did him. Brawls were always breaking out around him, but he rarely joined in them. He probably broke up more fights than any athlete who ever lived. He'd pick up people and throw them aside or hold them at arm's length."

Player Paul Silas says, "I was about to get into an altercation with Happy Hairston one time and I felt someone from behind put his arms around me and lift me up. I'm a big man, you know, but it was like a vise clamped on me. It was Wilt. It was an awesome feeling, and I was absolutely helpless. After that, I knew his strength was real."

Tom Hawkins says, "I haven't doubted his strength since I was taunting him one time and he told me to grab hold of a basketball with both hands and hold my body stiff. When I did, he gripped the ball in his hands, he crouched down, he sprang up, and I felt him lifting me right off the floor. I mean I'm no featherweight. I'm six-five and two hundred fifteen pounds. It was an unbelievable feeling. When we got to the basket, I let go, and he dunked the ball. I feel like he'd have dunked me with it.

"He didn't lose his temper often, but when he did, wow! He picked up Bailey Howell once and threw him through the air from the top of the key to midcourt, and Howell was another big guy."

His teammate Al Attles was in on that one, and Wilt carried him off to cool him off. He picked up Al the way a father would a child and walked off with him. Another time the writer saw him lift and toss Wayne Embry, who may have been the beefiest player ever.

Chick Hearn recalls, "I saw him throw Bob Lanier three rows into the stands one night, and Bob probably is the biggest player in basketball today. I never saw him have a fight, though I know he had one or two. Tom Meschery challenged him one night, but Wilt wouldn't fight."

Meschery says, "This was a tough game in the early days and there were guys who wouldn't take anything from anyone. Tom Heinsohn and I were two of them. Tom and I both challenged Chamberlain and we're still alive to talk about it because he didn't take us up on it."

Mendy Rudolph, the former referee, recalls, "Zelmo Beaty yanked at Wilt's pants one night and Wilt's arm shot out and Zelmo flew across the court like he'd been shot from a cannon. I thought Wilt might have killed him, and I rushed to Zelmo and told him not to move, not to twitch a muscle, until a doctor could get to him. Somehow, he survived."

Rod Hundley remembers, "Once in LA one of my Laker teammates called Wilt a nigger from the bench when he was with Philadelphia.

He challenged the whole bench. I remember him saying, 'C'mon, who said it? I'll take you all on.' And no one moved a muscle. Or called him 'nigger' again."

No one played Wilt tougher than Clyde Lovellette, who drove two of Wilt's teeth up into his gums with an elbow Wilt's rookie year. Chamberlain remembered. In the 1964 playoffs,

65

Clyde was working Wilt over when a foul was called on him. Clyde confronted Chamberlain, contending he, Wilt, really deserved the foul. Wilt exploded with a straight right hand to Lovellette's lantern jaw. Clyde went down as though hit with a hammer and had to be helped off the court.

There are those who say Wilt wouldn't fight because he was afraid to fight, that all his talk about not wanting to hurt anyone was a cover-up for cowardice, but most who watched Wilt over the years believe otherwise because they saw him wade in to break up brawls, and those who saw him clout Clyde still speak of it with awe. It is a legend in the league.

Asked about it in the dressing room that night, Clyde, rubbing his sore jaw, said, "Hey, I don't want to say anything to make him mad." Asked about it since, Clyde, later an Indiana sheriff, said, "Wilt hit like the heavyweight he was."

Wilt admits that he developed his technique of grabbing a rebound with one hand and smacking it into the other hand to make a sound like a gun going off to intimidate people. He also jammed the ball down through the hoop with force for the same reason.

Rod Hundley recalls, "I treasure a picture of myself cringing with fear and covering my head with my hands as Wilt is going over me to slam the ball through."

John Havlicek has said, "There isn't a player who played Wilt who wasn't afraid Wilt would ram the ball through the basket right into their faces. Players just peeled away."

Former Laker trainer Frank O'Neill says, "Wilt rammed the ball through the hoop so hard he was always hurting his hands and fingers. He tore the tendons in his fingers many times until they were twisted out of shape. He played in pain all the time. It hurt when he grabbed a rebound, but he never griped about it.

"Wilt may have griped about a lot of things, like the play of his teammates and things like that, but he never complained of pain. He even played in the playoffs once with a broken hand, the one we won, and didn't tell anyone. But he'd grab those rebounds like he was going to squeeze the air out of the ball, and no one could get it away from him."

Bill Sharman says, and other coaches and players agree, "You can argue about Wilt's ability in this area or that, but there is little argument about him being the best rebounder of all time. He beat Bill Russell and everyone else game after game and year after year off the boards. I think he improved later in his career when he was with us at what he did with the rebound when he got it—making the fast outlet pass to get a fast break going, for example—but he always could get more rebounds than anyone else."

George Kiseda says, "I don't care if you're eight feet one, you have to work for rebounds, and Wilt paid the price in pain others would not pay. Jabbar won't pay that price, but Wilt paid dearly. I agree he had bad, hard hands. Wilt hated to hear that. But his strength made up for it."

Paul Silas, the best rebounding forward of recent times, says, "Wilt took up so much space under the boards and he was so strong and hard to move out of position, he was hard to beat to the ball. Sometimes, of course, you might anticipate the rebound better or get into position better, but Wilt was smart, much smarter than people realize, one of the smartest players ever, and he always seemed to have a sixth sense of where the ball was going and where to go to get in position for it.

"If Wilt had a weakness, it was that he had to gather himself for a leap. He wasn't a quick leaper, and he couldn't go right back up a second time the way some can. But he usually got the ball the first time."

Wilt has said, "When I wanted the ball, I got it. I don't care how rough it was underneath or how it hurt, I hit those boards. I also blocked more shots than anyone ever realizes. I was blocking shots before they kept count."

Jerry West says, "The toughest adjustment many college stars have to make when they come into pro ball is to stay on their game when big guys like Wilt block their shots. It was scary the way he'd ram the ball right back into your face or swat it into the seats, and it was embarrassing, but if you changed your shooting style, you were dead.

"You just have to learn to accept a certain amount of blocked shots. The shooter has the advantage. He knows when he's going to shoot, and if he shoots quickly, it's hard to block it without goal-tending it. But Wilt was so big it was hard to get the ball up over him."

Red Auerbach says, "Only one guy knew how to block shots and that was Bill Russell. I call Wilt Chamberlain and Kareem Abdul-Jabbar swatters. The only player who knows how to block a shot properly today is Bill Walton." Rick Barry says, "Russell took the ball away from you. Wilt took only the shot, since he swatted it out of bounds and you got the ball back." John Havlicek says, "Russell was the best shot-blocker, but Wilt was next best."

Paul Silas points out, "Wilt was stronger, Russell was quicker. In close to the basket, Wilt was much more intimidating, but Bill had a wider range and he blocked shots ten feet to either side of the basket and still got back." One Laker adds, "You just didn't dare go in for layups on Wilt, but you do on Jabbar. Our appreciation of Wilt has gone up since he's gone and Jabbar has come in because we realize now how much more intimidating Wilt was. There's no comparison."

Jerry West says, "Defense is as important as offense, but most don't realize it. I was a good defensive player, but famous for my shooting. But I'm prouder of my defense than of my offense. But no guard, no other player can control the game on defense the way the big center can. Frankly, Russell was the most dominating defensive player ever. He worked at it more than Wilt did. But later in his career, when Wilt concentrated on it more, he was almost as good.

"The thing was, he created a team defense. I could take chances on steals and things like that because I knew Wilt was behind me, blocking up the middle, and anyone who got by me still had to get by Wilt. He took the under-the-basket game away from our foes."

A Laker adds, "Jabbar simply does not work at defense the way Russell did or Wilt did. Jabbar is more offensively oriented. After his early years, Wilt began to balance his game defensively and offensively. With his height and quickness, Jabbar is a good defensive player, but he is not nearly what he should be. Wilt was slower, but bigger and better. Not as good as Russell, but who was?"

Alex Hannum once said, "If you concentrate on one phase of the game, you're going to be better at it. Russell was devastating on defense, but he was ordinary on offense. Wilt went both ways well."

Frank McGuire says, "Teams came to depend on Wilt on defense as well as offense. For a guy who was supposed to be pacing himself and not going end-to-end, he somehow did a job at both ends."

Bill Sharman says, "Teams could gamble on aggressive defense with both Bill and Wilt behind them. Bill was the best on defense, but Wilt was also outstanding offensively."

Wilt says, "The press and the people don't seem to know it, but I think that in basketball it was well known I was as good defensively as offensively, and offensively I was the best."

One of the things Wilt did on offense that was not noticed much was set screens. When teams started to work off Wilt by giving the ball to him and going for shooting position, he was enormously effective. In his early years, he would turn to shoot, but later he would look for the pass first. The Laker photo file is full of pictures of Wilt holding the ball in one hand, blocking a defender while a teammate slides by him.

West says, "If he had moved up and down, side to side more, he would have been more effective, but even standing still in the pivot we used him well. Sometimes, he clogged up the middle, however."

Wilt says, "I was supposed to be selfish, but I'm the only center who ever led the league in assists, and I got more assists than any center ever. I was a shooter, but I passed off."

Wilt's stature as a pure shooter is controversial because of his poor record from the free-throw line. The best hit 90 percent of their free throws. Other good ones hit 80 percent. In Wilt's best year, he hit 61 percent. In his worst year, he hit 42 percent. Three other years he hit 44 percent. In his career he barely bettered 50 percent.

He shot more free throws, 11,862, and missed more, 5,805, than any pro ever. He shot underhand and overhand, one-handed and two-handed, from in front of the basket and to the side of it, from right on the line to behind it, hard and soft, and nothing helped.

It troubled Wilt from the start of his career. Early in his pro days, Warrior owner Ike Richman hired an expert, Cy Kasselman, to help. It didn't help. Ike hired a psychologist and a hypnotist and paid Wilt $100 an hour so Wilt would take treatment, but it didn't pay off. Another expert, Bunny Levitt, tried and gave up. Bill Sharman was the best free-throw shooter in early NBA history, but when he coached Wilt he couldn't correct his faults. Sharman says, "By the time I got to him it wasn't a physical problem. If he had been grooved one way early in his career, he could have been effective, but he developed a mental block."

The writers ridiculed Wilt and the fans hooted him about it. "He hated to go to the line," a teammate comments. "He was embarrassed by it. And he should have been. He wouldn't have been roughed up so much if he'd hit free throws. As many points as he scored, he still cost his teams ten games a season by his failures to score on free throws. There isn't a player in the league who ever regarded Wilt as a shooter or even as an athlete because his inability to sink shots standing alone ten feet from the basket betrayed him." This is the consensus.

Wilt says, "I couldn't shoot underhand in the old-fashioned way Rick Barry still does because bending down bothered my bad knees. Weight-lifting may have made me too strong. But I always had a tendency to shoot too flat and too hard one-handed, which is why I started standing back from the line. It wasn't so bad when I was shooting from the field, jumping and

70

shooting down, but it was bad standing still at the line shooting up.

"Also, Phog Allen at Kansas taught me to put English on the ball to spin it off the backboard on my field shots and I spun my free shots too much. I could see the problems. If someone like Neil Johnston had taken the time to teach me when he was coaching me early in my career I might have overcome it. But he couldn't be bothered.

"After a while, I'll admit I became psycho about it. It bothered me that people paid so much attention to this and so little to the rest of my game when I was scoring so many points from the field. I had a better shooting percentage from the field. The best ever, in fact. As far as that goes, I must have been a ninety percent free-throw shooter in high school. I got screwed up somewhere along the line and couldn't straighten out. I practiced. Hell, I won bets from West and other good free-throw shooters by hitting nine out of ten in practice, ten or fifteen in a row at times. But I'd get in the game and it would be the same old thing, so I started to say the hell with it.

"Sure I was embarrassed by it, but I'll tell you one thing, I didn't miss many in the clutch. I don't know if I concentrated more under pressure or not, but when games were on the line and other guys would have choked, I came through."

West says, "He was the worst free-throw shooter I ever saw, but he did do better in the clutch, and he did do well in practice. As far as that goes, he was a super practice shooter. Early in his career he was accurate with a jump shot and a fall-back shot, and later he used a finger-roll shot, reaching up to the basket, but he could even hit outside set shots in practice. In games, however, he primarily got points from right underneath the basket, which is why his shooting percentage was so high."

George Kiseda says, "Wilt used to shoot straightaway one-handers from twenty feet in practice and he never did in games. I asked him why, one time, and he said because the day of the seven-foot forward was coming and he wanted to be ready. That was his sense of humor, but the fact is he never practiced his game shots in practice, he just fooled around. He was hell in games of 'Horse.' "

Rod Hundley asks, "How much practice do you need for a dunk shot? He had other shots, but most of his points came on dunks and taps and stuff like that from right underneath."

Bob Cousy says, "Wilt came into the league with a good jump shot from around the key, and his fallaway was almost unstoppable, but you wanted him under the basket, not outside." Tom Hawkins says, "I saw him bank ten or eleven of those fadeaways in a row. But he was criticized for it because it carried him away from the basket." Frank McGuire notes, "Because of the criticism he eventually stopped using it, but when he was with me he hit fifty percent of them and that was good enough for me."

Although he seldom showed a hook shot which was the trademark of the big centers when Wilt showed up on the scene, Wilt insists, "I had all the shots. I beat the butt off Baylor and all the rest in shooting practice, shooting all kinds of shots. But in games, I just used those that worked the best for me."

But Rick Barry says, "He may have been a better shooter before I saw him, but he didn't have many shots when I faced him. He didn't need shots. That finger-roll nonsense was just a reaching layup. He could go through people and over their heads and put the ball in the basket. Don't call him a shooter, call him a scorer." A majority agree.

As a scorer he was unsurpassed. Officials legislated against him, widening the free-throw lane from 12 to 16 feet and lowering to three seconds the time a player could spend in there, but it didn't stop him. His most prominent records include 100 points in a game, 4,029 in a season, and 31,419 in a career. Runner-up Oscar Robertson is almost 5,000 points behind on the career count. Throw in 3,607 points in playoffs and Wilt's pro total comes to more than 35,000 points.

Wilt led the league in scoring seven straight seasons. No one else has led it more than three times. He averaged 50 points a game one season. Jabbar's one-game high has been just 55. No one else has averaged even 40. Wilt averaged close to 40 the entire first half of his career. The last half he shot a lot less, but still concluded his career with an average above 30, a record for 10-year men. Jabbar is fractionally higher, but must endure awhile.

Wilt took 63 shots in one game and none in a couple of others later. He averaged almost 40 shots a game at his peak, but fell off to 14 near the finish. He was always accurate, however. He led the league in accuracy nine times, five times in a row. Only in his first season did he hit less than 50 percent of his shots. No one had ever shot 50 percent previously. Four seasons he surpassed 60 percent. His 72 percent one season is the record. His 54 percent for his career again is shaded so far only by Jabbar.

Wilt scored 50 or more points in 127 games, 60 or more in 32, 70 or more in 6. He has the 5 highest single-game totals of all time, 15 of the first 16, and 43 of the first 50. Elgin Baylor's 71 is the sixth highest total; he appears in the first 50 three times, and is the only other to appear more than once. Mikan's high was 61 and that is 30th. Jabbar's 55 doesn't even make the first 50. Russell doesn't even make the book.

Wilt's career total of 23,924 rebounds stands 2,200 higher than Russell's and almost 10,000 ahead of anyone else. Throw in 3,913 in playoffs and you push Chamberlain's pro career count to close to 28,000. He led in rebounding 11 times, Russell only 4 times. Wilt's one-season total of 2,149 and average of 27 are records, also. His career average of 22 is stunning. He broke Russell's one-game record of 49 with 55 in a game against Russell. He hauled in 40 or more 14 times, and 5 came in games against Russell. However, his 10 highest totals did come in home games. Still, of the 40 top games, Wilt had 22, Russell 14.

No lifetime statistics are available on blocked shots, but Wilt and Russell certainly are the top two.

Wilt is seventh in career assists with 4,643. Russell is not anywhere near the lifetime leaders. Wilt is the only center who comes close. In fact, there is not even a forward in the top ten.

All but Wilt are or were guards. Wilt set a record for centers with 630 assists one season, then surpassed it with 702 the next season when he became the only center ever to lead the league in this category.

Wilt's statistics are spectacular, yet many observers are of the opinion that he should be even farther ahead of his competition. George Kiseda comments, "Bill Russell spent his entire career in Boston, while Wilt went from town to town. Russell was much more popular than Wilt and he got a big break from the scorers. Russell got breaks in Boston you wouldn't believe. He didn't do as well on the road as he did at home, but he did better than Wilt. We kept track of rebounds for a while and the difference between our totals and the 'official' ones were scary. And the guards got the assists, not the centers. They played Wilt with a rigged deck, but couldn't take his points away from him."

Many agree. Wilt, for one. "I rarely got a fair count," he has commented.

Nevertheless, the numbers are numbing.

Pete Newell was just one of many who pointed out, "Whatever Wilt set out to do, he did. At first he wanted to score more points than anyone ever, and he certainly did that. It's amazing that he also was able to outrebound everyone ever, too. When he wanted to prove he could pass as well as shoot and was unselfish, he set assist records. When he concentrated on defense, he dominated in that. There really never has been another performer who was so completely able."

Wes Unseld was one of several players who observed, "I had success against Wilt at times because he was under wraps at times, but I always had the feeling he could do anything he wanted whenever he wanted."

Fred Schaus says, "It's unfair to expect a player to perform at his peak eighty or more games a season, season after season, but when Wilt turned it on, he just tore games up."

Former Laker publicist Jim Brochu notes, "Sometimes Wilt would do nothing for forty minutes, then turn it on and turn a game around in a few minutes. He could do it when he wanted."

Dave Cowens says, "I don't know why he didn't turn in on me and go to the basket more, because I couldn't have stopped him, but late in his career he just didn't."

Tom Hawkins was one of several who said, "He was driven, as if he always had something to prove. The spotlight was on him every time he stepped on court, and it got hot at times."

Wilt has said, "If I scored thirty, they asked why I didn't score fifty. If I scored fifty, they asked why I shot so much. If I didn't shoot, they asked me why I wasn't putting out. I played defense and they didn't notice. I led the league in assists and they said I was selfish.

"I am the only player in the history of this sport who ever changed his game completely season after season just to suit my teams, and yet they said I was selfish and I wasn't a team player. It was stupid, but when they asked me not to shoot, I didn't shoot. I am the best shooter ever and a better shooter than West or Baylor, so it was stupid to pass to them, but I did it, and it still didn't satisfy anyone."

Eddie Gottlieb says, "When Wilt was scoring fifty points a game he was the best player in the history of this sport, and it didn't make sense to stop him from shooting." Frank McGuire agrees, "They say Wilt was more effective when he passed off, but I say you're better off having a fifty percent shooter shoot than a forty percent shooter. If his teammates couldn't see that, they were the ones who weren't playing team ball."

But Rick Barry says, "Wilt was the single most selfish player I've seen in this sport. He didn't stop shooting until he got older and injuries caught up to him. He didn't change his game for his team; he did it to survive. And whether he was leading in points or assists, he always had to get the credit. I'm glad I didn't play with him because I don't think I could have."

Barry was braver than most players, who were reluctant to be quoted. One said, "The numbers are for the birds. Wilt piled up the stats, but when it counted, he didn't come through."

Another said, "He was the biggest player this sport ever had, but he disappeared when the game was on the line." A third said, "He'd play lousy, but pile up the stats, and you were surprised when you read them later because you knew he hadn't put out."

Bill Russell says, "The only numbers that matter are wins and losses. My personal statistics did not compare to Wilt's, but my teams surpassed his. If I knew one thing about playing this game it was that you have to play it as a team. I don't care if a man is a thirty-percent shooter, if he's in a position to take his best shot, you have to give it to him. If you don't take care of your teammates, baby, they won't take care of you, they won't be there when you need them. Wilt took care of Wilt. Wilt speaks of wisdom, but he was no mental marvel."

Jerry West admits, "I don't want to rap Wilt because I believe only Bill Russell was better, and I really respect what Wilt did. But I have to say he wouldn't adjust to you, you had to adjust to him." A teammate mutters, "There haven't been many players who wanted to play with him." Another says, "He won the statistical titles and lost the team titles."

Red Auerbach adds, "All I can say is look at the list of champions. Our Russell teams are there eleven times, Wilt's teams twice." Another coach comments, "He won more games and lost more titles than any player in history."

Columnist Dick Young comments, "Any way you cut it, Wilt was a loser."

Ah, there is the rub. It has been said again and again and again—Wilt is a loser.

In Wilt Chamberlain's first varsity season in high school, his heavily favored team lost the city championship contest, though it went on to win the next two.

In his first varsity season in college, his heavily favored team lost the national championship contest, and when it failed even to make the title tournament the next season, he quit.

In his first season as a professional, his team was not favored, but was given a good chance to go all the way. However, it lost the semifinals to the eventual and usual champion, Boston.

It lost before it got to Boston the next year, and to Boston again the following year. By then, Bill Russell was regarded as superior under pressure, and so a superior center.

Wilt considered himself superior to Russell, but regarded Russell's Celtic teams as superior to Wilt's teams. "I outplay him, but his teams outplay mine," mourned Wilt. He admired Russell and they remained personal friends off the court.

After his teams lost to Russell's Celtics again, he was traded. And his new team promptly lost to Russell's Celtics again. Finally Wilt's team became better than Boston. But lost to them again. Finally beat them. Then lost to them again. And Wilt was dealt off again. And lost to Russell again. Wilt won another one after Russell retired, but lost others.

In neither deal did Wilt's team get much for him. It hurt him that he was sold so cheaply. "I have been blamed for the failures of my teams. I have been held responsible for things that were beyond my control. I have been criticized for a conduct that was not at all unusual. I stood out, so I was singled out," Wilt has said.

"I always felt I should be paid what I was worth. That's fair, isn't it? I have lawyers and businessmen around me, but I always made my own deals without ringing in agents or people like that. I was always willing to talk face-to-face with the owner. I would play if no one was paid. I am one of the few superstars who enjoys summer games on playgrounds and in little gyms. I have heard Kareem plays these games sometimes, but I don't think Elgin or Jerry does. I know most don't. Without being paid, they won't. But as long as teams are making money, I want my share. I never held a gun to any owner's head."

Rick Barry has said, "The problem was, Wilt always had to be paid more than anyone else, and he wasn't always worth it. I was criticized for going after money, but I never got what Wilt got." Jerry West has said, "I'm not sure how much Wilt would play without being paid. I don't see him playing now that he is not a pro. But I think he earned a lot of money with what he did." Even Bill Russell has said, "I think Wilt blazed a trail and opened up the owners' pocketbooks for a lot of players."

Jack Kent Cooke has said, "There may have come a time when Wilt wanted so much it would have been bad business to meet his demands, and there never was a time when he came cheaply, but Wilt was worth every dollar I ever paid him." However, one owner says, "Wilt was a million-dollar property who wasn't worth a dime in the end. Dealing with him, a man paid a price in blood. For all Wilt did, he just didn't do enough. And in the end, he didn't come through for you."

Some of Wilt's problems were personal. As he toured with

the Globetrotters summers, Moscow one year, Paris the next, and then began to go around the world on his own, he became increasingly sophisticated. He was an intelligent but basic man, who considered himself superior to many in many ways beyond basketball. While he really liked Eddie Gottlieb and Ike Richman of the Warriors and other owners he encountered later, he did not like others.

A bachelor, he constantly bragged about his prowess in sex, saying he had "copped" this showgirl there and this movie star here. Neil Johnston used to say sex was bad for an athlete and warned his players, especially Wilt, about "messing around with women." Wilt laughed at this. But later in his career he had a problem when both he and his coach were dating the same woman. She was white and the coach was white, while Wilt was black. On the other hand, she and Wilt were not married, while the coach was.

Wilt built up or tried to build up a reputation as a "stud," but he resented talk that he was "a black stud" with all its implications of supposed prowess peculiar to blacks, just as he resented being spotlighted strictly because of his size.

Once in the L.A. airport while Wilt was sitting and waiting to take a plane, a white woman went up to him and handed him her infant child. She then stepped behind the bench and had another person snap a picture of them together.

"I want to send this to my husband in Vietnam," she explained to the startled Chamberlain.

Wilt did not draw color lines. He dated black women, but white women, too, because there were more of them to date. His friends were white as well as black. This bothered a certain number of both blacks and whites. But they were wrong in this, not Wilt. He did not run with ballplayers and this bothered some of them. Off court, he slipped into shadows. There were blacks who were offended because he was not front and center fighting for their rights, but he did things they did not notice.

Once this writer received an in-depth interview with Wilt for a story in *West Magazine* of the Los Angeles *Times.* When the story appeared, a black columnist in town sent Wilt and me long letters of outrage that Wilt had given a story to a white writer instead of a black. This writer felt bad about it, but Wilt did not. It was a story he was interested in doing and he had not been especially interested in the writer.

Asked about being approached by members of militant black groups, Wilt shrugged and said, "I send them on their way. I believe in blacks, but not in violence. I am a leader, not a follower. I will do things, but only my way. I refuse to be pressured into joining groups because it might look good. I don't wear masks. I do what I want to do, not what others want me to do."

When Wilt supported Nixon for President, it alienated liberals and blacks, but Wilt saw in Nixon a man who was overcoming the label of "loser." He was flattered by Nixon's attentions. And, of course, as some of us see it, he was bound to be different and independent, doing the thing you might least expect him to do. At the same time he was building a business empire that gave employment and economic opportunity to blacks.

Much of this was behind the scenes and not generally known, but it added to the antagonism many felt toward Wilt and spilled over into the court, subtly influencing the feelings many had about him.

Wilt was always blamed for his teams being beaten. It was said he passed up practices whenever he pleased, would not work when he did put in an appearance, often loafed in games, did not come through in the clutch, played worse in playoffs than during regular-season games, but blamed his teammates for his defeats.

He was, it was said, destructive to team morale, an arrogant individual, who held himself apart from and above his teammates, did what he wanted, when he wanted on court, and could not be coached. It was said he was so important to his owners that he was responsible for the firing of several coaches. He was, it was said, for all of his awesome statistics, overrated and overpaid.

80

There is, it appears, some merit to all of this. Johnston, his first pro coach, said, "He is at times almost impossible to deal with. He is difficult to coach." But now Neil, Dolph Schayes, Alex Hannum, and Bill van Breda Kolff refuse to comment on coaching Wilt.

One gets the impression Wilt is as intimidating off the court as he is on it. Mature men seem fearful of arousing his wrath. One coach who asked anonymity said, "He breaks a coach's spirit and takes his courage away from him. He leaves them less men than they were."

Another said, "A lot of coaches are cowards. They are paid less and are less important than the players they have to handle, which makes it impossible to handle them. Coaches are always being fired, so they take any job that is offered them, no matter how hard it will be to succeed, and they humiliate themselves by hanging on no matter what.

"It's true in all sports. Managers and coaches will go to work for owners who will not let them do their jobs, blame them when the jobs are not done right, embarrass them, and ignore them when they beg for one more season, one more chance.

"Wilt was the worst player I ever dealt with. By comparison, our owner wasn't too bad, but only by comparison with Wilt. If you asked Wilt to do something, he wouldn't do it. If you didn't ask him, he might. He had no team spirit whatsoever. You couldn't count on him."

On the other hand, Frank McGuire says, "If a coach couldn't control Wilt, it is the coach's fault, not Wilt's. It is the job of a coach to control players. If he can't, then he shouldn't be coaching.

"It is the mark of a good coach that he makes the most of the talent on his team. If a coach got less from Wilt than he had to give, then the coach did not do his job.

"If Wilt is willing to talk about his coaches, and he is, why aren't they willing to talk about Wilt? I think perhaps they are trying to protect their reputations.

"I consider Wilt coachable. That was my experience."

Bill Sharman adds, "All superstars are difficult to coach. Rick Barry was. Wilt was. Elgin Baylor was. Even Jerry West was. They are special people. They are high-paid and high-strung. They have extraspecial abilities and they have developed styles that made them superstars. They are reluctant to change.

"But, approached properly, and shown the wisdom of the way you want them to play, they usually are willing to go along with you. Wilt went along with me, and when it worked, he was happy with me. You can't keep all your players happy, but you can the ones that matter most. That is a coach's job. I had no complaints with Wilt."

Joe Mullaney says, "Wilt had to be treated differently from the other players. I wonder now if one of my problems wasn't not explaining the situation properly to the other players. It is easy to say that a coach treats all players on a team alike, but it is hard to do. You have to make exceptions for stars. It is not just that your job depends on them. It is that they are special.

"We won a lot of games with Wilt, but we did not win the ultimate title with him. I blame myself, my other players, injuries, the fates, as much as I blame Wilt, maybe more. Actually, I don't blame Wilt for not taking us to a title, except that he was a part of our winning and so he was a part of our losing. But Wilt performed wonderfully well and courageously for me and I can't complain.

"Wilt isn't easy to coach, but it isn't supposed to be easy to coach. By blaming Wilt, a coach may be blaming himself."

A long time ago, one of Wilt's first coaches, Blinky Brown, said, "Wilt will always listen to his coaches, but he'll make up his own mind about what he's going to do." Another said, "Wilt will listen, but he hears only what he wants to hear."

Wilt says, "I had good coaches and I had bad coaches. That is my opinion and I am entitled to it. Frank McGuire was the best. Alex Hannum was very good. Joe Mullaney and Bill Sharman were good, too. Some of the others were not so good. But I did not fire them. I never told an owner to fire a coach in my life. I haven't known many owners you could tell what to do.

"I don't think I was so hard to handle. Animals are handled, not men. I could be coached. But I knew basketball, too. If a coach told me to do something I knew was stupid, I wasn't going to do it. If a coach could show me the sense in something, I was always willing to try something different. I changed my style several times to suit my teams and my coaches—sometimes when I wasn't so sure it was right.

"I have my own life-style. I carried a heavy weight on that basketball court. I had to pace myself to play well for full games, game after game through the long season, without sitting out like most players. I found it hard to unwind after games. It took time. I have insomnia. It took time for me to fall asleep. I got to bed late, and I couldn't be getting up early to practice. I can't practice so hard I leave my game on the practice court. I don't need a lot of practice, playing eighty to a hundred games a season.

"If a coach couldn't understand this, that wasn't my problem. It was my responsibility to myself to make the most of my ability, not waste myself in nonsense. I don't care if a coach complains about me. I can't see what coaches would have to complain about. I don't care who the coach was or what I thought of him, there wasn't a one I didn't give my best. A lot of players make a show of doing what coaches want, saying 'yes, sir' to them, and putting on a show in practice, but none of them gave more than I did in games."

It is true that many players we observed would bitch about Wilt behind his back, but praise him to his face. It happened constantly. Also many players like Elgin Baylor and Oscar Robertson who had differences with Wilt decline to discuss them now. David Shaw, who wrote Wilt's book with him, admits, "I never got any good anecdotes about Wilt from any of the Lakers. They were all terrified that no matter what they said he might interpet it as a negative comment."

One former Laker says, "He played on the same team with

you, but he was never your teammate. He might do something for you, but he would never do anything with you. He had a few friends on his teams, but very few. He went his own way and did his own thing. On the court, he did what he wanted to do. He didn't do it for you. We had to bust our butts in practices while he goofed off if he even showed up. We hustled hard in games while he coasted. But he piled up the stats and there was always a crowd around him after the game. We did all the work and he got all the credit. You had to hate him."

A former Philadelphia teammate says, "When you wanted him, he wasn't there. He piled up points on patsies, but came the clutch he disappeared." Curiously, Wilt has asked, "Who says Wilt has to get the ball in the last minute of a game? Wilt never said it." Another says, "He never wanted the ball when a game was in the balance. He was afraid of looking bad by blowing a last shot. He protected himself so he could blame everyone but himself for defeat."

However, Jerry West says, "There are not many players who ever wanted the ball in the clutch. I did. That was my reputation. I didn't make all my last-second shots by any means, but I made enough to know I could. I had confidence in myself most players don't have. Wilt was no better, no worse than most. He came through his share of times. I'm not afraid to talk about him. If I felt like rapping him, I would."

Tom Hawkins confirms, "West was special. He was the greatest clutch shooter I ever saw. I don't know who even comes close. But I was a player and I know most players did not want the ball in tight spots. They really didn't. No way. No one wants to look bad. I think Wilt was that way partly because he knew he'd be the first player to be blamed for any defeat.

"I didn't want the ball in a tight spot. But then I wasn't a shooter. I had no confidence in my shooting. I would have welcomed the opportunity to defend Rick Barry coming down-court with the ball with the ball game in the balance. Defense was my game. And defense was Wilt's game. It may have been offense at first, and he was a great scorer, but he never was a great shooter. He was a great rebounder and shot-blocker at all times, even the toughest of times. I never saw him disappear on defense in the clutch."

Dick Young, the New York columnist, has said, "Defense doesn't take a fine touch. Offense does. Wilt was the greatest offense in his sport, but when the chips were piled high on the table, he folded his hand." Lenny Shecter, the late writer, once said, "Wilt was overrated and overpaid because he did the least when it mattered the most. He choked in the clutch."

Wilt has said, "I'd score forty points and take down forty rebounds and assist on ten baskets and block ten shots, and if I didn't make a basket in the last second, I was blamed for a one-point defeat when half of my teammates maybe didn't do a damn thing. It was unfair, really.

"The more I would do, the more I was expected to do. Not only by the press but by the players, too, and sometimes the coaches. I've been criticized constantly and passed around like a piece of crap. There is a lot of jealousy in sports. Among owners, too. A lot of people were jealous of what I could do.

"It spilled off court, too. I attract attention, but I don't ask for it. I do talk to writers because I know they have a job to do and I'm not afraid to speak my mind because that's my way, but a lot of time what I say has been twisted and slanted and I've been made to look bad.

"I live my own life. Most of the players are married. If they go home to their wives, I'm not going to go with them. If they don't, I'm not going to play a part in that game. I'm not married because I'm not ready to settle down. If I did settle down to one woman, I would want to be faithful to her. That's my code of conduct. What others do, however, is none of my business. To each his own.

"I have always had interests beyond basketball, anyway. I don't want to be with players all the time and I don't want to talk basketball all the time. And I don't know many players who run with other players. Sports is too competitive. Players stick knives in teammates' backs all the time.

"I know who is talking about me behind my back. I am aware of those who build me up to my face and tear me down behind my back. I know by instinct who I can trust and who I can't. I can't be concerned about cats I can't trust. I always just played the game as best I could and then went my own way.

"I could care less about criticism from other players, from coaches, from sportswriters, or from fans. I know inside of myself what I have done."

Philadelphia sportswriter Jack Kiser says, "Wilt always knew who was honest with him and who wasn't. He seemed to have a sixth sense for it. The only player he couldn't see through was himself. He always claimed he didn't care about criticism, but he showed constantly that he was thin-skinned about it and sensitive to it.

"He may have been justified in many of his complaints. No one has put his picture in perspective, has taken his career season by season, and his life and added up the pluses as well as the minuses. On balance, he may do better than most believe."

Wilt has said, "There has not been an easy season in my career. I have had great success, yet year after year been made to look like a failure. There has not been an easy year in my life. I have accomplished a lot, but some people like to make little of it. I have had a good life, yet many see me as a bad guy.

"The world is made up of Davids. I am a Goliath. And nobody roots for Goliath."

Bill Russell has called it "The loneliest life in the world." He has described it as "a world of bright lights and screaming emotion and vast amounts of money . . . and deep wells of loneliness." He has said, "You fall far into it and all your life struggle to come back up." He also has said, "The spotlight burns you and leaves scars on you."

What he was talking about was the world of sports in general and of the NBA in particular, because he knew that best. He has said it is a gypsylike life, traveling from town to town under pounding pressure, that it was both a privilege and a curse to be a superstar, that the stars bear the biggest burdens, and he has known few who weren't hurt by it.

He spoke to Wilt about it, befriending him. They did not put one another down.

Russell says, "Money motivates you, but so does ego. I'm not sure which matters more. You want to win, but that is a matter of ego. You want to win, but you don't want to look bad doing it. You want to win, but you want to play a part in it. Few will sacrifice themselves."

It is not clear that Russell did. While winning, he did what he could do best. Winning, he took credit for it. His statements are as egotistical as Wilt's, but because he has a more beguiling personality and maybe most of all because he won so much, he is considered more kindly. He has said, "Losing made money matter more to Wilt."

Maybe. However, Paul Silas points out, "Wilt was a giant off the court as well as on. He was businesslike and he wasn't afraid to fight for right. He did a lot to raise salaries for players throughout the league, and he blazed a trail for blacks. He made it clear whites didn't deserve more money unless they were better than blacks. It may not have been his intention, but he led us. He knows this and takes pride in it. We have talked about it and he knows what he did."

It is argued that pro basketball limits its audience because it has become a black man's game. Sadly, there may be some truth to this. Most top players today are black, but most people are white and most monied fans are white. A white fan may not identify with a black player as well as with a white. Originally, owners took only the top blacks. Then a quota system developed so that teams could keep half their rosters or more white, and start at least one or two whites.

Today, no such quota system can be detected, except that in fringe cases a white may be preferred to a black player. However, some owners who deny they operate prejudiced systems have admitted privately they wish white superstars such as Jerry West, Rick Barry, and Dave Cowens were more common.

Broadcaster Brent Mussberger of CBS-TV, which carries NBA games, has admitted that his bosses could, but might be reluctant to, meet Barry's request for a similar salary to forsake playing in favor of commentating because it would take one of the few white superstars out of the sport and thus might decrease the popularity of the telecasts.

Wilt Chamberlain has said he feels loyalty to the Globetrotters not only because they were willing to pay him a top price and give him an alternative place to play, but because they paid blacks to play when no one else would. The Globetrotters did not pay their players a lot, usually, but they were willing to pay a lot to land Wilt, who was an unusual attraction.

Abe Saperstein, originator and proprietor of the Globetrotters, had offered Wilt $12,000 to come right out of high school to join his touring team. However, Abe also owned a piece of the Philadelphia Warriors; and his buddy, Eddie Gottlieb, who owned the biggest piece of the Warriors, persuaded Abe to retract the offer.

Gottlieb worried that Wilt would develop bad habits and might be tempted to continue as a clown. He also figured college championships would come to Wilt and enhance his gate appeal. He convinced Saperstein that the potential payoff was higher with the Warriors.

Gottlieb did not work too hard at getting Wilt into pro ball out of high school because that was not done at that time. Anyway, Wilt, too, thought he'd capture college crowns; he was flattered by the attention paid him by university recruiters, and he looked forward to his college career.

However, when Wilt grew disenchanted with Kansas and college ball, and disappointed by his failure to take a title, and dropped out with one year of eligibility left, Gottlieb tried to get his fellow owners to accept him a year ahead of schedule. He failed. They were willing to wait to lose to him.

Gottlieb agreed with Saperstein that Chamberlain should not be permitted to embark on any risky, rival exhibition schedule of his own, and backed a big-money bid for Wilt to spend the year with the Globetrotters. Saperstein already had lost his stars Goose Tatum and Marques Haynes, who, protesting low pay, had formed their own troupe of traveling clowns, the Harlem Magicians.

Tatum, the clown prince of the club, never made more than $35,000 a year before moving out on his own. He had hosted and befriended Wilt in Kansas City, Tatum's hometown, and he offered Wilt a long-term contract in which he might make as much as $100,000 a year if he pulled in enough patrons. Wilt was tempted, but Tatum never came up with the cash.

However, Saperstein countered with a contract calling for $45,000 with bonuses that would bring it to $65,000. With Gottlieb, there was the lure of much more money when Wilt went into the NBA and put the top pros in their place. Wilt wanted to strut his stuff in the NBA, and he wanted to ally himself with the NBA people.

He signed with Saperstein. The contract was announced at the higher figure. When he did go into the NBA, he was given a contract that called for $35,000 with bonuses that brought it to $85,000, though it has been believed to be $65,000. In any event, the signing was announced at the lower figure. Saperstein wanted the promotional appeal of a high-salaried superstar, but Gottlieb did not want to promote higher salary demands from his other players.

Abe had agreed not to keep Wilt more than one season. But when Globetrotter attendance increased 20 percent with Wilt, he went after Wilt with offers that eventually came close to $100,000. This angered Gottlieb, they argued, and their friendship never was the same again. Saperstein once said, "It is hard to be in business with friends and keep things friendly. Either your business or your friendship has to suffer."

However, Wilt wanted to play pro ball with the best in the business and to establish himself as the best, to take teams to titles, and to send his salary soaring above anything it might be with a touring team. He could still make money on the side on tour and spent part of every summer until 1968 touring with the Trotters. Eventually, there came a time when they could not pay him the sort of money he was worth; he tired of it, and stepped off to the side of the road.

Jack Kiser recalls that Al Cervi was coaching the Warriors when he watched Wilt with the Globetrotters one night. Although Cervi was having a bad season without a solid center, had developed an ulcer, and had been pressured by his wife into retiring even if he was not fired, Al admitted, "It's a temptation to try to stay because that guy can turn a team completely around."

Cervi wondered if Wilt would not be a coach's dream, but he became a nightmare for Neil Johnston, who got the coaching job in the fall of 1959 when Wilt became a Warrior. Wilt was critical of Johnston, who he feels was jealous of him both because of games in which Wilt had embarrassed him in the Catskills and because he realized Wilt would easily surpass his records and salary.

Wilt has said, "Johnston was óne of those guys who had given faithful service to an owner, who rewards him when he comes up with a bad knee or something by making him coach, even if he isn't qualified." Kiser confirms this, saying, "Neil was a nice guy, but he had a big ego. Wilt had one, too. They clashed. I believe Neil really was jealous of what Wilt could do.

"They had trouble from the preseason period on. Neil fined Wilt $500 for something at halftime of an exhibition game in Kansas City, and Wilt told him he couldn't make it stick. Instead of going out for the second half, Wilt went to Gottlieb, got out of it, and then went to Johnston and told him where he could stick his fine. Well, Johnston's authority with the team just disappeared at that point. He became bitter about it and denied it, but everyone knew Gottlieb, not Johnston, coached the club."

Gottlieb denies it. "Johnston coached. Wilt played. I tried to keep clear, but I was drawn in between them at times. And there was a personality conflict," Eddie admits.

Without Wilt the previous season, the Warriors had won only 32 games, lost 40, and finished last in the Eastern Division, 20 games behind Boston, which finished first and went on to win the playoff championship. The Warriors did not even make the playoffs. However, with Wilt, the Warriors went to 49-26, and soared to second place, only 10 games behind Boston, which went on to another playoff laurel after eliminating Philly in six games in the semifinals.

The Warriors had some good players—Paul Arizin, who could shoot; Guy Rodgers, who could pass; and Tom Gola, who could do a little of everything—and Wilt made them a good team, but they could not be compared with the Celtics, who surrounded Russell with a powerful forward like Tom Heinsohn, All-Time All-Pro guards such as Bob Cousy and Bill Sharman, and explosive players like Frank Ramsey and Sam Jones coming off the bench.

Wilt's first NBA game was against the Knicks in New York, and a capacity gathering in old Madison Square Garden watched him hit 17 of 20 shots, some from outside, pour in 43 points and take down 28 rebounds to lead a 118–109 victory. The Knicks had a poor center, Charlie Tyra, and he could not contain Chamberlain. Knick coach Fuzzy Levane conceded later, "He was scary."

Wilt's first game at home in Philadelphia was against Detroit and towering, awkward Walter Dukes. Chamberlain got 36 points and 34 rebounds to lead a 120–112 triumph before a record crowd that went wild.

Wilt's first game against Boston and the best of centers was in Boston in the fourth game of the season. He outscored Russell, 30–22, but was outrebounded by him, 28–35, and his team lost to Bill's, 115–106.

Wilt was angered when write-ups of the game contended he had been embarrassed to have a shot blocked by Russell and had suffered a shocking experience. "I didn't do that bad," Wilt grumbled.

The next time he battled Bill, Wilt outscored him 45–15, and outrebounded him, 35–13, and the Warriors won, 123–113. Russell said, "Wilt is the greatest rookie ever and I only wish I'd been as good when I began."

However, the pattern of that season was that Wilt won the statistics and Bill's Boston team won the games.

Wilt's statistics were awesome. He scored 50 or more points seven times with a high of 58 and totaled 40 or more rebounds five times with a high of 45. He set new league records for total points, 2,707; average points, 37.6; total rebounds, 1,941; and average rebounds, 26.9. He was named not only Rookie of the

Year, but first-string All-Star center and Most Valuable Player, an unprecedented sweep.

Still, it was a difficult campaign for the rookie, climaxed by being beaten by Boston in the divisional playoff finals, and many seemed to forget he was not Superman and was a rookie. Heinsohn roughed him up so much that Wilt lost his temper in the second game and punched at Tommy, missed, hit teammate Tom Gola on the arm and hurt his hand. Although Wilt tallied 50 points in one game, the Celtics won in six games, four victories to two.

Wilt blamed his injured hand for holding him back, but mainly he blames his teammates. He points out Rodgers missed two free throws when the Warriors were two points back at the finish of the final game. He points out Rodgers had one point in one game, none in another. "He choked," Wilt later wrote. Gola fouled out twice, too, Wilt adds. And Woody Sauldsberry twice, too. Arizin was the only player aside from Wilt who played to his potential, Wilt wrote. Wilt averaged 30 points, seven below his seasonal average, and 25 rebounds, two below his seasonal average.

Wilt had been roughed up all season. On a Sunday in St. Louis, Lovellette walloped Wilt in the mouth with an elbow and knocked two of his front teeth up into the roof of his mouth. Wilt calls Clyde one of the "dirtiest" players in the league and says it was "deliberate." Wilt says he hurt horribly and developed an infection, but that Johnston didn't seem concerned, and not only kept him in the game but continued to play him the next two games.

Jack Kiser comments, "Wilt was really hurt, but Neil left him in St. Louis. The doctor in Detroit took the teeth out, and told Wilt to go to a hospital for treatment, but Neil played him. Wilt called me to his room to complain. His face was swelling up. He wasn't able to eat anything but orange juice and soda. He drank a gallon of 7-Up to keep going. I guess he wasn't going to quit until Neil said it was OK.

"We got to New York and he was unrecognizable. Willie Naulls elbowed him accidentally and Wilt went to the sidelines. Our team doctor, Simon Ball, had come from Philadelphia, and he took one look at Wilt and ordered him to a hospital. Neil grumbled about losing him, but had to let him go. The doctor told me later that Wilt had to have a blood transfusion and a normal man would have died, but Wilt not only had played, but was back playing after missing only three games while surgery brought him back to normal.

"Neil was a decent man, but where Wilt was concerned he seemed to have a blind spot. Now, I am known to wear a hair shirt myself; I can't condemn Wilt the way others do. He had his faults, but so did others around him. He and Neil never had any respect for each other, and if Wilt lost respect for coaches after that incident, I don't blame him. Wilt may have been at fault fifty percent of the time.

"Neil was not a good coach. He wanted Wilt to play the way he had played, not the way Wilt played. He wanted Wilt to run end to end like a madman forty-eight minutes a night, and move all over to set screens on offense and shoot hooks. And he ridiculed his free throws instead of trying to improve them. Wilt literally ran from fouls so he wouldn't have to go to the line. It wasn't a good team. Rodgers couldn't shoot outside. Arizin could, but he took forever.

"Wilt carried the club, but the players resented him. They'd pat him on the back and tell him how great he was, and when he turned around they'd bitch how he was hogging the glory. Wilt knew. I think the only guy he trusted and could confide in was Rodgers. Guy talked Tom Gola into accepting a subservient role to Wilt, but at first he complained he felt like the caddy to a golf star.

"Arizin was in a world of his own. Early to bed, early to rise, play the game and go to bed. He was like a Marine doing drills. Someone once said he was the only absolutely straight guy he ever saw in the NBA, the only one who never cheated on his wife.

94

"Arizin was super as a shooter and a person. He never said anything bad about anyone. He never said anything to Wilt at all. The old pro was as much help to the rookie as a pimple."

Wilt finished that first season, wrote his story for *Look,* and announced his retirement. He said players were picked to be coaches without coaching experience, and the coaching was poor, the games were rough, the officiating was awful, the travel was terrible, the schedule was too long, he had proved everything he had wanted to prove, money didn't mean that much to him, and he was going to go elsewhere to find an easier life.

Bob Cousy snorted, "Now we can go back to basketball."

At first Wilt denied some of the story. Then he said he had meant what he had said. Then he was offered a three-year $250,000 contract and decided he'd come back after all.

Gottlieb brought Johnston back, and Wilt was not very far into the new season when Neil, hinting Wilt might be afraid of Lovellette, said that he was not covering Clyde closely enough.

"I'm trying to rebound and cover my man, too. You never tell Arizin or Gola or anyone else they have to cover their man closer," Wilt complained.

"They're not making sixty-five thousand a year like you are," replied Johnston, who did not know Wilt was making even more.

Wilt exploded and snapped at Johnston, who snapped back. They argued verbally, but did not throw any punches before others got between them and parted them.

All season, others had to get between Wilt and Johnston. Wilt withdrew into himself and became moody. He started to skip practices. Johnston was powerless. Gottlieb sided with Wilt. Wilt came alive only in games.

In one game, he tallied 67 points against the visiting Knicks, just four short of Elgin Baylor's league record. In another game, Wilt, facing Russell, gathered 55 rebounds, surpassing Bill's league record by six.

For the season, Wilt set new records with 3,033 points and 2,149 rebounds and averages of 38 and 27, respectively. It was, as it turned out, his career record in rebounding. Still, Wilt was bitter when he wound up second to Russell in the All-Star vote and fourth to Russell, Pettit, and Baylor in the MVP vote.

He was commanding on court, but his army was in disarray behind him. "We were divided into Wilt and Johnston factions," a former Warrior reports. "Both behaved badly."

Gottlieb got into it. He invaded dressing rooms several times. Once, he hollered, "You're not a team. I could get ten guys off the street and they'd play together better than you guys."

Yet the team didn't fall far from its previous season's pace, winning 46 and losing 33, and finishing second, 11 behind Boston. But Boston was outstanding, setting a league record with 17 wins in a row and finishing at 57–22.

Philly never got back to Boston in those playoffs of 1961. They fell in the first round, a short series, three straight losses to Syracuse, which was wiped out by Boston en route to another Celtic title.

Syracuse had finished 14 games behind Philadelphia during the regular season, but the Warriors seemed disspirited in the playoffs. Wilt averaged a few less points and rebounds than he had, and had no big games. Later he blamed Gola for not scoring and fouling out, Rodgers for fouling out of the first two, Arizin the last two.

Wilt admits he, himself, wasn't too inspired.

Gottlieb got rid of Johnston, then, who for the first time complained publicly that Wilt was uncooperative and couldn't be coached. "It's tough to coach a team when one man gets so many privileges. How can a coach control a team when one player is in charge?" Johnston asked angrily.

He seemed willing to go, though he had nowhere to go, and never was successful coaching anywhere else, either. He concluded, "Wilt has everything but a championship. There will have to be a change in him and the team before it happens."

Wilt countered, "We could never have won a championship with Johnston." He complained that Neil's comments made him look like a "prima donna," and insisted they'd had only one disagreement—the one over defensing Lovellette—in two years.

Much later, however, he admitted they had other disagreements, running disagreements, and many of them.

Wilt denied that he had discussed Johnston with Gottlieb, but later claimed Gottlieb had come to him and all but apologized, saying he admitted his mistake in hiring Johnston, who had botched up the basketball team, and all but begging forgiveness of his star.

Wilt was glad to see Johnston go, in any event. Even Neil's friends ran out of bars to avoid Johnston when he walked in, Chamberlain claimed.

In just two seasons, the first controversial chapter in Chamberlain's professional life closed. Forever after, whether Wilt did or did not get along with his coaches, he would be considered a player who was hard on coaches.

Frank McGuire pointedly remarks, "The biggest thing I had
going for me when I came in to coach Wilt Chamberlain was
I had never been an NBA All-Star, I had no scoring records to
be broken, I had never been underpaid as a player, and there
was no way I could be jealous of Wilt."

Wilt was so happy to have another coach, and one who had
proven he could win a championship when he won one from
Wilt's team in college ball, that he went out of his way to
welcome him, and was on his best behavior with him, as though
to prove he could work with a good coach.

McGuire was a good coach. A New Yorker and the son of
an Irish cop, Frank had been a success as a college coach at St.
John's and North Carolina, and was widely respected as a
coach who could make the transition to pro ranks. Many did
wonder, however, how well he or anyone else could get along
with Wilt.

McGuire admits, "Many of my friends and many people
whose advice I sought in this sport told me I was making a
mistake to leave a good college job to go pro, especially with
Wilt. There was a lot of money, but not much security. The life

was a lot tougher and the players more demanding. They said if I couldn't control Wilt, the team would come apart. And that Wilt would cut me up in little pieces."

Clair Bee, the Long Island coach and McGuire's rival in New York, told McGuire he'd find Wilt either a coach's dream or a nightmare. But Joe Lapchick, McGuire's mentor and predecessor at St. John's, said Wilt was waiting for someone to bring out the best in him.

A con man in the kindest sense of the word, McGuire wanted to take up the challenge. He said, "The challenge of this job is finding out what makes Wilt tick. In college, I brought in a kid as a freshman at the age of eighteen or nineteen and molded him, season by season. In pro, I'm dealing with guys twenty-five or thirty and set in their ways. Wilt's twenty-five. In some ways he's a man. In some ways he's still a boy. I've got to find the key. I know he can be better.

"You fake until you find your way. Most coaches know the game. Psychology is more important than X's and O's. You're dealing with individuals. Unless you can find a way to motivate them and get them to playing one way together, all the tic-tac-toe crap you put on a blackboard with chalk is meaningless. Well, Wilt was the most outstanding individual I ever encountered, and I had to get to him to lead this team and rally the rest around him."

His first meeting with Wilt was at the Coco Inn at training camp in Hershey, Pennsylvania, where the smell of chocolate fills the town. Wilt recalls McGuire had a file folder full of $400 worth of reports on him, but that Frank was throwing it away. As McGuire remembers it, he said, "You're supposed to be tough to coach, but maybe you haven't had a coach who treated you like a man. Well, we're starting from scratch. If we treat each other with respect, we should do all right." Wilt remembers it essentially the same and says he was impressed.

The one thing McGuire stressed was, "The coach has to coach and the player has to play. I do not want yes men. If you disagree with something I do, argue about it. And I will listen.

But I have to have the final say. And if you don't do as I want you to do, you won't play. We will not have many rules, but the ones we have you have to respect." Which is essentially what he told his players at the first team meeting.

McGuire met with Wilt off court at every opportunity. He talked to the other players. Unlike more coaches than you might imagine, he decided how he wanted his team to play and set up a strict pattern for them to follow. He gave them a style to stick to. George Kiseda says, "McGuire denies it, but he laughs when he does. He dedicated the season to Wilt and the playoffs to the team." McGuire smiles and says, "Well, I wanted Wilt happy, and I felt we could use the season to prepare for the playoffs."

Wilt's defense was satisfactory, but his offense was solo stuff. He was moving around the court and taking those fadeaway jumpers that took him away from the backboard. McGuire asked him to go to a low post close to the basket, stay there and forget the fadeaways. Wilt refused, figuring the fadeaway was his best shot and one that proved he didn't have to have size to score.

McGuire countered by pointing out that inside Wilt could not only shoot his own shots but follow the misses of his teammates. He promised Wilt his teammates would set him up, and swore Wilt would score even more this way.

"With you scoring thirty-eight points a game, the team fell short. If you score fifty, that will be the difference between losing and winning," McGuire said.

"Fifty!" Wilt said. "My man, you're mad." Even Wilt didn't believe it was possible.

Others did. Laker coach Fred Schaus said, "Wilt might average seventy-five a game someday." Old pro Jim Pollard said, "If Wilt puts out he might score a hundred in a game one of these nights."

McGuire held a basketball up prior to practice one day and chalked it off into sections. One big chunk was, he said, Wilt's. The smaller pieces he apportioned to the other players. "Feed

100

Wilt and we win," he said. "Sacrifice yourself for your team."

Some took convincing. Guy Rodgers asked, "If my scoring average goes down, will you sit alongside me when I go in to talk contract next year?" McGuire said he would. Rodgers' scoring average went from 12 to 8. Wilt's went from 38 to 50.

McGuire was aware Wilt prized his statistics, though Wilt never has admitted it. In Boston, where Russell's rebound totals and Cousy's assist totals soared, McGuire had college coaches keep track of statistics during Philadelphia visits. One was Joe Mullaney, then at Providence.

In part, these showed Wilt had more rebounds, Russell less than reported officially. This was the important part in McGuire's con game. He had Philadelphia writers publish them. He showed Wilt how he was interested in him and the justice so often denied him.

Wilt nodded knowingly, having found an ally.

McGuire encouraged Wilt to shoot. Wilt did not need much encouragement. Wilt averaged almost 47 shots a game that season, a record no player dare approach. His teammates teased him that his arm was about to fall off, but Wilt ignored it. One wanted to erect a statue of him waving for the ball.

Wilt still shot his fadeaway, but not as often. He still roamed, but not as much. He sacrificed defense for offense. Underneath, when he got the ball, he was unstoppable.

On the second Friday of December, 1961, with only 4,022 fans in the stands to see a doubleheader at Philadelphia's Convention Hall, the NBA's scoring record holder, Elgin Baylor, and his heir-apparent, Wilt Chamberlain, met in a nightcap matchup that remains memorable.

It was the Lakers versus the Warriors, but the stars stole the show. Wilt outscored the acrobatic Baylor, 28–16, in the first half, and the Warriors led by nine. But Baylor threw in 16 points in the third period to put the Lakers in front by two.

Chamberlain came back with 15 in the fourth quarter, but Baylor banged in a basket at the buzzer to tie the game, 109–all, and send it into overtime. At the end of regulation play, Wilt had 53 points, Elg 47, and the 100 points between them was a pro record. But they were just beginning.

In the first five-minute overtime, Chamberlain outscored Baylor, 9–3, but when a basket by Al Attles was ruled to have come too late, the teams were still tied at 121.

In the second extra session, Baylor outscored Chamberlain, 9–6, but when Elgin, after being fouled by Wilt, missed one of two free throws at the finish, the teams remained even at 133.

In the third overtime, Chamberlain outscored Baylor, 10–4. Less than two minutes into it, Wilt was fouled by Tom Hawkins as he went over him to hit a basket. He made the free throw; and the three-point play surpassed Baylor's record one-game total of 71.

Jerry West, who tallied just 32 points, came through in the clutch with big baskets, however, and the Lakers finally put the Warriors away, 151–147, although Wilt wound up with 78 points to 63 for Elgin. This also added up to a two-man record of 141.

It was typical in a way that the Warriors would lose with Wilt setting a scoring record.

However, Wilt's new mark had an asterisk alongside it because it had come in triple overtime compared with Baylor's regulation-time achievement. McGuire raged, "If he ever gets a break from the refs he'll score a hundred some night."

Fred Schaus says, "It was just a matter of time until he broke that record and every other one. He was hitting his fadeaway fantastically well and couldn't be contained underneath.

"Both my centers fouled out on him in that triple overtime and I wound up with Rudy LaRusso on him, but no one could contain him. He was awesome."

He scored 61 in his next game. A few weeks later, he tallied 73 against the Chicago Packers to top Baylor's regulation-time record by two. Four nights later he had 67 in one game. Twice in February he had 67 in games. Then on the second of March he exploded with his infamous 100.

This was in Hershey, one of the many barnstorming stops the

pros made outside their own cities at that time. It was a small building, but contrary to common belief, the court was regulation length. The crowd was small, only 4,112.

There was an amusement area outside, and Eddie Gottlieb and Ike Richman were playing a target-shooting game. They were scoring 400 to 500 points a game. They had checked and found 1,800 was the record. They knew Wilt liked to bet, so they tried to sucker him.

Wilt was invited to try his luck and they bet him he could not hit 1,000. He took the bet and won. They raised the score and doubled the bet. He beat them again. The score and stakes kept rising. Finally, they bet a bundle he could not beat 1,800. He hit 2,000.

Wilt has written about it and Gottlieb confirms it. "It was nothing, but it was like it was a sign it was his night, and he beat us out of a bundle," Eddie recalls.

Wilt says, "I'd been up until the wee hours on a date. I hadn't had any sleep, and I was bushed, but as it turned out, it was my night."

The Knicks were terrible, a last-place team, and they determined the only way they could win was to run Wilt ragged. McGuire read about this, and in the dressing room before the game challenged Wilt to run right with them.

The Globetrotters played a preliminary game against a team of pro football players. Some of them stayed around to watch Wilt, and this may have inspired him some. In any event, he came out working harder than usual, looking for shots, shooting more.

Wilt has said, "We didn't plan anything special or expect anything extraordinary. When you're averaging fifty a game, you have to work. On nights you get the shots and they fall, you'll score more. This was one of those nights and it just built up."

McGuire says, "It was a while before the realization of what he was doing sank in."

Darrall Imhoff started at center in place of the injured Phil

Jordon for the Knicks. Darrall was a defensive star at Cal, and he's complained Jordon ruined his reputation by begging out of the game. By the end of the first quarter Wilt had 23 points, Imhoff had five fouls, and Cleveland Buckner came in. Imhoff says Buckner went home to Mississippi after that to forget the experience. At halftime, Wilt had 41, though the Warriors were only ahead by 11, at 79–68.

Although Wilt claims he wasn't conscious of 100 until he got close to it, Dave Zinkoff, veteran public-address announcer for Philly, recalls, "After a while I started to call out Wilt's total loud and clear on every basket. Everyone knew what was happening." One of the things that was happening was Wilt was being fouled repeatedly, but was hitting his free throws as he never had before or has since.

Wilt tallied 28 in the third period to reach 69 and put 100 within reach. McGuire remembers thinking, "Wouldn't it be nice if Wilt got a hundred." Eddie Donovan didn't think so. The Knick coach told his team in a time-out, "There's no way that big SOB's gonna' get a hundred against us." He told his team to foul Wilt at every opportunity. Willie Naulls, a Knick, but a friend of Wilt's, was so mad he said, "I won't play a part in that crap." Donovan said, "Sit down." Naulls sat and later drove back to Philly with Wilt, laughing about how ridiculous the Knicks were.

An angry Richie Guerin led the attack on Wilt. Referee Pete D'Ambrosio recalls, "I remember thinking how glad I was the game was in Hershey because there weren't too many fans to complain about the excessive number of fouls we called." The ref says he wasn't surprised as Wilt's total mounted because he had worked high school games in Philly where Wilt once tallied 90 in 32 minutes.

As the last 12 minutes of this 48-minute game ticked away, the fans started to pull for Wilt to pull off the fabulous feat, but Philly publicist Harvey Pollack says, "The support wasn't that great. The applause was at best polite." There weren't many writers at the out-of-the-way game, but those who were there agree that with no rooting interest everyone just sort of watched with wonder.

Of course, 100 is just a number, but it is a magic number and 99 somehow wouldn't have been nearly as much. Warrior player Tom Meschery recalls, "Wilt wasn't about not to get the hundred. He was flyin' for that damn ball. He was going for every pass and rebound within reach." Imhoff recalls, "Buckner scored his all-time pro high of thirty-three because Wilt wasn't playing defense, only offense."

Scorekeeper Dave Richter recalls, "I started to run out of room in my book for Wilt's goals, started to make smaller and smaller X's, and wound up in the margins." With 7:51 left, Rodgers passed to Wilt, who flung in a fadeaway from the foul line to give him 79 and a new regulation-game record. With five minutes left, he reached 89.

He did not score then for 2 minutes and 15 seconds as the Knicks kept the ball away and the 100 seemed to be getting away. But then in rapid succession he sank three free throws and two fadeaways to reach 96. York Larese looped a pass to the hoop which Wilt went up to dunk for 98 with 1:19 left.

Playing with passion now, Wilt intercepted the inbounds pass, but missed a jumper from the foul line. The Knicks got the ball and held it until a shot missed. The Warriors went on offense. Wilt went into the pivot. Joe Rucklick fed Wilt, he turned and shot, but missed. He grabbed his own rebound and threw it back up, but missed.

Ted Luckenbill grabbed the rebound, passed it out to Rucklick, who lobbed the ball toward the basket. Wilt went up, grabbed the ball, and stuffed it through the hoop with both hands. That was it, 100 points.

There were 46 seconds left, but fans came onto the court and had to be cleared off while Wilt's teammates went to him to congratulate him. Even some of his depressed rivals shook his hand. He was not taken out, but did not take another shot. The Warriors won going away, 169–147, and Wilt was cheered off the court. In the dressing room, he said, "When I hit my first

105

ten free throws I thought of setting a free-throw record, but that's the only record I thought of until late in the game. I took too many shots not to score a lot, many of them bad shots. I could not have done it without my teammates setting me up."

Rodgers, who had 20 assists, said, "It was easy. Give the ball to the big guy and he puts it in." Wilt's one-game records included 63 field shots, 36 field goals, and 28 free throws in 32 attempts. Later, McGuire said, "I can remember the first time one of my teams scored a hundred. Then one of my men, one man, scored a hundred. It was fantastic and never to be forgotten." But Wilt says, "Hey, my man, anyone can have a big game. Walt Wesley once scored fifty in one game."

One man who remembers well is Imhoff, who received a wire of congratulations on his defensive performance from former teammates. Protests Darrall, "I only played twenty minutes and he only scored about twenty-five on me. When I went out the first time, he had eighteen, and when I came back, he had eighty-nine. And I didn't last long when I came back before I got my sixth. We had four other players with five fouls and another with four. I've taken an unfair rap, but what the heck, no one could stop him that season. He was at his peak."

"It's consistency that counts in a player," Wilt points out. "I'm prouder of my fifty-point-four average that season than of my hundred in one game, because consistency did it." McGuire says, "He did not hit fifty every game, but he did in forty-six games. I do not think he had a bad game from the first game to the last. I think it's so much malarkey when some say he was more effective feeding others than scoring fifty a game. He was never more effective than when he averaged fifty, but he just didn't have as good a team around him as he did at times later."

McGuire turned it into a team. He went with six men most of the way. Paul Arizin tallied 22 a game, but Rodgers and Gola sacrificed themselves to complement Wilt. McGuire pulled Gola out of the backcourt and made a small forward of him to help out up front. He added a rugged rookie, Tom Meschery, to help out up front, too, and moved another rookie, scrappy Al Attles, into the backcourt.

Wilt never has forgiven McGuire for cutting a close friend, Carl Green, in order to keep one of his college players, Larese, who flopped. However, Wilt found his best friend in basketball in Attles when McGuire kept the fifth-round hustler instead of first-round "Pickles" Kennedy, a Philadelphia favorite from Temple. Wilt respected McGuire's courage.

McGuire says, "We talked basketball. I asked advice of Wilt. I knew he liked that and I learned from him. He was smart as any player I ever knew. I let the players pick their guys they were going to guard. Hell, they picked the ones I wanted them to, anyway.

"I asked Wilt that he get to every practice on time, and he not only didn't miss one, he was usually early. Of course, he didn't do anything when he got there, but I bought the explanation that he had to save his legs.

"I didn't push him on his free throws. I said, 'Hey, Wilt, if you hit all your free throws we'd never lose. It would be too easy, and it wouldn't be any fun.' He liked that.

"I didn't get into Wilt's private life except to see that he got first-class treatment wherever we went. When we dropped into one dump and he complained, I got Gottlieb to book us into the best hotel. Wilt loved luxury, but he even gave me his suite one time when I took a smaller room for myself. You do for him and he can't do enough for you.

"He even tried to make a fancy dresser out of me. He said my wife wanted him to. He bought me a hat. One of those little Harlem hats. I looked foolish in it. But I loved the idea of it.

"Hey, we got along all right. I loved the whole year and I would go back and do it again in a minute. I love Wilt and I wish we could do it again."

It was a wonderful year for Wilt and he loved it and McGuire. He has said, "McGuire was tough, but fair. He was a brilliant strategist and a master psychologist. He knew how

107

to win, but he let us have a say in how to play. He treated his players as people and he looked after us. He didn't need the spotlight. He was the finest man and best coach I've known in basketball."

· There was some jealousy on that team. And disputes. Well, there are on every team. McGuire took care of them. According to Wilt, he had a run-in with Tom Meschery when they wound up with dates with two white girl friends and Tom didn't want to double with a black guy. But Wilt says it may have been a misunderstanding and they became friends later.

Wilt was thrown out of a game that season, the first of three from which he was ejected for arguing with officials in his NBA career. However, the eight and a half minutes he missed were the only ones all season. With overtimes, he set the enduring records of 48½ minutes a game and 3,882 minutes for 80 games. He became the only player ever to pass 4,000 points in a single season with 4,029. He also had 2,052 rebounds, the second highest total in his career.

Although Boston had to replace the retired Bill Sharman, Red Auerbach's Celtics were just becoming the deep, powerful team they would be. They burst from the gate by winning 23 of their first 26 games as they started the search for their sixth title in seven seasons. Settling into a new style, McGuire's Warriors floundered for a while before they got going.

In the All-Star Game at midseason, Wilt set a record with 42 points to surpass the 33 of his rookie year. He hauled in 24 rebounds to just miss the record 25 of his rookie year. Four times Wilt scored 20 or more points, four times he gathered 20 or more rebounds in these games.

This game, in which the superstars divide playing time and share the ball, is one in which high numbers rarely are reached. But Wilt loved this spotlight and always went at it as if it was his personal showcase.

At season's end, Wilt beat out Russell as the All-Star center for the third straight season, but was bothered because Bill beat him out as MVP. McGuire called it a "travesty." But Bill's

Boston team had won the pennant and 60 games, while losing only 20. Closing with a rush, Wilt's Warriors won 49, but still lost out by 11 games.

However, this time there appeared real reason to believe Boston's string of three straight playoff titles might be snapped. Wilt's Warriors appeared ready. They had beaten Boston four straight times at season's end.

McGuire surprised Syracuse in the first round with a strategy that had Wilt concentrating on defense and passing to teammates on offense. It was something he had thought about doing from the start of the season.

But when Syracuse took two of the first four games, McGuire returned to his seasonal style in the fifth and final game. Wilt tallied 56 points to set a playoff record as the Warriors won, 121–104. This qualified them to meet Boston, which had been waiting.

Rested, Boston bombed Philly in the first game, although Wilt outscored and outrebounded Russell. However, Philly bounced back to beat Boston in the second game. Wilt not only outscored Bill, 42–9, but came through in the clutch.

Philly trailed by ten points with ten minutes to play, but came on. Wilt stuffed a teammate's shot to tie it with four minutes left. He got to the other end in time to block a layup by Tom Heinsohn. Fouled on a follow-up shot, Heinsohn hit a free throw. But back at the other end, Wilt tapped in a teammate's miss to put Philly ahead to stay.

Boston won, Philly won. Boston won, Philly won. The teams alternated home sites and the home team won each time through the first six games. There were a couple of near riots in the fifth game, and at one point Sam Jones grabbed a stool and threatened to hit Wilt with it. The bitter rivals went to a seventh game in Boston for the Eastern Conference crown. It turned out to be a controversial contest.

Jack Kiser recalls, "Frank McGuire was streetwise off the sidewalks of New York. When he turned in his list of officials he approved for the playoffs, the one name that he carefully left off was Mendy Rudolph's. Mendy did not work any of the first six games, but just before the seventh game started, here he comes ready to referee. McGuire screamed bloody murder and threatened to pull his team off the court, but he was stuck."

The Celtics led 34–23 after one period, but the Warriors led 56–52 at halftime, and 81–80 after three periods. Wilt and Russell wrestled furiously into the fourth and final quarter, and Russell held Wilt to 22 points in the game. After a goal-tending call against Wilt and some long shots by Cousy, Boston led by 10 with five minutes to play, but the Warriors still almost won.

Thunder rolled from the stands through the frenzied finish. A three-point play by Wilt triggered a 9–2 Warrior spree that brought them within three points with three minutes to play. Wilt was fed in the pivot, but he was hounded so heavily by defenders he failed to get off a shot or make a pass and surrendered the ball on a 24-second violation. The Celtics missed a shot, but Russell blocked a shot by Arizin at the other end and the lead remained three with 2:20 left.

A jumper by Jones made it 105–100. A jumper by Arizin made it 105–102. Heinsohn shot from the corner and Chamberlain blocked it, but Rudolph called goal-tending to make it 107–102. Wilt says, "He was fifteen feet from the basket when I blocked the ball and there was no way it could have been goal-tending." Kiser agrees: "He hit the ball on the way up right back into Heinsohn's face, and it was nowhere near its peak, much less on the way down. It's one of the worst calls I ever saw, but Rudolph also called Wilt out of bounds with the ball right in front of me when he was clearly in bounds." Wilt says, "I was three inches inside the line."

That was with one minute to play after Wilt produced under pressure with two free throws to cut the count to 107–104. The Celtics stalled, shot and missed. The Warriors returned to shoot with 20 seconds left. Wilt took a miss, put it over Russell into the hoop, and was fouled. He sank his fourth straight free throw in the clutch and the Warriors had come back to tie at 107.

The Celtics had 16 seconds for a last shot. Sam Jones hit it with two seconds to go and the Celtics led, 109–107. After a time-out, Gola, from midcourt, tossed the ball at the basket and Wilt, but it was inaccurate, Russell deflected it, the buzzer blew, and Boston players did a victory dance as their fans came from the stands to embrace them.

McGuire, Wilt, and the rest of the Warriors departed in despair. McGuire's bitterness became anger, and he put a fist through the referees' dressing room door trying to get at Rudolph. Frank later gave Kiser a signed story, which was published, blaming Mendy for taking the game from them.

All sorts of rumors spread into stories that this had been a gamblers' game, but Rudolph was never charged by the league with anything worse than doing a difficult job, and he did it for years until illness sent him to the sidelines as a television colorman.

Today, McGuire will only say, "I just want to forget it." Wilt says flatly that he will always remember the series as the one in which Rudolph beat his team, but he complains about only two calls in one game. They were critical, but big basketball games often are decided on close, controversial, critical calls. It is a poorly constructed sport that must be at the mercy of officials. If you play it, you live with it.

Wilt also blames the injuries to Gola, who was hurt on and off all season, and fouls by Rodgers, who fouled out of three games, including the final one, for costing his side the series. He does not make much of the fact he scored less than half his average in the final game.

On the other hand, he came through in the clutch repeatedly in the last minutes of that last game. This is sometimes forgotten when other games in which he did not do as well are remembered. But in the end, the big game was lost again, which was a bitter blow to him. "It hurt horribly," he has admitted.

It was the most meaningful game of Wilt's pro career and is second in importance only to his sophomore-season title game during his college career. Again, Wilt's team might have won, but didn't. The label of "loser" was stuck to him firmly.

111

By the narrowest of margins, Boston's dynasty endured. They won the divisional final by two points, and then the league final by three points when the Lakers also carried them to seven games, and even into overtime. Frank Selvy missed a short shot that would have ended the dynasty.

The Lakers, too, were labeled "losers." There are those who think that if they had won that game, they would have dominated the NBA in coming seasons instead of losing to Boston again and again.

Laker coach Fred Schaus says, "We might have beaten them then. Before that, Philadelphia might have. They were close games and it could have happened. But Boston had the best team in basketball in those years and they were not going to lose many titles. They would have won ten of thirteen instead of eleven. Or nine of thirteen. But they'd have won a lot.

"We had top players, as did Philadelphia, but Boston had top players, too. Boston had more good players, better depth, capable players coming off the bench. It's a long, hard season. It's a long, hard grind in the playoffs. Boston had too much."

It is forgotten that Boston was an eleven-point favorite going into that final with Philadelphia when the Warriors almost stopped them at three straight titles. When they did not, the Warriors seemed to come apart. The disappointment deepened when Gottlieb revealed he was selling the franchise to San Francisco interests.

McGuire said he could not go because he had a palsied son in treatment that required him to remain in the East, but the fact is that after the Philadelphia protest over the officiating in that controversial and critical contest was disallowed by the league, he said he would never again coach in the NBA. He never has.

Wilt went with the Warriors, without McGuire, reluctantly, a brief chapter brought to a surprisingly swift conclusion, a brief era in his history and basketball history ended.

Supposedly it says on W.C. Fields' tombstone, in his words, "On the whole I'd rather be in Philadelphia." Whatever, the sentiments are clear: It is preferable perhaps only to death. The writer does not agree, rather liking the town. Others feel otherwise, slandering this city.

Certainly, Wilt Chamberlain did not endear himself to his hometown by asking aloud, "How could anyone love Philadelphia?" He asked privately to be traded after two seasons back in his hometown, but that was as much to get away from the Warriors as from the city. When a new coach was hired, he agreed to give him a chance.

The American Basketball League had begun in the fall of 1961. Abe Saperstein was behind it and asked Wilt if he was interested. However, the Globetrotter boss wasn't prepared to pay Wilt the kind of money he wanted. No one in the league was. The owners didn't rob the NBA of its stars, instead taking shadowed and fringe players. By the end of their first season they were close to collapse. Midway in their second, they did fold.

When Wilt was offered the opportunity to go with the Warriors to scenic San Francisco, he characteristically refused. He had gone to England to pick up a Bentley he had ordered and was in France when told by transatlantic phone by Eddie Gottlieb that the Warriors had been sold. He told Eddie he'd probably prefer to stay overseas and become an expatriate and live a life of leisure. He made Eddie call again and again, before, to no one's surprise, Wilt gave in and agreed to go. A $100,000 yearly salary for three years was the convincer.

Wilt has called Gottlieb "the only real basketball man among all the owners" he had. He really liked Eddie and seemed to feel sold out when Eddie sold the team. Gottlieb says, "Wilt was bitter, but it was the chance of a lifetime for me and I couldn't pass it up." It was said that "when Eddie bought into the Warriors for $2,500, he borrowed $2,800 of it." He became coach and manager of the team in 1946 when the franchise and the NBA began. He made some money, saved it, and five years later bought the team for $25,000. Now, a group of San Franciscans, impressed by the success of pro basketball in LA after the Minneapolis Lakers moved there, were so eager to compete with their rivals in southern California that they offered $850,000 for Wilt and the Warriors.

There was no way Gottlieb could let such an opportunity pass, especially when the bidders threw in a $35,000 annual salary for him to manage the operation the first season and serve as a consultant after that.

Wilt's first year in Philadelphia, attendance jumped 20 percent. But then it fell off again. Wilt was a bigger draw in cities around the league where he appeared only a few times a season than he was in his hometown where they could see him whenever they wanted and were used to his scoring. He was booed as a villain on the road, but fans did come out to root against him.

It is not clear why the Warriors played so poorly their first season in San Francisco. Arizin's retirement was significant but they started five of the six "regulars" who had performed so successfully their last season in Philadelphia.

114

Meschery was injured and replaced by Ted Luckenbill in the team's San Francisco debut at the Cow Palace, but Gola, Wilt, Attles and Rodgers started the historic tilt. With Wilt tallying 56 points, Detroit was demolished, 140–113.

The Warriors started fast and were in the divisional lead in mid-November. Then they fell from first place in a 127–115 loss to LA, despite 72 points by Wilt. They never regained the lead. Later, they suffered losses to LA in games when Wilt tallied 63 and 53 points.

This was the pattern: Wilt scored spectacularly, though not as spectacularly as the season before, but the Warriors lost. At one point they lost 11 games in a row.

Wilt's stature was at such a low ebb that although he was coming off a fabulous season and was on his way to leading the league in scoring and rebounding for the fourth straight season, he did not lead the centers in the voting to select the Western Division team for the All-Star Game at midseason. Walt Bellamy of Chicago did. Walt also had been selected as the center on one All-Star team at the previous season's end, and Russell had been named ahead of Wilt to the official league team, despite Wilt's 50-points-a-game average.

Reluctantly, Wilt could accept Bill being named ahead of him, but not Walt, and he was insulted. "There is no way that man rates ahead of me," Chamberlain remarked angrily. And there was not.

Wilt proved his point by playing superbly in the All-Star Game in Los Angeles, while Walt did little. And although Bellamy built up impressive statistical totals over a long career in the NBA, he was passed from team to team and wound up just another big man who was not, after all, "The New Wilt Chamberlain."

From midseason on, Wilt sulked. For a while after Willie Naulls and Kenny Sears arrived, he passed off to them a lot, averaged six or seven assists a game, and shot less than ever before, but when they had trouble putting the ball in the basket, Wilt went back to doing it. There were nights when he moodily refused to shoot and took only three or four attempts, but he averaged 34 shots a game.

Naulls and Sears figured to add scoring punch in support of Wilt, but disappointed. Team defense disappeared. Coach Bob Feerick had to try to rebuild the team and pull it together, but he never seemed able to get a grip on it. The Warriors were ten-plus players in search of a team. Players came and went.

The Warriors were faltering at the finish. Trying for a playoff position at least, they lost a critical contest to Detroit, 131–123, despite 51 points by Wilt, including a basket at the buzzer that sent it into overtime. Then their last hope passed when they lost in Syracuse, 163–148, despite 70 by Wilt.

Wilt played all 80 games, averaged 47½ minutes, 44 points, and 24 rebounds a game, but the Warriors won only 31 games and finished fourth, 18 games below .500, 22 games out of first, and 3 games out of the playoffs, which were won by Bill Russell and Boston once again, in 6 games with Los Angeles.

It had become clear at this point that unprecedented scoring by one player like Wilt simply wasn't enough to insure a winning team.

Bob Feerick was blamed for bad coaching because the club was not what it had been under McGuire or even, for that matter, Johnston, and Feerick was made general manager while Alex Hannum was brought in to try to get the team going.

Before he died in mid-1976, still manager of the Warriors, Feerick reported to this writer, "I don't believe I was entirely to blame for the disappointing season, but I'm willing to accept my share of responsibility.

"A lot of factors entered into it. We got most of the starters from Philadelphia, but not the outside shooter, Arizin, to complement Wilt and not the bench strength. Some of the old players were not happy with the move and did not play well. New players let us down.

"I liked Wilt as a person and admired him as a player, but he did not put into it what he might have. He would not practice and it was as though he was not part of the team.

"When you are winning, problems among players do not seem important, but when you are losing, they increase in importance. Most losing teams are torn by dissension, while winners laugh off differences.

"We had a bad building and San Francisco fans never got behind us. We did not get much break from media. What started as a promising situation deteriorated almost overnight.

"Wilt would not help a lot in public relations. He did not like to make public appearances. We were trying to put together a team effort to succeed in San Francisco, and Wilt was not a team man. And yet I really was awed by what he put on the court, and really liked him off the court."

Wilt fell in love with San Francisco, but San Francisco did not fall in love with him. Part of the problem was that when the Warriors were starting their first season in San Francisco in 1962, the baseball Giants, with such stars as Willie Mays, Willie McCovey, and Juan Marichal, were ending a pennant-winning campaign. Priding themselves on their sophistication, San Franciscans never have been able to unbend to the point of supporting sporting teams with passion. At that time, enthusiasm for one team, the Giants, was as much as they could muster.

In years since, their support of the Giants has deteriorated to the point where the team may move, just as the Warriors were driven across the bay into Oakland and a new arena there in the 1970's, where they joined the hockey Seals. Now the Seals have left.

The Cow Palace is a drafty barn unsuitable for major league sports, but San Francisco has done nothing more than talk about a new big-league building for many years. It is the largest city in the country without an adequate indoor facility.

Wilt was big box-office around the league during the Warriors' first season in San Francisco, but the team averaged less than 4,000 fans a game at home. The new owners, led by Franklin Mieuli, lost a lot of money, close to a million dollars.

"It was deeply disappointing," Mieuli once told this writer.

117

"We went to a lot of trouble and expense to bring the best in basketball to this city, and it didn't respond. Wilt didn't help a whole lot." Wilt has said, "I never played before for a team which lost more games than it won, and it was the most miserable season of my career."

He has said, "Mieuli knew as much about basketball as I do about phrenology." And, "Feerick couldn't coach pros." And, "Bay area writers knew nothing about the game." And, "The fans couldn't have cared less."

He also has said, "San Francisco is a sensational city. A beautiful city. A different town. Sophisticated people. Lovely ladies. A romantic town fit for a romanticist. The best in food and drink for a man of taste. European charm and California tradition. But no place for basketball."

He moved around a lot—Twin Peaks, Pacific Heights, other places, even living in a houseboat off Sausalito for a while—and liked the views of the fog-shrouded Golden Gate Bridge, the bay area, and beyond.

But he could not have cared less about the Cow Palace and the fans who responded to his performances with indifference. Sportswriter Bucky Walter says, "San Franciscans are proud of their city almost beyond belief. They like their heroes home-grown.

"They wouldn't even take Willie Mays to their hearts when he was playing at his peak because he was a New Yorker. They preferred Willie McCovey because he developed here. Wilt was an outsider and sort of extravagant for their tastes, but Rick Barry was something else when he came along.

"The second season was better because a better coach made the team better, and more entertaining," Bucky concludes.

Gottlieb got Hannum for San Francisco. Hannum had been a tough player and had become a tough coach at Syracuse. However, Hannum was homesick and his wife wanted to go home to California. When his Nats shifted to Philadelphia to become the 76ers, he left to return to southern California as a building contracter. Gottlieb talked him into returning to basketball in northern California.

This was a month before the new season was to start, and Hannum asked two questions of Gottlieb:

"Does Chamberlain demand to play the full forty-eight minutes of every game?"

"Absolutely not," Gottlieb said.

"Is Chamberlain going after points to insure his high salary?" Hannum then asked.

"Absolutely not," Gottlieb repeated.

"OK. You've got yourself a coach," Hannum said.

But Alex had asked the wrong man. Wilt did want to play the full forty-eight minutes of every game, and he did want his points, though as much for ego as salary. Actually Wilt thought that since he was the greatest scorer the game has had, it was a waste for him not to score.

When they met at training camp, Alex said he wanted Wilt to shoot less, pass more, concentrate less on offense and more on defense, play close to the basket at all times, and forget the fadeaway (as McGuire had), and come out of games for rests so he could go all out while he was in games.

Wilt grumbled about it. And he just didn't do it at first. He had never liked Hannum, anyway. Hannum hollered from his benches. When he was at Syracuse he used to holler at the refs that they were letting Wilt get away with murder and he used to taunt Wilt. And he sent his star, Dolph Schayes, out to work Wilt over. Schayes pushed and pulled Wilt and drove him to distraction.

Wilt has said, "When he was against me, Hannum used to complain I was walking with the ball and playing a one-man zone defense and in the lane too long, but somehow when he was with me he stopped saying anything about any of this."

Wilt and Alex argued all the time for a while. And Wilt constantly complained about Alex to others. Finally fed up with Wilt's second-guessing and individualism, Hannum

119

cleared the dressing room one time and challenged Chamberlain to a fight.

Alex was a tall, slender man who was giving away reach, height, and weight to Wilt, but he never backed down from anyone. Wilt supposedly decided it would not be wise to take on his coach. He admits the balding, scowling Hannum seemed menacing, but he says it was Alex, "as smart as he was strong," who thought better of the bout.

In any event, they did not come to blows, but sat down to talk about their differences. They agreed to try to respect each other's wishes and try to work together for the good of the team. Wilt respects courage on the part of his coaches and came out of the meeting feeling better about Alex.

This incident was not well known at the time, but since has been confirmed by Chamberlain. Alex always "forgot" it. In any event, it did not totally end differences between them, though Alex denies it, but they were able to work together after that.

To better their rapport, they started to see one another socially. Alex had a powerboat and Wilt loved to water-ski. Alex would take Wilt water-skiing and attain such speeds and steer such sharp turns Wilt laughingly wonders if Alex wasn't trying to kill him. Alex just smiles, but admits he'd never go driving with Wilt in the souped-up cars Wilt sped across the countryside.

Publicly, Alex admitted, "Actually, we're a conflict in personalities and in ideas. He thinks one way, I think another. But, I have never gotten such cooperation from a man. Wilt has done everything I've asked him to, and he's done it willingly—given me absolutely no trouble.

"I still don't know whether he likes me. I hope he does and I feel pretty certain he respects me as a coach. But whether he does or doesn't, he puts out for me, and I wouldn't trade him for Bill Russell.

"We're not a good shooting team. We have to get a lot of scoring from Wilt in order to win, and scoring is not Russell's

120

best department. In my opinion, Chamberlain has to do more things for us to win than Russell has to do for the Celtics. And Wilt is doing it. He's changed.

"I ask a lot of Wilt. I ask him to play like Wilt on offense and like Russell on defense. I'm not trying to stop him from shooting. When Wilt is against a center he can eat up, I want him to chew him up. But I want Wilt to give the other players the ball when they have their shots. I want to get the other guys into the game. I found out they had forgotten how to play without Wilt.

"I believe in pattern play and set plays. I believe in a running game and I've got my guys going, but you can't free-lance and improvise all the time. If we're missing chances, I call for a set play. If we have a man who can get open, I call his play. I want Wilt to take part in these patterns as part of the team. What good is it if Wilt scores seventy-five points and we lose?

"I think many people have the wrong idea about Chamberlain. They think all he ever cares about is how many points he scores. This isn't true. All the man wants to do is win. He'd rather score one point and have us win than to get fifty and have us lose."

Wilt did not see things exactly the same. He said, "My last season in Philadelphia, we won eighty percent of the games in which I scored fifty or more points. We won more games than the team has ever won. I'm not sure my shooting less will make us win more. When I did not score as well as usual, we did not win.

"I don't think I'm different as a player than I was. Defense has been my best thing since I was in high school, only nobody noticed. I've always blocked shots, rebounded, passed off to anyone who was open. But I don't want to waste my ability to score. I don't want to hurt my effectiveness.

"If the man doesn't want me to shoot, I won't shoot," he concluded ominously.

In the season opener in Baltimore, Wilt scored only 23 points, but the Warriors won. The next night in St. Louis, Wilt scored only 22, but the Warriors won another one. As the season moved along, Wilt shot less and the Warriors won more.

Writers raved about "The New Warriors," who were running, hustling, defending. One writer wrote, "Wilt Chamberlain has become a man." Another would write of "The Growing Up of Wilt Chamberlain." It was as if they were blaming him for failures from before, and Wilt did not like it.

Moodily he started to shoot less and less. One game he did not take a single shot even though his team was being beaten badly. George Kiseda's lead the next day was, "Wilt Chamberlain, the greatest offensive player in the history of basketball, proved last night that he also is the greatest defensive player ever because he became the first man ever to hold Wilt without a shot."

Kiseda recalls, "When I asked Wilt about it, he said he'd shot one hundred percent because he hadn't missed any shots. I told him zero for zero was zero percent. He said, 'Well, you figure it your way and I'll figure it mine. You writers always fuck up the facts anyway, and twist statistics to suit you.'"

Hannum hammered at Wilt, trying to reach him. He was aware Wilt had to be dealt with differently than others. Alex pointed out, "This man has emotional problems which most of us don't have. When you're as tall as Wilt . . . the only way Chamberlain can get any privacy is to lock himself in his hotel room.

"I think this is why Wilt used to take the fallaway jumper so much. This is the type of shot the average-sized player depends on, and Wilt did not want to take unfair advantage of his size. But I think he sees now that it is not to the team's advantage for him to shoot it."

Alex said he was annoyed when a wire-service story reported Wilt was leading the league with a "disappointing" scoring average of 31 points a game. "Disappointing to whom?" he asked. "The guy has been playing great basketball and doing everything a man can do. This makes me mad. I feel we ought to promote basketball as a game."

Wilt agreed and gradually began to accept Alex and play with more passion. "I don't agree with Alex on everything, but he's made a number of points with me," Wilt commented.

"You can't expect a man to change overnight," Alex said.

Wilt did make adjustments as the season went along. He began to shoot again. In one game against the Knicks, he missed his first shot, then hit his next 18 in a row to surpass an NBA record dating back a dozen years, one of the few scoring records that had eluded him. But he averaged only 20 shots and 36 points a game. He went from 20 games of 50 points or more to 10. He took almost 500 less shots and scored some 600 less points than the season before. He also took down 150 or so less rebounds than ever before, averaging just 22. He still led the league in scoring, but Russell led in rebounding.

Wilt fit into the team in time. Averaging only 41 minutes a game, he stayed fresh. He went from 275 assists the season before to 403. He set picks and passed off. It was a better team because it was strengthened by towering rookie Nate Thurmond and sophomore Wayne Hightower and because Hannum received inspired performances from his players. Formerly a center, Thurmond played defensive forward. With Wilt he led the Warriors to the best defensive record in the NBA.

The Warriors started slowly, progressed with the season, soared in the standings, took over second place in January, first in February, and protected their lead the last six weeks as St. Louis passed Los Angeles, sagging from injuries to both Baylor and West. The Warrior record of 48-32 was 17 games better than the season before, 2 better than St. Louis and 6 better than LA. "Hannum is the greatest coach I've had," said Chamberlain.

Despite Bob Cousy's retirement, Boston broke from the gate with 25 victories in their first 30 games, then held off a late rush by Cincinnati to win by 4 games the Eastern Division pennant for the eighth straight season. The new way worked for Wilt to the extent that he beat out Bill Russell in both the All-Star and

123

MVP categories, but did not win the latter because Cincy's Oscar Robertson did.

However, Boston took Cincy out of the playoffs fast, in five games. Meanwhile, after St. Louis beat LA, San Francisco took St. Louis out. It took seven games. The Hawks, with powerfully built Zelmo Beaty at center, beat on Chamberlain like a drum, but Wilt tallied 50 points in one game and the key points in the last game as the Warriors won it, 105–95.

For the first time, the old divisional rivals were to meet in the playoff finals.

Perhaps to psych out Chamberlain, Russell gave interviews that he was suffering so from arthritic knees he was not playing well and was so exhausted he had insomnia and was near to a nervous breakdown. He then went out and defensed Wilt so determinedly in the middle two periods that he held Wilt to 2 points in that time, as the Warriors fell out of it and lost by 14.

"Wilt was just tired," Russ said, seemingly with sympathy. Wilt nodded. He bounced back and outplayed Big Bill in the second game. Red Auerbach brought in Lovellette to try to contain Wilt in the last quarter, and that was when Clyde so roughed Chamberlain that Wilt felled him with one big blow, almost touching off a riot in steamy Boston Garden.

Boston won anyway, by 23 points. Surrounding Russell were Sam Jones and K.C. Jones, Tom Heinsohn and Tom Sanders, a young John Havlicek and veterans Frank Ramsey and Lovellette coming off the bench—and even Naulls, dealt earlier by the Warriors. The team was tremendous, deep, powerful, versatile, balanced.

Hannum hoped to do better at home and did in the third game, 115–91, with Wilt tallying 35. But Boston bounced back to turn off the Warriors in the next tilt, 98–95, despite 27 points and 38 rebounds by Wilt.

Back in Boston, Auerbach's bunch made it six straight titles and seven out of eight by beating the Warriors, 105–99, despite 30 points by Chamberlain, who played in pain after gashing his hand on the rim. While Celtic supporters bore Russell off court on their shoulders, Wilt, his hand bound by a bloody bandage, slumped off sadly.

The loss spoiled the season for the San Franciscans. It disappointed them and disspirited them. It was as if all that had happened before had been a waste. They had not even come close to the Celtics and they sagged. Wilt went to Europe to forget. The others scattered. Hannum never was able to pull them together again. Athletes are high-strung and the confidence of this crew had collapsed.

Mieuli, colorful, likable, but a bit outlandish at times, had been strutting about like a bantam rooster, cock of the walk, and he took the defeat hard. He didn't like Hannum, and Hannum didn't like him. He didn't like Wilt, and Wilt didn't like him.

Hannum said, "I was never Mieuli's man, even when I was working for him. Franklin got stuck with me because Eddie Gottlieb brought me in." Nor was Wilt Mieuli's star. He was Gottlieb's. And then Eddie went back to Philly and Franklin took over.

Hannum summed it up when he said, "Franklin is a promoter and what he wants most to promote is Franklin Mieuli. The trouble with trying to work for Franklin is that he wants to be the main attraction, and he wants everybody to agree with him all the time. I think this is why I got fired and Wilt got traded." Hannum got fired after the following season. Wilt got traded halfway through the season.

The spotlight may not have been big enough for Wilt and Franklin both. And Hannum, too.

The trouble started in training camp when a doctor who did not know Wilt gave him his routine preseason physical and detected an irregular heart pattern on the electrocardiogram. Wilt told him he'd almost always suffered stomach pains, the cause of which never had been diagnosed, and the doctor thought the conditions might be connected. He ordered Wilt to the hospital.

Wilt was there four weeks while specialists ran tests, but he

125

didn't believe there was anything wrong with his heart. Finally, he called his physician in Philadelphia, Dr. Stanley Lorber, who told him he'd always had an unusual heart pattern and probably had pancreatitis. He suggested that Wilt return to Philadelphia for tests there.

Wilt jumped the hospital in California and flew to Philly. By then his case had been widely publicized in headlines in sports pages across the country. The rumor was the giant's heart was giving out. Lorber decided Wilt had pancreatitis, put him on the wagon, off the whiskey and wine Wilt liked, and onto milk and orange juice. Wilt accepted the diagnosis because he liked it better than heart trouble. And he began to read medical books, deciding he'd soon know more than the medical fraternity.

Released, Wilt rejoined the Warriors, who'd played five games of the regular season without him and lost four of them. Mieuli waited at the airport to welcome him back with a token of friendship. Following the previous season, Wilt had suggested their divisional title be rewarded with something different from rings as usual, like diamond stickpins. To his disappointment, Mieuli provided the usual rings. Now, however, Franklin held out a custom-made diamond stickpin.

Wilt stared at it expressionlessly, then asked, "What's this piece of shit?"

Franklin remembers it, as does Hannum, though Wilt seems not to. Alex has said, "At that moment, I think, Wilt was through with the Warriors." Mieuli has said, "I must admit it did not endear me to Wilt. He is not always a gracious gentleman and is far from my favorite player of all time."

Mieuli still owed Gottlieb for the Warriors. Wilt says he was owed on his salary and was bugging Franklin about it, and it had become a burden to him. Wilt says Mieuli had made up his mind to trade him before his market value went down, and ordered Alex, over his protests, to get him back in the lineup right away to play for points, although Wilt had lost 35 pounds and was not in shape. Wilt went back in and Bucky Walter

126

remembers, "He was sick, for sure. He got by on guts. He was sweating terribly and drinking ice-cold milk by the cartons in an effort to cool off."

In his first game back, Wilt played 33 minutes and scored 16 points. In his second, he played 48 and scored 37. Soon he was playing 48 and averaging 38. In his first six weeks he scored 50 or more six times. He scored 62 in one game, 63 in another. An elbow by Boston's John Thompson broke his nose, so Wilt had to wear a face mask, but after missing two games, he scored 40 his first game back and 58 his next game. He kept going.

He grew a goatee, too, the first in the NBA and a style-setter for other athletes to follow. Hannum, Mieuli, and others didn't like it, but Wilt couldn't care less. No one cared about him, so why should he care about them? The team was playing terribly, anyway. Wilt was back to shooting and the team was back to losing—games, fans, and money.

They had won 10 and lost 34, the last 11 in a row, when the All-Star Game came up in St. Louis. Mieuli and Hannum went to St. Louis with Wilt, and Wilt says Mieuli told Hannum, "I'm not leaving St. Louis till I get rid of that son of a bitch," and went from room to room in the headquarters hotel trying to swing a deal, any deal to dump him.

Hannum wasn't too happy about it, but Mieuli insisted he'd be better off with Thurmond—twenty-three, and five years younger than Wilt—at center and with several regulars in return for Wilt. But no one wanted to give a lot for Wilt with his reputation.

One team that would take him was Philadelphia. Eddie Gottlieb was back there; he had helped Irv Kosloff and Ike Richman buy the Syracuse team and transfer it to Philly. They wanted Wilt back on his hometown team.

As it was announced, the trade, made around midnight after the All-Star Game, in which Wilt tallied 20 points and totaled 16 rebounds and his West team lost by one point, was Wilt to the 76ers for Lee Shaffer, Connie Dierking, and Paul Neumann, plus $300,000 in cash.

What was not announced was that the deal included settlement of monies owed Gottlieb from the original sale and owed Wilt on his seasonal salary, and no other cash may have exchanged hands.

Shaffer had not even reported to Philadelphia that season and he did not report to San Francisco. Dierking and Neumann reported, but played poorly. Dierking was traded, later Neumann. Thurmond was always hurt and never quite as effective for the Warriors as expected.

After the trade the Warriors lost 6 more in a row to run their losing streak to a record 17 straight before winning, but won only 17 of 80 all season, the worst record in the league in more than a decade.

And Hannum was fired.

Mieuli, a bearded motorcycle driver, is an eccentric among owners, but a decent guy who just didn't make it with Wilt. Franklin fell in love with Rick Barry the following season and he remained loyal, his torch burning brightly even after Rick left Franklin for the ABA. Until Franklin could get him back, he kept Rick's jersey hanging in his office.

Of the Wilt trade, Mieuli once told me, "The deal didn't work out well, but I've never regretted it."

Wilt did regret it to the extent that he did not want to leave San Francisco. In fact it was not until 1976 that he sold his last home there. One burned in a flash fire. And back in 1965 he threatened retirement once again. But Gottlieb talked him out of it once again, with the help of promises of future favors from Richman, and to no one's surprise, Wilt headed "home."

"It's a hurting thing to leave the city you love," Wilt sighed. "I guess it was the money. I really don't know for sure, but that must have been why they did it.

"What I do know for certain is that in San Francisco I found a place I would like to call home. As you know, I've seen most of the world. It is either here or New York that I would like to plant my roots.

"The 76ers made a bad deal trading for me because I am

considering retiring after this season. I explained to Ike Richman and Irv Kosloff exactly how I feel. They are both close friends and associates. It gets to a point where money isn't everything.

"I'm sorry some hold me responsible for what happened, as if I had anything to do about the move. It's been my cross to bear that I've been singled out as a villain ever since I started to play. I've learned to live with it, but sometimes it still hurts. It's the old story that no one likes Goliath."

So he went, humbled momentarily at having been bought at a bargain rate. Athletes are traded, but most will tell you it makes them feel unwanted, unappreciated, and unloved. Wilt did.

Someone said he was "The Littlest Giant."

The late Abe Saperstein at the time confided the deal between the 76ers and Warriors was "a lot of poppycock." He said, "I'm firm in my belief Gottlieb was interested in both clubs. He maintained his offices in Philadelphia all the time he was in San Francisco, and just shifted back.

"When I was a major stockholder in the Warriors, Chamberlain was under contract to me and the Globetrotters. When I transferred Wilt to the Warriors because they needed him so badly, the deal was he was to revert to me later. It was verbal, not written. That was my mistake. Eddie and I broke over it.

"When they bought my stock, they didn't haggle about price because they had a purchaser, a patsy in the form of some San Franciscans to buy the club for big money. When they couldn't come up with all the cash because the club was losing money in San Francisco, Gottlieb got out and got Wilt as settlement.

"Franklin Mieuli didn't fight it. He didn't like Wilt and Wilt was pressing him for salary owed him. Franklin has a team that is losing on the court and at the box office, and he doesn't need Wilt with his salary hanging over his head and nothing to show for it. He has the kid Thurmond to play, anyway.

"Irv Kosloff and Ike Richman are each supposed to have half of the 76ers, but I'd be surprised if Gottlieb doesn't have a piece. And he's still under contract to the Warriors. They yanked Wilt back to settle with Mieuli.

"I don't think any money changed hands. They just took it out of one pocket and put it back in another. It was all in the family. The NBA family. That's the way the NBA does business.

"Having been identified with the fellows involved, I know how those eastern schemers operate," he concluded.

Gottlieb has said, "We were just doing business."

Eddie was not supposed to be part of ownership in Philadelphia, but it was he who kept the long-distance lines busy talking Wilt into returning to Philly. Chamberlain liked Gottlieb and Richman. According to Chamberlain, Richman promised him half of his half—25 percent—of the Warriors on his retirement. It was supposed to be a bonus—cash free—but was a verbal commitment, not a written, contracted one, because NBA rules prohibited players owning pieces of teams. Richman was Wilt's personal lawyer. Wilt had no special relationship with Kosloff.

Richman said, "This was a great deal, maybe the greatest deal in sports history." He would not discuss his business arrangement with Wilt except to say that "He is a person with whom you can reason. He is a great man, who will not do anything foolish. He does what he thinks is best for all concerned. He always has been honest and sincere. I have never had any reason to feel other than optimistic about further dealings with Wilt. I know him for what he is, a person who is as big mentally as he is physically. And I am willing to go along with him, as is Mr. Irv Kosloff."

Wilt told him, "Ike, I'll play right away if you want, but I'm in no shape to play. I'm not a piece of chopped liver."

Ike offered him a week to work his way into shape, though he needed him on the court and at the box office. Richman reported, "He's been frustrated and gloomy. This is a young man in the prime of his life who until this season has enjoyed good health and immeasurable success.

"Now he has been sick. While he was hospitalized, his team went into a tailspin. He began playing because he felt an obligation to his coach, his teammates, and to the owners and people of San Francisco. He did not want to leave because the Warriors were struggling on an eleven-game losing streak and he wanted so much to help break it.

"We'll wipe the gloom away quickly. Everyone is enthusiastic about his return to this town, his town, where he belongs."

Everyone except Wilt, perhaps. He'd had an apartment in New York for several years. After the trade, part of the agreement that brought him back was that he could live full-time in the big town and only commute to Philadelphia, without having to participate in a lot of practices.

Gottlieb concedes, "We had an agreement. Why not? Why can't a man live where he wants? As long as Wilt was with the team for games, why did he have to live in Philadelphia? What did Wilt have to practice? He had bad legs, anyway. He'd tell you that. The coach didn't care. Coaches have to make adjustments, anyway."

The coach was Dolph Schayes. For the record, he said, "There's a myth that Chamberlain is uncoachable. It's ridiculous. I think quite a bit of Wilt as a person. He is very coachable. He will build morale on a team that already has a high morale. He's still a young man who wants to play on a championship team. I feel he has a good chance to be on a champion this year."

Privately, Schayes said other things. "Why did this have to happen to me?" he asked one writer.

Wilt wondered why it had happened to him. As a player, Schayes had handled Chamberlain roughly. And he'd written a magazine story calling Chamberlain "immature, stubborn, a crybaby." Wilt denies he bothers to read what is written about him, but he seems to see everything and remember everything ever written. Wilt admits one reason he didn't want to return to Philadelphia was because Schayes was coaching. He was, Wilt has said, like Johnston, "a great player who became a lousy coach." He was, Wilt has admitted, "a warmer man than Johnston." In fact, "too nice a guy to be a good coach."

Schayes was as nice off the court as he was mean on it. George Kiseda agrees: "He was too nice a guy to be a successful coach in pro basketball. The players considered him a pussycat. They made fun of him behind his back. They ridiculed him. They did not take him seriously."

One of those players confesses, "We did not consider him a coach to be taken seriously. We ridiculed the way he walked and talked. We did a number on the poor guy, which was a pity."

Asked about it, Schayes debated weeks before he decided he did not want to talk about it.

To Wilt, Schayes seemed to be just another old player who had come up lame and instead of being shot was made coach. This was the pro way, Wilt wrote in a *Sports Illustrated* article, "My Life in a Bush League," which came out before this season even ended. The players on that team expected Wilt to take over and Dolph to diminish in authority, which is what happened.

Schayes had been a fine free-throw shooter and he had written of Wilt's poor free-throw shooting, "It's ridiculous; any high school player could do better. He's just too lazy to practice. That's all it takes—practice." He asked Wilt to practice free throws. For a while Wilt did—400 or so a day. He hit 80 percent of them. In practice. He hit between 40 and 50 percent in games, about half as many. Schayes surrendered. So did Wilt. After a while he seldom practiced free throws or anything else.

It was a talented team. It had a forward who could shoot, Chet Walker, and one who could rebound, Luke Jackson, and guards who could shoot from outside, drive and handle the ball, Hal Greer and Larry Costello. Johnny Kerr was not a scoring center, and that was what the team lacked until Wilt turned up. However, Wilt with his reputation was not welcomed. Contrary

133

to what Schayes said, morale was low. The team was disorganized and uninspired.

Ironically, Wilt's return to action came against the Warriors. It was in Philadelphia, but in the smaller Arena, instead of Convention Hall, which was busy with a bowling tournament. Although it was publicized, no one expected the crowd that came out. The Warriors had been averaging less than 4,000 fans a game, but 10,000 turned up. Traffic jammed on Market Street. After 6,140 had fought their way in, police closed the doors and had to barricade the rest of the frustrated fans away.

Inside, when Wilt was introduced, he received a standing ovation that lasted almost a minute. In the game, his every move was met with cheers. When the team won, Wilt and his mates were cheered away. Wilt admitted he was moved by it. It was not until later that he learned Ike Richman, seeking to inspire Wilt and a warm feeling between him and Philadelphians, had handed out enough free tickets in churches, schoolyards, shops, and on street corners to fill Municipal Stadium, and even organized groups of youngsters with banners and noisemakers to create a racket.

Let down, Wilt has sighed, "I still like to think some of it was genuine."

That was the Warriors' fourteenth straight loss. The 76ers went into Syracuse to play the Celtics and broke Boston's string of 16 straight wins, one shy of the Celtics' own league record. Wilt blanked Bill Russell on 15 field shots. Returning to Philadelphia for a rematch with the Celtics, a record crowd of 10,381 packed Convention Hall. Wilt outplayed Russell and the 76ers won again.

They won 9 of their first 11 with Wilt, but then both guards, Greer and Costello, were injured, and Wilt suffered another attack of pancreatitis and played in discomfort. The 76ers fell back to finish at 40–40, 8 games behind Cincinnati and 22 behind Boston, which won its ninth straight Eastern title on a 62–18 record.

Wilt missed seven games that season, but in the games he

played he averaged 46 minutes, 34 points, and 22 rebounds. He won the scoring title as he had every year, but he lost the rebounding title to Russell. He finished second in the All-Star center vote to Russell and only fifth in the MVP poll, captured by Russell, whose Celtics remained dominant.

Boston was out of reach of Philadelphia long before Wilt arrived, but with Wilt the 76ers were given an outside chance of an upset in the playoffs. First, they had to get by Cincinnati. But Robertson had a sore foot, so the Royals were a soft touch. The 76ers won the short series with three victories in four games, Wilt's free throws winning one of them in overtime.

Wilt's story "My Life in a Bush League" broke during the finals and created unsettling controversy on the 76ers. He was fined for it, but he paid a heavier price in the anger of his coach and of players who resented his criticisms. At first Wilt denied a lot of it, especially the title. Later he admitted he had called the NBA "bush," but swore he had been promised the story would not be published until after the season, and said the writer, Bob Ottum, apologized. Ottum says flatly that Wilt approved the story and no apology was in order from either himself or the magazine.

Red Auerbach's Boston team with Russell somehow always escaped controversy. They were a team, together. Everything revolved around Russell, but he was an unselfish player. No one dominated the scoring. Sam Jones averaged almost 26 points a game that season and that was the all-time team record. A defensive star, K.C. Jones, teamed with him in the backcourt. Bob Cousy and Bill Sharman were gone, but their replacements were less individualistic. Up front Satch Sanders and Tom Heinsohn provided muscle. John Havlicek had replaced Frank Ramsey as the supersub who stirred things up coming off the bench. A swing man at both forward and guard, the hustling Havlicek was second in scoring on the club. Willie Naulls also subbed spectacularly in spots.

But the key man may have been Auerbach. Other coaches may have been as knowing, but Red was more imaginative and inspirational than most. There is some chemistry that enables some men to communicate with and impress men more than others; it is the key to success in a coach, and Auerbach had this invisible, subtle quality.

More than anything else Boston had, it had desire. The Celtics were a collection of talented players used wisely and well by Auerbach, but what set them most apart from their rivals and won the close games and close series for them was the desire to remain the champions. Other teams are content to win a title or two, but the great teams remain somehow hungry. The more they win, the more they want to win.

Proud, poised professionals, the Celtics were cool in the clutch. They stayed in games and set up victories by outhustling the hungriest of their rivals, outscrambling them for rebounds, diving for loose balls, wading in, accepting punishment and paying a price in pain to continue on top.

They had built one of sports' dynasties and so were comparable with the Yankees, Canadiens, and Packers in baseball, hockey, and football when they dominated their rivals for prolonged periods. The Celtics won their eighth straight NBA title and ninth in ten years by routing a crippled Laker club in five games in the finals in 1965, but they really won it when they won by a narrow margin in seven games in the semifinals for divisional laurels from a Philadelphia team that had superior individual talent, possibly Boston's first foe that did.

In the opener in Boston, Wilt tallied 33, but Russell outrebounded him, 31–30, and Boston won, 108–98. Wilt blamed the Boston fans and Celtic full-court press which, he said, demoralized the 76er guards, who threw the ball away again and again. Demoralized, Greer scored 27 in defeat. In the second game in Philadelphia, Wilt outscored Bill, 30–12, and outrebounded him, 39–16, and Philly won, 109–103, despite 40 by Sam Jones.

In the third game back in Boston, the Celtics won, 112–94. Wilt blamed the pressing defense again, but admits he played poorly. He outrebounded Russell, 37–26, but was held by Bill

136

without a basket until there were only a few seconds left in the first half and Bill had bombed Wilt for 15 points, himself. By that time, the 76ers were out of it.

In Philadelphia, the 76ers sent the fourth game into overtime on a toss-in with one second left and a disputed 35-foot shot by Greer that Auerbach claimed came after the final buzzer. The 76ers then won it, 118–116. Wilt had 34, Walker 21, Greer 27, and the Philly sharpshooters were bothering Boston.

The Celtics took the series lead again in Boston with a 114–108 victory. Wilt totaled 30 points, but got only 21 rebounds to 28 for Russell and blocked only 2 shots to 12 for Russell.

The 76ers squared the series again in Philadelphia with a 112–106 triumph as Wilt outscored and outrebounded Russell under pressure, despite playing most of the last quarter with five fouls.

So the seesaw series went to a seventh game. With the home team having won each game to that point, the advantage was with Boston on its Garden court. Close to 14,000 fans turned out to see what turned out to be a classic contest.

There was bedlam in that building throughout the game. The Celtics tore into the 76ers at the start and stunned them as they sped to a 30–12 lead which seemed to settle it fast. However, Philadelphia made a comeback and, with Wilt leading the way, cut into the margin little by little until they took the lead in the third quarter.

Boston bounced back to take a seven-point lead with less than two minutes to play in the final period. But the 76ers simply put the ball in Wilt's hands and he came through in the clutch. A tip-in, two free throws under pressure, and a "Dipperdunk" over Russell, six straight points, and it was 110–109.

Boston took the ball with only six seconds left to kill. Russell inbounded it with Walker defending him. Spotting a teammate to one side, Russell lobbed the ball toward him, but it hit a wire supporting the backboard. Philadelphia's ball. Bill could not believe it.

Russell went to one knee, pounding his fist on the floor,

saying, "Oh, my God, oh, my God, it's their ball." He started to scream at the ref that Walker had crossed the line, had hit the ball, anything. He said later films showed Walker had crossed the line, which was illegal, but had not hit the ball.

Philadelphia took a time-out to plot the last shot. Rather than throw it directly to Chamberlain, Schayes decided to decoy by having Greer give it to Walker, who would then turn and toss it to Wilt. Meanwhile, the Celtics convened around Auerbach, who asked, "What do we do now?" No one had an answer for him. "Play defense, but don't foul," he decided. "Watch Wilt, of course."

Russell went out to watch Wilt. He admits, "Suddenly I could see we were men, not supermen. I figured I'd spend the summer trying to explain how I'd hit that wire. I figured we'd blown it. I only hoped Wilt would blow it."

It never got to him. With everyone standing in a sudden hush, Greer lobbed the ball toward Walker as Russell leaned against Wilt. But Havlicek, who had been laying off the play, gambling that the pass might go to Walker, suddenly darted between Greer and Walker, reached out, and deflected the ball. Boston announcer John Most screamed again and again in the din that developed, "Havlicek steals the ball! Havlicek steals the ball!"

Sam Jones grabbed it and hugged it as the buzzer blew and bedlam broke out. As the Celtics were mobbed, the 76ers stood around as though they could not believe what had happened, before finally starting to take the slow, long walk to their room of despair. Wilt had 32 rebounds, 30 points and his fourth playoff defeat to Russell's Celtics in six seasons as a professional.

It just didn't seem in the cards for one of Wilt's teams to win. Yet, Richman remained faithful. He signed Wilt to a three-year contract at $150,000 a year. It was reported to be $100,000 a year. Bill Russell went to Walter Brown and said he was winning when Wilt was not, and whatever Wilt got, he wanted a dollar more. So Walter signed Bill for $100,001 and Bill bragged about it all the time. To this day he laughs and says he owes Wilt something for making him rich and the good story goes on and on, but Wilt just smiles.

If Bill brags, so does Wilt. It is not typical of him that he has been silent about salary, but he has been, and told David Shaw he would not discuss dollars and cents even in his book, though he did hint he received larger amounts than reported. He just smiles and knowingly winks. But reliable reports from inside and in some cases court records reveal he was making more than usually reported in the press.

But if Russell never caught up to Chamberlain in salary, Wilt never caught up to Bill in crowns, though he did beat him once, one season. He was on his way to it after he returned to Philadelphia in the 1975–76 season, though it took time.

The following season two impressive rookies provided depth the 76ers had lacked as Billy Cunningham arrived to complement Jackson and Walker in the front court, and Wally Jones came in to team with Greer and replace Costello in the backcourt.

Wilt averaged 33 points, 24 rebounds, and 5 assists a game and he missed only one game. He again led the league in scoring and rebounding and was seventh in assists with 414, the highest total ever for a center. He was both All-Star center and MVP. Hal Greer averaged 22 points. Others contributed consistently.

Yet Wilt suggests Schayes spoiled the season for them to some extent. If someone made a mistake in practice, his side had to run laps. Then, softhearted, the coach evened it out by having the other side run laps. Which is one reason Wilt hated to practice. One way or another, he had to run laps.

Wilt says that when he got permission to miss a practice during the playoffs, the only one he missed that week, Wilt stresses, because he had the flu, Schayes did not excuse him when reporters asked where Wilt was. "Who knows?" Schayes is supposed to have said.

According to Chamberlain, Schayes' strategy consisted largely of faking fouls. "We've got to really make them look real to the referees," he is supposed to have said, having been an actor of no mean ability himself in his playing days.

It was nonsense, suggests Wilt, who would be blamed when Schayes later was fired. After seven seasons, Wilt was on his way to his sixth coach. It was ridiculous, suggests Wilt, to blame him for the incompetence of his coaches. Or the demands of owners, who did not know what they were doing. Who, too often, hired the wrong coaches for the wrong reasons.

A teammate says, "Dolph wasn't too bad. He wasn't good, but he wasn't too bad."

Schayes could not have done too bad a job as coach. The Warriors were almost unbeatable after midseason. They were unbeatable their last 11 games, including 2 with Boston. They won 55 games and lost only 25 to beat out Boston by one game for the Eastern title and cut the Celtic string short of 10 straight.

But in the playoffs it was another story. This time it was Boston that had to battle through a first round to reach the divisional final, and they barely beat Cincy, three victories to two, to get there.

Once they did, they promptly trounced the 76ers, seemingly sluggish from a 13-day layoff, by 19 points in Philadelphia to wipe out Philly's home-court advantage in the series.

It never got to a seventh game. Boston won the second game, too, by 21 points. When Cunningham and Larry Siegfried squared off, Wilt pulled the Boston player away. Russell intervened, and he and Wilt squared off. They fought with words, not fists, however.

Frustrated, Wilt had a big third game, but after leading by 24, the 76ers barely won by 6.

Boston bounced back to win the fourth game by 4 in an overtime in which Philly tallied only one basket.

Wilt erupted with 46 points in the fifth game, but Boston won decisively, 120–112, to finish it.

Later, in the locker room, Philadelphia sportswriter Joe McGinnis pointed out to Wilt that he'd missed 17 of 25 free throws and asked him if he felt he'd cost his team the game. Wilt glared at him. McGinnis repeated the question a second time. And a third. Wilt exploded and went at McGinnis, but was held away by teammates. Wilt said he wanted to kill the writer, who lived to write a best-seller, *The Selling of the President.*

It was another sad ending to another spectacular season for one of Wilt's teams as Russell's Celtics went on to win a final from LA again in seven savage games.

Inspiring them, Auerbach had announced he was retiring from coaching to concentrate on managing. He lit his last victory cigar to celebrate eight straight league titles and nine in ten seasons. He was one Wilt never would defeat, now.

There was still Russell, who was named player-coach, the first black coach in major league sports. It might have been Wilt. Ike Richman used to talk about it. But he never got around to it.

Schayes, who had been voted Coach of the Year, was fired. Kiseda says, "You figure it out. I guess the sportswriters who voted were more incompetent at their job than Dolph was at his. But he may have been the worst coach I ever saw, despite his record in the regular season."

Wilt later wrote that "Auerbach outcoached Schayes something terrible" in that series. It was the coaching, then, that did them in that time.

All that was needed, then, was a good coach. Maybe. That is the way it worked out. It wasn't Wilt, although he said, "I think I'd make a good coach." Rooting courtside for Philly in Boston in December earlier, Richman had a heart attack and died. So Wilt lost a faithful friend and a booster, and he was not at that time, when he might have been, made the coach.

Kosloff didn't offer Wilt the job. Kosloff said he knew nothing about Richman's promise to pass on 25 percent of the 76ers to Wilt. So he didn't offer to make him an owner, either. Following his failures with Franklin Mieuli, Wilt had about had it with owners.

He even sympathized with coaches when he wrote, "Here are the NBA owners, with diamond rings on their little fingers and cigars in their mouths, and they want winners. Do what you have to do, coach, baby, but boot me home a winner. Don't talk to me about personality problems, coach, just show me that big box score. Don't come to me with the song and dance about a tired team. I know the season is too long, but what the hell, baby, win, win, win.

"A gentle, softhearted coach against this kind of background is like a little old lamb in there with hungry lions. Schayes, for one, has that woolly look."

Reenter into Wilt's life Alex Hannum. No lamb he, though a gypsy, bouncing from owner to owner and team to team. In control with Richman gone, Kosloff made changes. He brought Jack Ramsay from St. Joseph's to be general manager and Hannum from oblivion to be coach, back east from whence he had fled a few years earlier.

That summer of 1966, Wilt lost another friend, Abe Saperstein, who died. His inheritors, fearing for the future, contacted Chamberlain in Europe and offered to sell him a piece of the Globetrotters' operation if he would become playing president. Wilt liked the sound of the title, but he preferred his fancy salary to an investment in basketball.

He also had an idea that with Hannum the 76ers might win it all and he would be a winner at last.

That was the way it worked out. The talent was there and Hannum pulled the players together. He gave them a style and stressed unselfishness. He didn't care if Wilt lived in New York or practiced in Philadelphia, but he asked Wilt to rebound, block shots, work on defense, sacrifice offense, play a low post, pass off, shoot selectively. Wilt was willing. What had he to lose?

"Don't be afraid to praise your teammates," Alex said.

Wilt did. He says he got closer to those teammates than any he ever played with. For the first and only time in his career he felt part of the team. It was a team. Wilt averaged 24 points

142

a game, Greer 22, Walker 19, Cunningham 18, Jones 13, Jackson 12.

Wilt took only 14 shots a game, but he hit 68 percent of them, and he passed off for almost 8 baskets a game. He was only third in the league in scoring but also third in assists. He was first in rebounds with 24 a game and probably first in blocked shots with about 10 a game.

Merv Harris, of the San Francisco *Examiner,* one of the most perceptive of experts on basketball, insists, "This was the best basketball team I ever saw and probably the best of all time." Len Koppett of *The New York Times,* another analyst of great perception, agrees, saying, "It had everything."

Losing only one game to Boston, the 76ers won 15 of their first 16 games. They lost one at Cincinnati, then won 11 more to go to 26-2. They lost another to Boston, then won 11 more to go to 37-3. They lost to the Knicks in Pittsburgh, then won 9 more to go past midseason at 46-4. Eased off, they won 22 of their last 31 to finish at 68-13, an .840 pace, surpassing all prior records.

The Celtics won 60 to match their second highest total ever and still finished 8 games back.

"Hannum is the greatest coach I've ever had," Wilt said.

Incredibly, Wilt says the 76ers "were probably a little overconfident" going into the playoffs. They lost their first game to Cincinnati in the new system in which the pennant-winner no longer received a first-round bye. But then they bounced back to beat the Royals three straight to remove them. In one of them, Wilt totaled 19 assists, tying Bob Cousy's single-game playoff record. Meanwhile, Boston knocked off the Knicks in four games.

The Celtics were an aging team and lacked the leadership of Auerbach, but Russell remained to inspire the rest. The smart money remained behind Boston. Didn't the Celts always beat Wilt's teams? Not always. Not this time.

Wilt dominated this series, loping up and down the hardwood courts, a giant among giants who seemed small in the spotlight when you watched them from the distant, dark reaches of the big buildings.

Fouled when it was not called, he'd spread his legs, turn his palms to the ungiving gods, tilt his head back and look to the heavens as though wondering why. Then, shaking his head in disgust, he'd shamble back to the play on his long, thin legs.

He went for the ball in explosions of energy, his long arms reaching, his big hands grabbing it as though it were a melon. Shooting or blocking shots, he showed startling strength. Renewing their classic confrontation, he battled Bill Russell.

"He was better than Russell now," wrote Len Koppett. "Hard for Russell to handle. His quickness sapped away by age, Russell resorted to strength and psychology, manhandling Wilt, talking to him, trying to talk him out of it, but Wilt now was not listening to him."

With Convention Hall occupied, the series opened in Penn's Palestra, and Philly blasted Boston by 14 points after leading by 25. Chamberlain outrebounded Russell, 32–15, got 13 assists, and left the scoring to Greer, who had 39, Jones, who had 24, and others.

The numbers, as usual, tell only a part of the story. When Russell was rallying his Celtics, Bill shot and Chamberlain blocked it, grabbed it, and fed out for a fast-break basket. Then Havlicek shot, and, on the rise, the ball ran into the wall of Wilt, who one-handed it and threw a baseball pass the length of the court for another basket.

That stemmed the tide.

Later, Wilt stood above the reporters, pulling on his black silk underwear, answering their questions. Did he hope to beat Bill this time? "We hope to beat Boston," Wilt said. "This is team ball, not one-on-one." Did he fear Russell? "I fear no one," Wilt said. "I respect Russell. He is a great player and a good friend." He had spoken to Russell just before the tipoff. What had he said? "That's personal," Wilt snapped.

In the other room, Russell said, "He told me I'd done a nice job of coaching." Smiling, he added, "I did. He also told me he

144

was going to spoil it tonight. He did," Russell said, breaking into that cackle which is his laugh.

The second game was in Boston, a nationally televised Sunday afternoon contest. Philadelphia fell behind, but Chamberlain rallied his teammates. They pulled well ahead and, after a rebound-jumper and driving three-pointer by Wilt, led by 10 with three minutes to go.

Then Boston, its fans screaming, went on a tear, and with Wilt committing critical fouls, the Celtics surged to within one point at 103–102 with almost two minutes left. Here is where all in that ancient arena and most others would have bet that Wilt and his side would choke.

They did not. Shooting, Wilt was fouled. Reluctantly, he lumbered to the foul line with the fans hooting at him. Akwardly, he put one up, it missed, and the fans howled. But he made the second. "You big bum," complained a courtside patron. Wilt went back to business.

Boston got the ball, shot it, and missed. Wilt rebounded it in his massive hands and the Garden grew quiet. It was Boston that choked, if that is the word. They missed their shots, while Philly hit to win 107–102. In the last minute, a Celtic tried a full-court pass and Wilt went up and with one fist punched it 100 feet into the air.

Afterward he was asked if this series would prove he was the greatest. "If I'm the greatest," he said, "I'm the greatest, win or lose."

Back in Philly, Boston broke to an early lead, but with Wilt taking a playoff record of 25 rebounds for one half, the 76ers were in front by intermission. He wound up with a one-game record of 41 rebounds, and the 76ers beat back Boston again and again in the second half. The Celtics got to within one, but three long baskets by Wally Jones hurled them back again. Four behind with two minutes to play, the Celtics started to foul to get the ball. Greer put in five free throws in short order. Then Wilt hit two. The 76ers won, 115–104.

Thus, three straight. Charitably afterward, Wilt smiled and

said, "I thought Russell played his best tonight. I never knew Bill to move so well." In the other room, Russell now had nothing to say.

On the brink of not only elimination but an embarrassing sweep, Boston went back home and won one, 121–117. Wearily, Russell remarked, "Wilt hasn't had a bad game yet. I hope he has one next game. We won one and we're not through yet."

They were, though. They gave it up only grudgingly. Wilt came out onto the court laughing and the Celtics came out steaming to an 8–0 lead. It went to 10 points, 12, 15, as the Convention Hall fans booed and threw eggs and garbage in their disappointment.

Booed, though far from the first time, Wilt burned, and brought the 76ers back, little by little. They caught up and it was seesaw, with the crowd roaring, until the 76ers went ahead with about 15 minutes to play. From then, they just turned it on and tore the old champions apart.

With Wilt leading Russell in points, 29–4, rebounds, 36–21, and assists, 13–7, the 76ers slaughtered the Celts, 140–116, to finish them off in five games, ending the dynasty short of 10 straight years.

Removed in the last minute to a standing ovation, Wilt would not acknowledge it. He sat on the bench drinking a paper cup of water, expressionless, ignoring the crowd and the photographers who came up. Wilt looked lonely.

"I don't think there's a happier guy in the world than Wilt right now," said Hannum in the dressing room later. But Chamberlain was sitting by himself in the trainer's room and he did not seem happy. To carry on now, Jeremy Larner later wrote, would have been to admit how much losing had hurt before. To have let the crowd give him happiness, he'd have to let them take it away again another time. He would not be a captive to the cheers of the crowd.

A photographer approached. "Leave me alone," Wilt said sourly, sucking on a cigarette, alone with his thoughts. But they would not leave him alone. The writers got to him. "Are you

146

relieved," he was asked. "At least," sighed Wilt, "we do not have to go to a seventh game." And then he was dragged into the delirium of the main room.

In the midst of celebration, Wilt was strangely subdued, as though he had lost too many times for this one win to make up for it. Sweat streaming down his skin, a calm Wilt was not about to let the press see him celebrate.

"We had the better team, so we won," he said. "No, I am not surprised. The better team always wins. No, I am not satisfied. We are not the champions yet, you know. We still have to win the finals yet."

And he went off into the night.

Ironically, it was San Francisco's Warriors who waited, Franklin Mieuli's team, with Nate Thurmond and now with new star Rick Barry. The Warrior coach was Bill Sharman, who followed when Hannum was fired.

Hannum and Wilt have to be excused if they had thoughts of revenge. Also if they feared failure. The greatest of ironies for Wilt would have been if Boston had been beaten, but the Warriors were not, and the title did not follow.

The first game was in Philadelphia. Thurmond gave Chamberlain a battle under the boards. The 76ers led by as many as 19 points in the first half, but were caught in the last minute of the second half.

It was tied when Barry drove off a pick by Thurmond. As Wilt left to pick up Barry, Rick threw to Thurmond. As Rick remembers it, "I'll never know how Wilt got back to Nate, but he did, and clobbered him as he shot. The whistle never blew. The ref, Earl Strom, was standing right there, but never made the call. I couldn't believe it, Thurmond couldn't believe it. We were deprived of both the easy basket and the free throws. The game wound up tied and we lost by six in overtime.

"I believe we deserved the victory, and if we'd gotten it, I believe we would have had the upper hand and would have gone on to win the series. Instead we were so depressed we let down and were beaten by thirty-one in the second game."

147

Wilt got only 10 points in that second game, but got 38 rebounds and fed off as others shot.

Barry roused his side with 55 points in the third game before 14,000 fans in the Cow Palace and the Warriors won, 130–124. Wilt got 28.

Wilt got only 10 points again in the fourth game, but rebounded, passed, defensed, and the 76ers won again, despite 43 by Barry, 122–108.

The 76ers were expected then to end it early, back in Philly for the fifth game.

Although Barry got 26 in the first half, Philly led. He was held to 10 in the second half, and after three periods, Philly led by 12.

But, in the last 12 minutes, Thurmond threw a defensive blanket over Chamberlain, the 76ers made only 3 of 17 shots, and the Warriors roared past to win, 117–109.

Now with the sixth game in San Francisco, the Warriors were in a position to square the series and send it into the seventh game, which Wilt dreaded.

A record crowd of more than 15,000 fans convened in the Cow Palace. It was close all the way and noisy all the way. With 30 seconds left, the 76ers led by one.

As Rick recalls it, "Walker was guarding me but Wilt was waiting. I faked a pass to Thurmond. When Wilt went to him, I faked right on Walker, rolled left around him, and went up to shoot.

"As I did, Wilt took the single most enormous step I have ever seen a man take and was back on me before I could change my move. I couldn't believe it.

"He leaped and got his big hand in my face. I went off balance and threw the shot up and it never came close.

"I scored forty-four in that game, but missed that two-pointer that would have won it. When they grabbed the ball and scored at the other end we were beaten by three.

"I feel that if we'd gotten the foul on Thurmond in the first game and I'd made the shot in the sixth, or even either one, we'd have won the series, but Wilt turned it around. Even not admiring him, I have to admit he turned it around. We never got to a seventh game, but they were lucky to win."

Another Warrior said, "Wilt would have choked."

But he didn't.

John Simmons of the Oakland *Tribune* says, "I remember that first call well. Wilt really laid into Nate, but Strom was saying, 'All ball, all ball, no block,' as if to justify his call. He never got the ball, he got Nate."

Bucky Walter says, "It was a key call and Wilt admitted to me later it was a foul."

Merv Harris says, "Wilt made a super play at the end of the sixth game. He never got credit for it, but there's clutch on defense as well as offense, and he came through many times. Although it only went six, it was as close as a seven-game series."

Winners by 125–122 and champions, the 76ers ran off to the silence of disappointed San Franciscans. Wilt did drink champagne in the dressing room, and hugged Hannum, but he seemed the least excited of the celebrants. Memories of past pain remained with him.

He said, "I'm happy. That's all. I'm happy." And sat down and stared at his large empty hands, while tumult raged around him.

Later, he pointed out, it was not called "Wilt's win," but, "a team victory." He wondered, "Why wasn't it a team defeat when 'Wilt lost' before?"

He noted that Barry was not blamed for his side being beaten while he scored big. "Why was I blamed when my team lost when I scored big?" he asked.

That was the way it was.

The fact was, the less he shot, the better his team did. With Wilt shooting less than ever, his team finally won the title.

Ah, but was it a better team? Or its foe worse?

For Wilt, there was personal satisfaction. Later, wistfully, he observed, "When I was a little boy, I used to think of myself

149

as climbing a high wall. Some people were helping me up, but a lot of others were holding me down. Sometimes I wondered if I'd make it all the way. In 1967, I guess I did."

But he was thirty years old, far from boyhood dreams. And there is, of course, always someone trying to knock off the king of the hill, and there was with Wilt always someone, it seems, trying to drag him down. Or something. Circumstances, whatever.

11

He stood high above the basketball world, but the crown rested uneasily on his head. It was as if Wilt Chamberlain had learned over such a long period of time to live with defeat that he did not know how to handle victory.

He did all he could from game to game, but got too little credit for victory and too much blame for defeat. Now that he had won the big game, was he expected to win every game?

In a curious comment quoted in *Sport* magazine, he said, "In a way, I like it better when we lose. It's over and I can look forward to the next game. If we win, it builds up the tension and I start worrying about the next game."

He escaped to Europe, as usual, but with the championship in hand returned to bargain with Irv Kosloff. The 76er owner refused to consider surrendering 25 percent of the team because of anything Ike Richman might have promised Wilt.

In fact, Kosloff said some race horses Richman had bought in partnership with Wilt had been bought with 76er money, and the franchise had the rights to half of the stable, which was a winner. Wilt was furious. Threats flew as they argued through that summer of curious discontent. Kosloff finally agreed to

151

settle with Wilt, though not for anything near the $2 million or more Wilt figured "his share" of the 76ers was worth

Wilt was tied down by a year remaining on his contract, but he and Kosloff agreed to replace it with a one-year contract calling for a $100,000 raise to $250,000, with Wilt free at termination. That was kept a secret.

That was it. Kosloff hoped to get another title season out of Wilt, but both knew he was leaving at season's end.

Wilt had missed almost the entire preseason period, but Hannum said, "I would rather have Wilt report a month late and come in satisfied, than have him here early, but unhappy." And defended him: "If he can't get the money he wants coming off the year he had, when can he get it?"

He insisted, "Chamberlain may have achieved his goal of becoming a champion, but he has such pride the challenge of staying on top will keep him motivated."

However, Wilt has admitted, "I didn't go into the season with any great enthusiasm." Incredibly, he said he had no goal so had to make up one to motivate himself—leading the league in assists.

He reported at Allentown, Pennsylvania, where the 76ers were about to play their last exhibition game. He walked into the dressing room to find it almost deserted. "Where is everybody?" he asked Alex.

"You've been away, but basketball teams usually go on the court to warm up before a game," Hannum said.

It started to come back to Wilt so he started to change into his uniform. Finding that the shoelaces were in backwards in the shoes that had been carted through West Virginia, Tennessee, Puerto Rico, and Pennsylvania, in hopes someone would put them on, Wilt gave the equipment manager a one-minute lecture on the science.

The No. 13 jersey was missing, and he didn't like that, either, but he took the No. 20 from a rookie, who had to wear another one inside out.

As the team returned from its warmup, Bill Melchionni wel-

152

Doing the bugaboo, Wilt attempts a free-throw while Phoenix players (Dick Van Arsdale, right) and teammate Elgin Baylor look on, looking like they expect he will, as he often does, miss. *(Wen Roberts, Photography, Inc.)*

Left: Wilt leans down hard on head of Boston's John Havlicek (17) as he one-hands a rebound in 1973. *(Wen Roberts, Photography, Inc.)*

Seemingly horrified Wilt watches Sam Jones' lucky shot fall through the basket, after having bounced high off the rim, to win seventh and final game of 1969 playoff finals. Lakers' John Egan (21), Keith Erickson (24) and Elgin Baylor (22) watch with wonder while Celtics Em Bryant, left, and Bailey Howell, right, start to celebrate. Sam himself right center, isn't even looking. *(UPI)*

The man who never fouled out of an NBA game, Wilt Chamberlain uses subtle restraint on Knick Dave DeBusschere to permit Jim McMillian to drive by in 1973. *(Wen Roberts, Photography, Inc.)*

The awesome spread of the 7′ 1″ Chamberlain convinces Knick Jerry Lucas it would be wise to pass off in 1973 contest. *(Wen Roberts, Photography, Inc.)*

Above: Kareem attempts to hook one over Wilt, but the big hand is over the basket ready to goal-tend the attempt. *(Wen Roberts, Photography, Inc.)*

Left: Wilt embraces Lew Alcindor (later to become Kareem Abdul-Jabbar) in typical defense posture in first confrontation in 1969. *(Wen Roberts, Photography, Inc.)*

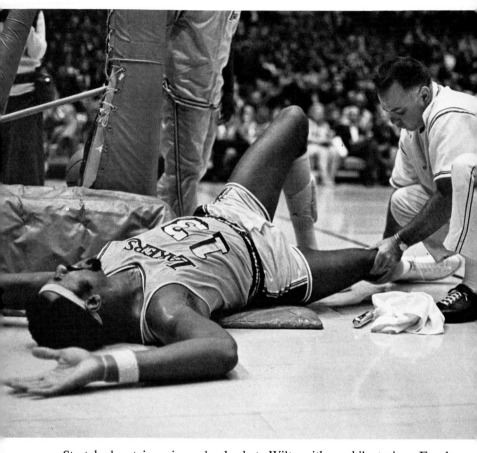

Stretched out in pain under basket, Wilt writhes while trainer Frank O'Neill examines knee that has just been torn apart late in 1969. *(Wen Roberts, Photography, Inc.)*

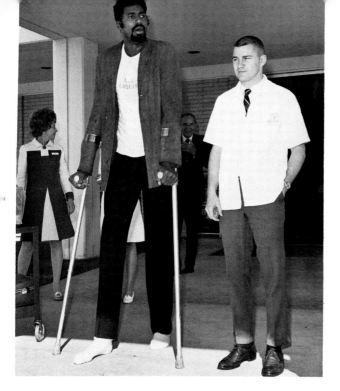

Above: On crutches following surgery, Wilt leaves the hospital in Inglewood. (*L.A. Lakers*)

Right: Under trainer O'Neill's care, Wilt works out to strengthen his knee on stationary bicycle. (*L.A. Lakers*)

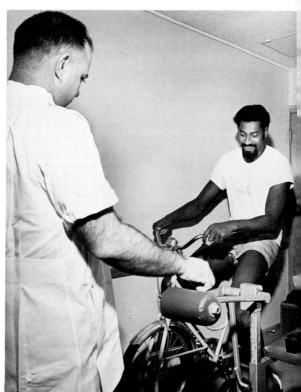

Side by side, the classic centers, Wilt and Kareem. *(Wen Roberts, Photography, Inc.)*

Right: Wilt finger-rolls one in over surprised Jabbar, after coming back from knee operation. *(Wen Roberts, Photography, Inc.)*

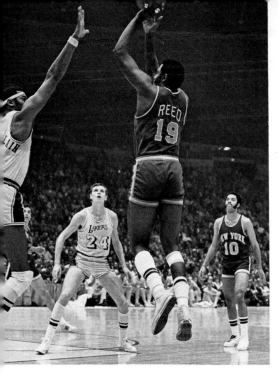

Left: Wilt goes up to attempt block on Willis Reed shot in 1972 championship finals. Laker Keith Erickson is at left, Knick Walt Frazier at right. *(Wen Roberts, Photography, Inc.)*

Right: The Los Angeles crowd cheers Chamberlain away after title triumph. *(Photography, Inc.)*

Right: Coach Bill Sharman congratulates Wilt near end of championship contest in 1972. *(Photography, Inc.)*

Far right: Standing above heads of media, Wilt is interviewed by Tom Hawkins in new champions' dressing room. *(Photography, Inc.)*

Wilt at the Victory Party in the Forum Club. That's assistant coach K. C. Jones, center, and Dr. Robert Kerlan, right. *(Photography, Inc.)*

The Most Valuable Player of the 1972 NBA playoffs, Wilt Chamberlain accepts a car from *Sport* Magazine in New York, but traded it in for a station wagon big enough to hold his three Great Danes. *(Los Angeles Lakers)*

Coaching the San Diego Conquistadors in the American Basketball Association, Wilt looks like he wishes he could play. He was prevented from doing so by Jack Kent Cooke and the Los Angeles Lakers, who retained playing rights to him. *(Clay Scott)*

"The Big Dipper" with his "Little Dippers," the girls volleyball team that the volleyball enthusiast sponsored and with whom he toured. *(James Roark)*

Wilt with his Great Danes outside his magnificent mansion in Bel Air. *(James Roark)*

comed Wilt and asked how much he had settled for. Wilt told him and Bill said, "Do you realize that there are people in Mississippi who have to work two hundred and fifty years to make that much?" Wilt laughed.

Another 76er said, "I think Wilt ought to throw a party and at each place setting there should be a check for ten thousand dollars." Wilt said he'd think about it.

Before they went out, Hannum said, "Wilt, you sit with me the first quarter and I'll fill you in."

"You want to do me a favor?" Wilt asked.

"I'm afraid to answer," Alex said.

"How about the second and third quarter, too?" Wilt said.

But Hannum sent him in after one period to placate the crowd. He got 12 points and 12 rebounds before he retired for the night. A rookie center for the Knicks outscored him. Wilt said, "I never heard of him." A teammate said, "You still haven't met him."

Hannum said to a reporter later, "I thought he looked in pretty good condition."

Hearing this, Wilt said, "I'm in shape for water-skiing."

Hannum said, "That's not the game we play."

Hannum was unhappy, too. He no longer was satisfied to just coach. He wanted to manage, too, but the 76ers had a manager, Ramsay. Hannum said that when he signed he had "an agreement that Kosloff would consider my nominee for general manager. . . . A few weeks later Kosloff told some friends of mine, 'Well, I didn't have a coach and now I have two.' Translated, that meant he had signed Jack Ramsay. I was furious."

Entering this second season, Hannum apparently had decided he could not continue beyond it with Ramsay. He later insisted, "I found Jack to be a fine person and a fine general manager." Ramsay has said, "We got along just fine. I just wanted to keep winning."

But Wilt said, "Alex had little respect for Ramsay. During the final weeks of the season, Alex was spending as much time looking for another coaching job as he was working with the

76ers. You could see he was distracted and not concentrating —and he later admitted as much to me."

Wilt adds, "It was pretty clear to me that Ramsay wanted to be head coach and general manager. It was also pretty clear that one of the first things he wanted to do was get rid of me."

Jack Kiser says, "Hannum wanted Ramsay's job, and Ramsay wanted Hannum's job. Wilt wanted the coaching job, too, but Ramsay didn't want Wilt. Ramsay has to be the star on Ramsay's teams.

"He never had an All-American at St. Joseph's. He didn't want Wilt on the 76ers. Later, when he coached at Buffalo he couldn't get along with Bob McAdoo and Ernie DiGregorio. Now that he's going to coach in Portland, he won't make it with Walton.

"The situation in Philadelphia going into the 1967–68 season was just beautiful!" he concludes sarcastically.

George Kiseda says, "It was as if no one on that team could deal with success. Everyone wanted more money, more power, more prestige. Everyone wanted all the credit for the past season's success, and no one was willing to sacrifice for success in the new season.

"Hannum had personal problems. His marriage was in trouble. His wife was not well and wanted to return to California. He was feeling out Oakland and Los Angeles interests about the possibility of becoming a manager or coach with an ownership interest in the new American Basketball League.

"Ramsay wanted to become coach, as he would at season's end. He seemed to feel winning with Wilt was almost like cheating. He had never really won anything at St. Joseph's, but he had become successful to some extent with small, quick clubs, and he wanted to prove he could succeed with the same type of teams in pro ball."

Maybe Hannum received too much credit for turning Wilt and his team into a winner. Everyone resented it, it seems. Wilt no longer went out of his way to talk of Alex as the greatest coach he ever had. Later, he complained of how Hannum

154

harassed him, wanting him to do this and then that when Wilt knew better than anyone what was best for him.

A lot of the publicity went to Wilt, and the good players grumbled about a bad situation where they did not get the credit they deserved. One says, "A lot of us felt whatever Wilt did he did for Wilt, not for us and not for winning. The numbers alongside his name mattered more to him than those showing wins and losses alongside the team name."

There was too much talent on the team for it to lose many games. It won 60 and lost only 20. One loss really rattled Wilt. It was late in the season in San Diego, and if the hosts lost they'd remove from the books the record of 17 straight defeats Hannum had suffered in San Francisco. After the game the night before, Wilt stayed in LA—with his parents, he says—and when he got to San Diego the next day he found Greer and Cunningham hung over from a party the night before and playing golf at their Vacation Village motel. When Wilt wondered why they were committing this sin, Billy said, "It's the Wilt Chamberlain Memorial Golf Tournament," and Wilt blew up. The 76ers lost that night, and Wilt sadly observes that if San Diego had lost, they'd have gone on to lose 33 in a row because they lost their next 15.

The harmony on the 76ers had gone sour. Wilt was so intent on winning in assists, he was passing up sure shots for passes. When his teammates missed shots off his passes, he got angry about it. A couple of times he went to a teammate with a hot hand and told him he was going to give him the ball exclusively because the other guys were wasting his passes and he wouldn't win the assists title that way. A couple of games he did not take any shots at all. When these were lost and writers blamed Wilt, he screamed bloody murder: "What do you want from me? First you say I shoot too much, then you say I don't shoot enough!"

Hannum later recalled, "A writer asked me if I was concerned and I said, hell, yes. I was concerned that he'd forget how to score. Now we're on a plane to Chicago the next day.

Wilt sits down beside me and shows me the paper. 'You read this?' he says. I tell him I did. 'Did you say this?' he says. I tell him I did. His beard bristled, but he didn't say another word. The next three games Wilt scored about sixty points a game." Alex laughed. "You never know what'll motivate him."

That year, assists did. His only high-scoring game the last half of the season was 53 against LA, and he says he did it to impress the Lakers because he had decided he wanted to live there and play for the Lakers the following season. He averaged 24 points and 23 rebounds a game, lost the scoring title, won the rebounding title, and won in assists with 702, an average of 8.6 per game.

"It may be my greatest accomplishment," he has said.

The playoffs that year were not. Philadelphia had beaten Boston by eight games for the divisional laurel again, but the rematch in the postseason was something else. Before they even got into it, Wilt was saying his team had proven over the long season it was the champion, and it was stupid to have to play playoffs and have to prove it all over again.

The 76ers had to go six games to get by the Knicks in the first round. Wilt said it was because he had a sore foot. And it didn't help that Cunningham fell, fracturing his forearm in the third game. Two points behind, Wilt missed five free throws in a row in the last half-minute in that one, but Walker tied it and the team won it. Walt Frazier injured his leg when the Knicks led by 16 points in the fourth game, and after that the Knicks were finished.

So it was Boston and Philadelphia again. The day before the opener at Philadelphia's Spectrum, Martin Luther King was assassinated. According to Koppett, proprietor of the league's playoff history, managers Auerbach and Ramsay met the day of the game with player representatives Russell and Chamberlain and agreed that, since a crowd was on its way, they would play that night but would postpone Sunday's game for memorial observances.

Chamberlain says Boston players met, but Hannum didn't

think to call the Philadelphia players together. He says that when they got to the game—the six remaining "regulars" were all black—they were grief-stricken and bewildered, and it showed in the defeat that followed. The Celtics shot well and won by nine.

After a five-day break, the series resumed, and the 76ers bounced back to win three straight. The old men of the Celtics seemed doomed. But they rallied to win one in Philadelphia and put some pressure on the 76ers. Then in Boston the Celts won again, and suddenly the series was tied and the pressure really was heavy on the 76ers. They never had won a seventh game, and the Celtics never had lost one.

In Philadelphia, before 15,000 persons the third Friday night of April, 1968, the game was close to the finish. But in the fourth quarter only two shots were credited to Wilt and both were taps, not shots. Russell sank a free throw to make it 98–95, Celtics, with a half-minute left. Walker shot, but Russell blocked it. Greer grabbed the ball but missed his shot and Russell rebounded it. Sam Jones was fouled and hit two free throws at the finish to settle it.

Russell ran off with his first coaching championship, while Wilt walked off with his sixth playoff loss to Bill's Boston teams in seven postseason meetings over nine years. The 76ers no longer were champions, but Boston would be for the tenth time in twelve years after beating the Lakers once again in the final.

Last year was already but a bittersweet memory for the dethroned, disspirited 76ers that mid-April night of 1968. The writers and broadcasters, whose job was to do the obituary on the Philadelphia team, got to Hannum first and one of the things they kept asking him was why Wilt hadn't shot down the stretch.

Obviously bone-tired and bitter, Hannum kept saying he didn't know, he just didn't know, it was just the way the flow of the game went, the situation called for set plays that just happened to go away from Wilt.

When the reporters got to Wilt, the big guy, head hung, said he didn't know why, he just didn't seem to have the ball, they just lost that's all, they just lost.

It was not until later, George Kiseda remembers, that he thought to go to the fellow Hannum had keeping, among other stats, the number of times the ball went into the pivot. The numbers showed that where Wilt usually got the ball 40 to 60 times a game, his teammates passed to him only 4 times the last 12 minutes, as if forgotten or mistrusted, in this critical contest when the 76ers lost so much by so little.

Well, they would not be the same team after this. Hannum, who will not talk about it today, was on his way to Oakland to become manager and coach of the new team in the new ABA, while Wilt, who now said Hannum was the second best coach he ever had, was on his way to Los Angeles to become the controversial star of the third team in his NBA career, trying to make it with new teammates and another coach.

Thus the third stage in Wilt Chamberlain's professional life closed.

12

What was Wilt Chamberlain really like? Once, Alex Hannum wrote, "He's just like any other seven-foot black millionaire who lives next door." Wilt liked it so much he used it as the subtitle to his book. He was set apart from others.

For Wilt Chamberlain, it was not enough to get off the court; he had to get away from the arena to relax. There were coaches he liked and coaches he did not like. He admired Frank McGuire most, but never developed a personal relationship with him beyond basketball. The one coach he came closest to away from the arena was Alex Hannum, but it only lasted as long as they were on teams together. He would, however, have dinner or a drink with Hannum, McGuire, Bob Feerick, when they came together in different towns.

There were players he liked and players he did not like. He was close to Guy Rodgers, who fed him in his early years, and later to Al Attles, whom he admires and who is admired by all. Wilt has had friendships with several players, but few personal relationships beyond basketball.

Wilt often was paid for published articles in which he was critical of coaches and teammates. For example, he has written of Rodgers, "Unfortunately, Guy was a light-skinned, straight-haired black man who seemed to wish he was white instead. He deliberately hung around with the white players, not the blacks, and he'd go out of his way to avoid using ghetto phrases and mannerisms. That just pissed the blacks off and contributed to a racially tense atmosphere."

Wilt was set apart from most other players in matters of publicity and special privileges granted and pay and importance to the team and was subjected to many jealousies.

He makes friends beyond basketball, and while he is always surrounded by people, he basically is a loner and an individualist. He once said, "I treasure my individualism above all my other traits. I hope to maintain it at the highest peak possible.

"I'm happy to go along with a group when it is doing something I want to do, but if someone says, 'Hey, let's go to a movie,' and it's not a picture I want to see, I am not going to go just because everyone else goes. If I feel a Richard Nixon is the best man to be president, I am going to support him, no matter what others say. I am not a fence-sitter and when I take a side, right or wrong, it's my side, and I'll stand up for it.

"Most people do not dare to be individuals. They go along with the popular pastimes and the will of the majority because it is easier to follow than it is to lead. I lead my own life and it does not bother me if I do not blend in with the crowd. In the things I have had published I have spoken my mind about people and players and situations because I believe I have had experiences and been sensitive to them and have things to say about them which should be heard.

"Most players are afraid to speak about other players. I'll speak about Baylor, but Baylor won't speak about Wilt. That is nonsense. We all have a right to have our say whether we like what is said or not. Players are super-sensitive to criticism. They are more out in the open than most people in other professions and their careers are always on the line. But in basketball games I'm gonna pass to a player whether I like him or not. My feelings are one thing, my job another.

160

"Sadly, all players are not like this. They develop cliques. Coaches play favorites. Frankly, I am not enamored of the locker room fraternity. I know coaches and players say one thing in public and another in private. I have one view of myself, others have other views. To me, mine is all that matters. To them, theirs is all that matters. I don't care. I have become immune to criticism. I am outstanding and so subject to criticism more than others.

"I wish it was different. We play eighty or more games a season, depending on the schedule that season. Perhaps a hundred with playoffs, not counting exhibitions. We travel from town to town, airport to airport, hotel to hotel. In the old days, we played a lot of little towns and bad arenas, sometimes stayed in bad places. Even today, all teams do not go first class.

"The games are hard. After a while, it is difficult to stay inspired. The demands of owners, media people, and fans take a lot out of you. It is difficult to get away from the sport for even a day. On the road just killing time between games poses problems. It is not an easy life. We are well paid for it, but money is not everything. And the glamour and excitement wear thin.

"The better the relationships among owners, coaches, and players, the better the life, but it seldom is what it might be."

Wilt took a while to accustom himself to the difficult life of a professional basketball superstar. When he threatened retirement over the years, he was really dreaming of an easier life in which no one would tell him what to do, enemy fans would not boo him, rival players would not tear him down, he would have friends rather than jealous teammates, he would be welcome wherever he was without demands made on him by his audiences, and success was his always.

Well, we all have our dreams. He was larger almost than life, so his dreams may have been unrealistic.

He liked his early bosses enormously—Eddie Gottlieb, Ike Richman, and Abe Saperstein. He trusted them as he trusted few others later. He sometimes mentioned that they were white Jews, showing neither religion nor race mattered to him. He

161

also always said he liked and trusted Frank McGuire, an Irish Catholic.

His relationships with his first teammates were flawed. One says, "He was really something when he came in, and it was as if we were nothing and he was going to make something of us. No one wants to be 'saved.' No one wants to be a spear-carrier. He had the ball all the time and all the headlines."

Another says, "He was arrogant, always bragging. He got the smarts and started to throw around ten-dollar words. It took a while to get used to him."

A third says, "He was sensitive, suspicious. He would do for you, though. He was generous. He could be good company. Once he relaxed and let you know him, you liked him. He just couldn't relax everywhere with everyone."

Wilt says his happiest times in basketball were with the 76ers in Philadelphia in the 1966–67 season, not because they won the title, but because they were a compatible team. In fact, he says they won the title because they were not only talented but compatible. He remembers it as one big, happy family, with whom he played the pranks he loved to play, including one in which they taped the team trainer between mattresses and abandoned him in a parking lot. Billy Cunningham says, "We were always needling each other and we did have a lot of fun. Of course, when you're winning, life is fun."

Wilt is an active traveling companion. He loves to play checkers, cards, dominoes. He claims wide and varied knowledge, is a trivia buff, and will make up games of all sorts to play with players and writers on trips. He claims a command of the language and loves word games.

In his Grosset & Dunlap and Tempo book, *Wilt Chamberlain,* which chronicles Wilt's early career, George Sullivan recalls a bus trip from Syracuse to Philadelphia in which the players tried to figure the mileage, picked a number, and put a dollar in the pot. Wilt got out paper and pencil, figured the possibilities, and picked every number not taken between 283 and 336 miles. There was only $8 in the pot when he put in $44. As they got close, with Wilt watching the mileage indicator, it became clear he was going to win, although Eddie Gottlieb threatened to send the driver through side streets until the mileage reached his number. But it wound up on one of Wilt's and he won the money. When he was asked why he would risk $44 to win $8, Wilt said that 18 percent profit made for a sound business investment.

After that, Wilt often studied the distances of trips his teams would take and would make bets with unsuspecting teammates. Bucky Walter says, "He had a way with money."

Chick Hearn says, "He had a way of winning because he only bet on sure things. I played a lot of cards with him, but I didn't win a lot, even though I don't think he was a good card-player. He made safe bets and wasn't fast to pay off losses. He and Elgin Baylor weren't supposed to be buddies, but they played a lot together because they were almost the only ones who could afford the sort of money they played for."

Rod Hundley says, "If he beat you, he wanted you to pay off right away. But I beat him in gin rummy one night and he wouldn't pay. 'Yeah, we'll play it off,' he kept saying."

Santa Monica *Outlook* sports editor Mitch Chortkoff recalls, "I once bet him five bucks UCLA would beat the Citadel by fifty points. He said you can't give fifty points no matter who the teams are, and took the bet. UCLA won by fifty-six, but he never paid off. He said he wasn't serious.

"When he coached at San Diego my seat at the press table was near his on the bench. With ten seconds to go one game, he designed a play in a time-out and came back bragging what a sure two points it was. I said, 'Betcha a buck.' He said, 'You're on.' They hit one of those ABA three-pointers at the buzzer. He jumped up and said, 'Gimme my money.' I said, 'No way. You bet two points and that was three.' He flew into a rage. He made so much fuss, ushers stared at me thinking I must have been bothering him or something. Finally he stormed off saying he wanted his dollar when he came back. When he came back I gave him fifty cents and said we'd call it even. He wouldn't speak to me for days."

Wilt himself says that when he was still drinking before his stomach troubles no one could "drink him under the table," and that even afterward when he was sticking to 7-Up and orange juice or grape juice and had champagne and wine only on special occasions, he still won bets with his prowess. He says he once won a bet from Tom Meschery by drinking a quart of Old Grand-Dad in about two hours in a Geary Street bar. And after drinking Tom under the table on Puerto Rican rum later that night, took on Wayne Hightower in another joint and wound up having to drive both of them home.

Jack Kiser recalls, "I saw him win bets beating guys like Al Attles in practice races foul-line to foul-line. I saw him win a bet from Nate Thurmond in a bowling alley when he palmed a sixteen-pound ball downward for a full minute and wagered a thousand dollars against five hundred that Nate couldn't do it for thirty seconds. Nate couldn't. Wilt would casually toss off a line like, 'I used to average two hundred twelve,' and someone would say, 'You're full of shit,' and Wilt would bet him. The guy would ask him how he was going to prove it, and Wilt would whip out an old sheet with league averages that showed it. He was always prepared.

"I remember he once bet George Kiseda that he, Wilt, could press four hundred pounds or some such amount, and George said Wilt was full of shit because the world record was four hundred seventy-seven or something, so they bet and Wilt took him to the YMCA and did it. He was a con artist because he only bet when he could back it up, and he was an escape artist because if you trapped him into a bad bet he wriggled out of it somehow."

Kiseda says, "He was always challenging you, wanting you to doubt that he could do some fabulous feat. We wound up in the Temple hospital together one time. It had high ceilings. He reached up above his head and asked how far his fingertips were

164

from the ceiling. I said about four feet. He bet me he could put his hand on the ceiling. I didn't think he could, but he did, flat. He'd practiced first, to be sure. He said, 'Do you think Tommy Hawkins could do that? Or Johnny Green? Hell, only Valery Brumel could. Maybe Brumel,' who was the world record holder in the high jump at that time.

"He was teaching me to play dominoes and wiping me out. He said he was maybe the greatest domino player in the world, but he wasn't sure. I asked him if he'd ever played for any title and he said no, but he held the West Coast points record. Who keeps track of the West Coast points record in dominoes? How the hell would he know?

"I got to where I could do fifteen handstand pushups against the wall and I figured he couldn't because he wouldn't be able to get comfortable upside down and hadn't practiced. I walked into his room and challenged him. He figured fast I had him. The next thing I know he's challenging me to arm-wrestling. I mean who am I to take on that monster in arm-wrestling? But he lectured me for fifteen minutes on how I had an advantage in leverage because my arm was shorter. Which is funny because I later found out Bill Neider blamed defeats to Wilt on the fact that Wilt had an advantage in leverage because his arm was longer. Anyway, Wilt talked me into it and took me down in about two seconds. And to this day I don't know whatever happened to the handstand pushups.

"But I got to think of him as a good guy. He didn't run with sportswriters much, but he was always available and always good for a good story, and if he did go out with you or meet you outside, he always picked up the tab. He always carried a roll of bills that would choke a horse. Always with hundred-dollar bills on top."

Jack Kiser says, "It was always the same roll. He paid out of the other pocket. Just like he always carried the same bunch of fan letters with him with a rubber-band wrapped around them. I can remember saying to him, 'Hey, Wilt, I know you get fan mail. I've seen it. The least you could do is put a different letter on top once in a while.' And he laughed.

"But he was always good for a tab. Which is unusual for an athlete. You know, they've been hustled since they were high school stars. And people are always asking to buy them drinks. They're spoiled and seldom will treat, even though they make ten to twenty times as much as the people they're with. But Wilt would pay and he'd never make a show of it. He'd arrange with the head waiter in advance so no check would come to the table."

No one was about to rob Wilt, of course. The gunman who confronted this giant in a dark alley had to be crazy. Eddie Gottlieb once told Wilt that if he kept carrying his roll around, someone was going to hit him over the head and take it from him. Wilt smiled and said, "The guy who hits me over the head has to have a ladder, and if I see a guy coming at me with a ladder, I'll know what's coming and get out of there."

Wilt did go in the grand manner. On a preseason visit to Hawaii when they were with the Warriors, Alex Hannum was handing out $1.55 a day to the players to cover cab fare from their hotel to the arena, but Wilt told him he needed $5. "I'm Wilt Chamberlain and people expect me to tip big," he said. Alex said, "Fine, if you want to be Wilt Chamberlain, you can pay for the privilege from your own pocket. You'll get the same as everyone else from me." Wilt laughs about that.

Mitch Chortkoff says, "It wasn't easy for him to travel in the world. He has said and I believe he is the single most recognizable person in the world. A king or president might get lost in a crowd, but Wilt stands out. I remember when he and Baylor and West were equally famous, but getting on or off planes or going places they often wouldn't be noticed, and Wilt was always recognized and always had people coming up to him. Yet he wouldn't withdraw and sit and sulk somewhere, like many seven-footers. He'd be the center of attention and tell great stories and enjoy it."

Merv Harris says, "He was well traveled, witty, spoke several languages. His friends came from both the ghettoes and the

166

penthouses, from Harlem and West Philadelphia as well as Fifth Avenue and Beverly Hills. He could talk to anyone. He went after women, but he treated them with consideration and courtesy. He always had fine homes and was a warm and charming host."

This is a subject of dispute.

Rod Hundley laughs and says, "He always had to be the best everything—the best basketball player, the best card-player, the best cook, the top jock with the ladies. It's funny, but I never saw him with a woman. Not once. I'm not the only one who'll tell you that, either. I think he's the only player, married or unmarried, I never saw with a woman.

"Hey, look, he always treated me well. And I always treated him well. But he knows players talk about other players behind their backs, and I'm talking behind his back. I think he's a fraud. I remember once we went into this French restaurant and Jerry West told Wilt to order from the menu because he knew the language. Wilt had a terrible time and we fell on the floor laughing.

"Look, he's the most interesting player I ever met, but also the biggest egomaniac. I know egomaniacs because I'm one without having half what he has. When I was broadcasting radio in LA, Wilt was one player I could always get on the postgame shows when others couldn't be bothered because he loved to hold court for a half-hour. He and Muhammad Ali would make a match in bridge for Jack Kent Cooke and Charles O. Finley. I'd pay to listen in on that conversation.

"I had to double as traveling secretary, and Wilt was always coming to me with some childish complaint. He'd ask why we were traveling on this airline because the service wasn't good, or staying in that hotel because the beds were too short. Creature comforts were very important to him and he was impossible to please. There was only so much I could do.

"He always had to have the front-row aisle seat on the plane. And sometimes we'd get on a continuing flight and someone would already be in the seat and he'd want me to kick the person out. How the hell could I do that? His teammates would leave it for him, except maybe Elg, who wanted to taunt him, but other people didn't know. And Wilt was always checking out of our hotel and into one he liked better."

Laker broadcaster Chick Hearn laughs and says, "Wilt would sit in that front-row seat and stretch out his long legs and block the way to the rest rooms. Here he'd be stretched out asleep and ten other guys were sitting with their legs crossed. But no one was about to shake him awake. But I have seen strangers shake him awake to ask for an autograph. Unbelievable!

"I've seen people stand and watch him eat his food. I've seen him stand and sign autograph after autograph, and other times when he wouldn't do anything for anyone. I've seen him refuse to sign until a boy said 'please' and refuse to hand back the paper and pencil until a boy said 'thank you.' He felt he had to be approached politely or he did not owe anything to anyone.

"Well, let's face it. Many fans are not properly polite. And Wilt is more cooperative with them than, say, Jabbar or Russell. Russell wouldn't sign for anyone."

Wilt says, "If people approach me properly at the proper times I will give autographs. I don't know how youngsters are going to learn to say 'please' or 'thank you' if people like me don't demand it. I will not sign autographs during games or concerts I attend because if people like me don't show respect for performers, I don't know who will. I think when I was leaving an arena after a game it was proper to be asked for an autograph, and I have signed when other players were sneaking out. But I think it is unfair that I cannot attend a game without being bothered to the point where I don't enjoy it. I think it is unfair of people to bother me at the beach when I am playing volleyball with friends. I do not want to be singled out there and am entitled to relax. If I started, I would never stop.

"It is easy for some to say I have to pay a price for my prominence when they do not have to pay it. It is hard to live a life in which you cannot appear in public without being an

168

object of curiosity, you cannot go anywhere without being bothered by strangers, and you have to hide to have privacy."

Once in Philadelphia a lady asked him for his autograph while he was eating. When he asked her to wait until he was finished, she became enraged and started to swing her pocketbook at him. Dolph Schayes and others with Wilt pulled her away from him. He was furious, but what could he do, hit her?

Hot Rod Hundley remembers, "Once when were playing gin on a flight, a guy interrupts to ask Wilt for an autograph. Wilt said, 'Can't you see I'm gambling. I'm not going anywhere. Come back when I'm done.' And damn if the guy didn't watch and wait and come back the minute Wilt got up to leave the game. And damn if Wilt didn't sign for him.

"He pays a price for fame, but he doesn't always pay it pleasantly. He treats people poorly at times and is sometimes rude.

"Most players have little love for him. They live off him, but don't like it. We're all bloodsuckers. They'd laugh about him behind his back. Call him 'Big Musty' because he never seemed to take showers. When the players were in a hurry to get somewhere, they'd say, 'Don't worry, I'll take a Wilt,' which meant a quick pass under the water, or near the water, hit the deodorant and aftershave, and on their way.

"He is one of the best-dressed men I ever knew. Had to have special-made clothes and had a marvelous flair for colors and combinations and a wonderful wardrobe. But he'd go on a trip and turn up in the same suit day after day. Liked to travel light, I guess."

In fairness to Rod, it should be pointed out that others said the same things but preferred to do so anonymously. It is Wilt's lot that others seem to look for flaws in him. They'll mock him for misusing large words, for example.

One player who is willing to talk on the record is Bill Bradley of the Knicks. In his book *Life on the Run*, Bill says of Wilt, "He would imply that basketball was just a small part of his life, a life which encompassed presidents and queens, millionaires

169

and movie stars. . . . Homes, women, cars, money, only provided accompaniment to his primary quest—celebrity."

Wilt is sensitive to but accustomed to criticism. He believes the writers and broadcasters are largely to be blamed for his poor public image. Writers often speak to him sympathetically, then write unsympathetically. He has said, "The same questions, city after city, season after season, it's a drag. They twist what you say and write what they want, anyway."

It is true. Anyone who has traveled with a prominent athlete knows how unimaginative most reporters are, and marvels at that rare athlete who can remain responsive and gracious while being asked, often almost ordered, to surrender what free time he has to go over the same ground again and again.

One like Wilt often is asked insulting questions, and if he gives an embarrassing answer or is misquoted, he will be haunted by it, because no matter how many times he may deny it, or how he may change his mind over the years, other writers will find it in the files and it will be used forever.

Usually, Wilt makes himself available to reporters after games, win or lose, and he will talk, which is not true of many athletes. As all basketball reporters will tell you, Russell often was unavailable, while Jabbar usually has little to say. Cowens is sometimes surly, too. Wilt is not often available outside the arena unless he has established a rapport with a reporter, but then neither are many others.

He can be difficult. He has stood up many reporters who made appointments with him, but so do others. He will answer other newsmen without looking at them, obviously wanting them to go. The first time this reporter approached him, he asked for twenty minutes before a game. Wilt agreed. After fifteen minutes of talk, Wilt started to look at the clock. At twenty minutes, he said, "That's it." And that was it.

Other times, Wilt talked on and on. If he was interested in good questions, he wanted to give good answers. If the reporter seemed interested in his answers, Wilt was responsive. But if Wilt did not like a question, he would just stare at the reporter

170

and not answer, which perhaps is better than telling the reporter he is stupid, as Mike Marshall has done to many, or as Joe Namath has done.

Jack Kiser points out, "The writers often protect pet players. They did not rap Russell for not going to practices the way they did Wilt, although Russell missed as many as Wilt did. In San Francisco they did not knock Willie Mays for acting like an ass with writers and other people because he was supposed to be God, but they walloped Wilt for speaking his mind. He used to watch Jabbar asked about race and religion and politics and would comment that when he came up no one asked him anything because they thought ballplayers didn't think.

"He was the first ballplayer to speak his mind about more than sports, and if someone like Larry Merchant, who inspired the new breed of sports reporters with his thoughtful, honest, hard-hitting stories in Philadelphia, had come along with Wilt, it would have been wonderful. Unlike most players who say something, then hide behind denials, Wilt seldom denied anything he said. If he did, he probably didn't say it. He always was a source of information to me, he answered the hard questions, and he never lied.

"Yet few writers wrote about him with any insight or compassion for his place in the scheme of things, and many wrote of him as if he was a freak. He had every right to resent his treatment from the media."

Len Shecter wrote, "It would be a miracle if the bribery of his elders and the adulation of his peers did not spoil him. There has been no miracle." Jim Murray wrote, "He was put together in a laboratory by a mad doctor with a pair of pliers, a screwdriver and a Bunsen burner. If you look close, you can see the bolts in the forehead. You don't feed it, you oil it, baby."

Understandably, he became bitter. Joe McGinnis was not the only writer he threatened. Bill Sharman says, "I heard Wilt talking to a writer in a terrible way one day. Later, he told me the fellow knew nothing about the game. I said he shouldn't have talked to him as he did because the fellow had a job to do and someday Wilt might need him. Wilt said the day he needed that writer was the day he didn't want to play anymore. I said I guessed my job was different and I was dependent on the reporters to some extent. I asked Wilt not to bop anyone before I left the room."

The late Milton Gross of the New York *Post* wrote many complimentary columns about Chamberlain and became one of his closest friends in the press. Then, one day, Milt criticized Wilt in a column, and the next day, when he went up to Wilt and said, "Hi, handsome, what's doing?" Wilt said, "Don't write bad about me, then talk nice to me." Wilt said he didn't want to talk to him anymore and told him to get the hell out of the dressing room. Milt went, disappointed and dejected, and commented later, "I thought Wilt could handle a fair rap."

When Sharman became coach of the Lakers, many reporters wrote the same story, wondering, in essence, if this supposedly tough coach could cut it with this player who was supposedly so tough on coaches. This reporter wrote such a story for a small monthly magazine. It did not come out until the other stories had come and gone and been forgotten.

The Lakers were well into a record winning streak, and it was clear Sharman and Wilt were working well together. The timing was terrible.

I figured Wilt wouldn't see the story, but he sees every story written about him. His spies are everywhere. Wilt ordered me out of the dressing room, commenting, "the same old crap." He was right, too. I had done no worse than others, but it was a bad story that came out at a bad time.

Not wanting to create an unsettling scene at that time, I left, but returned the next game. Without warmth, Wilt always answered my questions later.

George Kiseda recalls, "When you wrote something he didn't like he let you know it. But he didn't stop talking to many reporters. We once had a personal disagreement and stopped talking to each other casually, but when I had newspaper questions to ask, I asked them, and he answered them. He didn't let personal friendship interfere with a journalistic relationship, and he seemed to respect a reporter's job. Considering who he was and the number of games in his sport, he probably was interviewed more than any athlete ever and he was always good copy."

Mal Florence of the Los Angeles *Times* says, "When Wilt first came to the Lakers I wanted a personal interview and he kept putting me off. But the minute I wrote something critical, he found time for me. I wrote that the Lakers seemed to play better without him than with him. The newspaper had just hit the streets when my phone rang with Wilt asking me what the hell I knew about basketball. I said, 'Not as much as you, big fella.' He proceeded to chew me out for a half-hour. He then gave me a marvelous interview. He'd try to bulldoze you at times, but I always found him honest. I think in retrospect we realize what a rare, good interview he was."

Merv Harris says, "When the Los Angeles *Herald-Examiner* went out on strike and I went to the Long Beach News Bureau, Wilt was about to affiliate with a travel agency. He called to ask if I would do the news releases and stories on it for a fee. It was a small fee and he wanted someone who would do a professional job, but he was also looking to give me a helping hand if I needed it.

"Later, when he wanted to contact the Lakers, he asked me to serve as his intermediary with Mr. Cooke. Still later, in July of 1973 when he was holding out on the Lakers, and he had refused the AP an interview, he finally agreed only if I did it, though I was not with the AP. I was about to become sports editor of the San Francisco *Examiner,* and I used an unsigned story in that newspaper because he gave me the scoop that he was about to sign with San Diego of the ABA.

"The thing is, Wilt often was, at one and the same time, serving and self-serving. But he was thoughtful."

Although it is not generally known, negotiations for Wilt to join the Lakers started a year before they succeeded. Wilt wanted to go to LA in 1967, but could not get out of serving

173

out the last year of his contracted agreement in Philadelphia. Once that was served, he was determined to depart.

Although it always has been assumed Cooke paid considerable cash—reportedly about $250,000—for Chamberlain, Cooke says he paid little. Players were sent as token payment—Darrall Imhoff, Archie Clark, and Jerry Chambers—but by terms of his final pact with Kosloff, Wilt was free to go where he wanted. For Cooke, getting Wilt was merely a matter of getting together with him on a contract.

As court records later confirmed, the contract was for three seasons at $200,000 a season, plus a paid life insurance policy worth $250,000, a loan at 4 percent interest for Wilt to buy $100,000 of Cooke's cable-television company, and a loan to cover investments to provide tax-shelter investments for Wilt set up by the company. Also, Cooke agreed that his company would at any time Wilt requested it buy back the latter two holdings at no loss. Wilt did make the loans, took on these holdings, and sold them back, at what turned out to be a profit.

Colorful and controversial, Cooke says, "I thought of obtaining Wilt Chamberlain from the day I bought the Lakers in 1965. I was told and then later saw for myself the one thing my team lacked was an outstanding center in a sport where a center is all-important. With Jerry West and Elgin Baylor we had two of the greatest players ever to play the game, but we were denied championships, often by the narrowest of margins. Chamberlain was the greatest center ever to have played the game, and when I heard rumors in 1967 that he was unhappy in Philadelphia, I inquired of Irv Kosloff if Wilt was available. He was not at that time, but I persisted through proper avenues.

"I have always believed that if someone wants something more than anyone else in the world wants it and is willing to work harder than anyone else, he will get it. Something infinitely more important than money went into the deal for Wilt Chamberlain: desire, persistence, and just plain hard work. I have made major deals in recent years for Kareem Abdul-

Jabbar, Rogie Vachon, Marcel Dionne, and I was able to make them because I was willing to work to make them. My name is Jack Kent Cooke, not Norman Vincent Peale. I have powers of persuasion, but I cast no spells on anyone. I am an ordinary fellow. The most successful men I've known in my life are ordinary fellows who are willing to work for what they want.

"I wanted Wilt Chamberlain in Los Angeles, and Wilt Chamberlain wanted to play in Los Angeles. Those two came together to make this spectacular sporting move possible."

Cooke invited Wilt to meet with him at his Bel-Air home. They met four or five times. The first time Jack had other representatives present, but Wilt politely protested. After that, they met alone. They agree that the first few meetings were informal ones in which they broke bread and discussed life, liberty, and the pursuit of happiness, the power of words and the wonders of the world. Cooke comments, "We discussed everything but basketball and a basketball contract, but this was always in our minds and we knew it. We struck a rapport and after that it was not too difficult to come to terms with Wilt in our final meetings."

The experience unnerved Wilt a little. They talked about cars and compared Bentleys. Wilt thought he had an edge in that his was air-conditioned and Jack's was not, until Jack took him out to his garage and pointed out a second Bentley and a Rolls Royce.

"His house has more rooms than a hotel," Wilt admitted in awe. "He has antiques and Old Masters worth a fortune. The butler removed an ashtray from my elbow for fear I'd knock it over. It turns out Jack's ashtrays are gold and cost $127 each.

"I found him fascinating. He is a brilliant businessman. Maybe a match for me.

"I was owed a piece of the Philadelphia franchise, but Irv Kosloff refused to provide it. I deal in franchises myself. I work in the travel agency business. And when I'm setting up a man

175

to work for me, I figure he'll do a better job if he has a piece of the action.

"Kosloff apparently did not respect me enough to make me a part of *his* business. Mr. Cooke did.

"I made my own deal. I make better deals than others would make for me. I am the only man who understands my true worth."

Cooke said, "A long time ago I lost a newspaper I wanted because my bid was too low. I learned a lesson. The value of something is not always what it seems to be on the surface, but what it is worth to you. I paid above the appraisal of value to get the Lakers, but I have turned them into a team worth much more now.

"You take the long-range view and look for future returns. As a business, sports is bad. I could invest in many other things that would produce more immediate profits at less risk of losses. But I can afford to indulge my interests, and the history of franchises is they appreciate in value.

"If Wilt wins a championship for me, he will be worth what I paid for him. Even if he does not, he may be worth it. I enjoy him."

Both can be charming companions and Cooke can, when he wishes, charm anyone. Wilt was flattered by Jack's acceptance of him as a social equal, which is, after all, not unreasonable. Wilt commands money that puts him on a par with many major businessmen. By now, he could move in high society among members who do not earn their living in anything approximating their underwear.

When the deal was done, Jack called a press conference on the floor of his suburban Forum, and when Wilt was introduced he came into a spotlight from behind closed curtains as though it were the second coming.

Although they later came apart with a flurry of lawsuits, Cooke and Chamberlain stood together on that day and many nights thereafter, a most imposing pairing. Though by then soured by and suspicious of owners, Wilt, who did not wish to

176

be owned, called Cooke, "One of the most intelligent and charming men I've ever known and a man who has done so much in business he has to be admired." Cooke, who would own only the world if possible, called Chamberlain, "One of the most intelligent and charming players I've ever known, a man who has accomplished so much in his profession it is greatly to be admired."

They sounded as though they had the same writer.

Cooke commented additionally, "Wilt has been, I believe, the most unfairly maligned athlete of my time," which Wilt, too, believes, of course.

Fred Schaus, who had become manager of the Lakers by then, says, "I don't know any athlete who was more maligned more unfairly. I think he brought a lot of it on himself because he was so outspoken. We'd shudder when he'd say certain things because we knew they'd create controversies. But that was his way and he was honest. I also think he was haunted by his history. For example, I don't know if he missed practices before he got here, but he didn't miss many here, yet he was always known as a player who missed practices. Too often players are judged by hearsay. I found him cooperative, but I did not ask a lot of him off the court. He sat for hours at a photo day once. I liked him."

Pete Newell, who succeeded Schaus, says, "I was very careful to ask only important appearances of him off the court, but he came through whenever I asked his cooperation. I know he did not like to do a lot of this. I know he liked to get out of the spotlight when he could. He never asked anything unreasonable of us. Usually his requests had to do with accommodations on the road, and you had to understand that he could not go where others could go without being bothered, had to spend a lot of time in his room, and had to have special situations set up for him. I understood this."

Jim Brochu, who was a publicist with the Lakers, says, "Well, let's face it, Wilt was difficult to deal with as far as publicity and public relations go. I was lucky Elg and Jerry were so cooperative with the writers and broadcasters and in going to media luncheons because I did not have to count on Wilt. And yet the writers will tell you that when they did get to sit down with him he was beautiful.

"He would scowl through photo days and then complain about how he looked in the pictures. I was in charge of the statistical crew, and he jumped on me all the time about him not being credited with enough rebounds or assists.

"He complained a lot. I remember he had room service one day in Milwaukee. A typical Wilt meal, he ordered a whole chicken, a plate full of shrimps, cheese, coffee, orange juice, pastries. I never saw so much. We could have fed the whole team. And he bitched because they'd forgotten some one thing.

"Well, you know, he was special, and he had to be handled with kid gloves. And yet, I liked him. I really did. And I think he liked me. And when we meet now it's like we're old friends. You just had to understand that Wilt was special."

Frank O'Neill was trainer of the team at the time. He says, "I remember when Wilt ran up a seventy-dollar meal tab for room service at the Ponchatrain Hotel in Detroit. He was angry about it, but he ate enough for three people, and prices are high in places like that. He said he had cheeseburgers. Well, he had three. And three plates of fries. And three quarts of milk. And three servings of ice cream. And, you know, he'd eat like a king, but he was all alone up there in that room, he'd be hassled if he went out. He was trapped, a prisoner of luxury."

Wilt hated to be kept waiting. Once in Chicago when TWA kept the Lakers waiting for a flight, he was so angry by the time they began to board that he said, "The way I feel right now, if I had a gun in my bag I might shoot somebody."

This was reported and he was called off the plane and questioned by a TWA official. Wilt was so angry he threatened to buy the plane. When the TWA official told him the FBI wanted him detained to be questioned about the "threatened hijacking," Wilt stormed away and flew the friendly skies of United instead.

Of course, many persons who made wisecracks about hijacking, bombs, and guns were regarded with understandable suspicion, but Wilt didn't see it that way. He points out proudly that Jack Kent Cooke supported him, complained the coach should have pulled the team off the plane, and ordered other airlines be used when possible in the future.

Trainer O'Neill admits, "He was demanding. And he did hate to wait. One day we were sitting on a bus in San Francisco waiting for Jim Price to go to Oakland to practice. Of course, going to practice was not Wilt's favorite thing anyway, and by the time Price showed up, Wilt was steaming. He read the riot act to the rookie.

"He used to bawl me out when he couldn't find his sweatbands or something, and they'd be right there, and I'd holler right back, 'They're right there, you big dummy,' or something like that, and I think he liked that. He liked me talking back to him. Of course, I was not a threat to him. I had those headbands made for him by Barney Tiernan,—who makes the uniforms—Wilt's first year here and they became big sellers.

"I did what I could for him. He always had to have 7-Up in the dressing room and by the bench. Cokes weren't good enough for him and it got to be a problem getting 7-Ups by the case and seeing that the other teams had it for us on the road. He'd drink a six-pack of cans during a game and more after a game. And the guys used to steal them to make him mad. He'd bitch about it. So Elgin would announce, 'I want Hires Root Beer from now on.' And someone else would say, 'I want orange soda.' And I'd say, 'Pretty soon I'll have a candy store here.'

"Oh, jeez, he and Elg just jawed at each other all the time. You know we'd had a lot of success with West as our leader on the court and Elg as our leader off the court, but when Wilt came in he had to be the big man both places. Now, I'm not putting Wilt down. I for one really like him. When I left the Lakers, he was one who took the trouble to telephone and say how sorry he was. When I ran into him in a restaurant one night

179

he came over to our party and bought everyone drinks and left the bartender a big tip and was wonderful to everyone. Later they said they were amazed because they'd heard how hard he was to get along with. But he had problems with other players.

"He and West had a sort of unspoken understanding. They respected what they each could contribute to the other on court, and West didn't care if Wilt was king off court. But Baylor was 'The Kingfish,' the one who made up nicknames for everyone, needled everyone, told the tallest stories, directed the action, and he didn't like it when Wilt came in, took over, and was determined to top him. They just didn't like each other.

"They were super, proud players, and they just rubbed on one another. And then, of course, our coach when Wilt came in was Bill van Breda Kolff, and Butch was as stubborn and explosive and strong-willed as Wilt, and both had to be the boss. There was no way they were going to make it together. These were not marriages made in heaven."

If you were to name the five or six greatest basketball players ever to an all-time, all-star team, Wilt, West and Baylor should be on it. When Wilt joined West and Baylor, some, including Cooke, commented they might never lose a game because never before in sports history had half the greatest players in their sport come together on one team at one time. Others, however, commented they might need three basketballs. Still others suggested separate dressing rooms. Some saw that it would take a master psychologist and strategist to blend these individualistic personalities with the different playing styles into an effective unit, and that the team at that time did not have the man needed.

When Jack Kent Cooke was completing his contract with Wilt Chamberlain, he called in his coach, Bill van Breda Kolff, and asked him what he thought of working with Wilt. Knowing the deal was done, Bill showed the enthusiasm he knew his boss wanted to see. "That's great," he said.

The season was not very far along when van Breda Kolff came storming into Cooke's office, complaining about Chamberlain, swearing, "Either he goes or I go." That was not exactly wise. Faced with a choice between a coach and a superstar, owners will side with the player. Coaches come cheaper.

Van Breda Kolff, who was not Cooke's kind of man, was going to go anyway, so he decided to go before he was told to go. He negotiated with San Francisco and Detroit. Fred Schaus says, "His deal with Detroit to go there the following season was set by midseason."

Cooke says van Breda Kolff and Chamberlain were conflicting personalities. "They simply were not temperamentally suited to one another," he comments. His manager at the time, Fred Schaus, admits, "There was no way those two could get along."

It must be remembered that van Breda Kolff had come into a difficult situation. Despite the presence of Baylor and West, Fred Schaus had won divisional pennants but not the playoff title. He had, in fact, lost four final series to Boston in seven seasons, two in seventh games, one by three points in overtime, the other by two points.

Schaus had played to his two stars, firing from a double-barreled shotgun. He had no domineering center and his strategy was to give the ball to Baylor or West and let them work for a shot. Van Breda Kolff came in to change the team to five-man tactics in which his stars shared responsibility with lesser players. The result was still another final-series playoff failure against the Celtics.

Now Wilt, the "loser" who had won one, joined forces on the Lakers with the "losers" who had yet to win one from Bill Russell's Celtics. And van Breda Kolff had three stars to try to work into a team concept. And he knew the new one was supposed to be difficult to coach. "I'm the coach and he's just a player," van Breda Kolff growled going in.

"Butch," as everyone called him, was considered a player's coach. He pushed his players hard, prodding, profane, but then prepared to party with them later. He once said all he asked of life was to play the game, have a couple of beers with the guys, and go home.

Intensely excitable, he raged during games—sometimes at refs (he led the league in technical fouls, ejections, and fines), sometimes at his players. He once followed Baylor down a corridor leading to the dressing room screaming, "Ten years an All-Pro and you make a pass no stupid rookie would make. Ten years an All-Pro? That should be ten years a dum-dum." Baylor went for him and they had to be held apart.

But Baylor and the rest came to see that when Butch called one of his players a stupid son-of-a-bitch, it was in anger, which he forgot fast. That very night, he might be drinking with the player. In fact, Baylor has recalled, "He used to run bed-checks to find out who was awake to drink with. Sometimes we had to help him back to his room."

Jim Brochu says, "The trouble between Butch and Wilt started in preseason training camp and continued through the season. Butch expected everyone to work hard in practice, and Wilt wouldn't. Butch couldn't approve Baylor and West working hard while Wilt walked around. I guess Wilt was used to special consideration, and Butch didn't believe in it. You know Butch, driving everyone like a drill sergeant, but Wilt wouldn't budge.

"Butch told Wilt he wanted him to play a high post and pass off to the other players who would play off him. And that was just the opposite of what Wilt had been told to do by coaches he liked, such as McGuire and Hannum, who wanted him in a low post close to the basket. Anyway, Butch didn't ask Wilt about it, he just told him. Wilt was used to being asked. He was burned up. He wasn't the sort to socialize with his coach, so he and Butch never relaxed over drinks."

Wilt said, at the time, "I would think that with the experience a Wilt Chamberlain, an Elgin Baylor, or a Jerry West has in this league, a coach who has a lot less experience would want to take advantage of it and talk things over. I am not easy to get along with, but I like to feel that any problem between two men can be resolved with two provisions: first, that both men are mature, and second, that they are able to sit down and talk. I have never had trouble with a coach, or, for that matter, any other person with whom I can talk."

Bill and Wilt seemed unable to talk together. When the team got off to a disappointing start, the bad feeling between them built up. The team was winning, but not as consistently or easily as expected. It was being rebuilt, of course, as well as reshaped, with the three traded players replaced, and it was almost a new team.

Chick Hearn recalls, "Traveling with the team, the two began to bend my ear complaining about each other. We get to

Atlanta and Wilt gives me the business about Butch at the airport, and then Butch gives me the business about Wilt at the hotel. Wilt calls and asks me to come to his room to do something about it. I hang up and Butch calls and asks me to come to his room to do something about it. I tell Butch I can't because I have some writers coming to my room, then I call Wilt back and tell him the same thing. Then I call Fred Schaus in LA and tell him I don't want to get in the middle of this thing and take sides, and he better catch a plane and fly in before it blows up. I was scared. So Schaus flies in and meets with them and soothes them a little, but only a little and only temporarily. I knew there was no way those two could get along in a million years.

"I remember another time. Butch had a rule that no one could bring food into the dressing room before a game. If Wilt had stomach trouble it was because he'd eat anything that stood still. He used to bring half a chicken into the dressing room and down it before a game. Butch bitched, so Wilt sent the clubhouse boy out for hot dogs. Butch called Schaus down and there's Wilt eating hot dogs. Schaus goes over to him and Wilt looks up, smiles, holds a half-eaten dog up to him and asks, 'You want a bite, Fred?' I mean, you know, Wilt did what he wanted."

Schaus says, "They both had to have their way and there was no way. They were so strong-minded and stubborn there was no way to their dying days either would give in to the other. And all I could do was get between them and try to keep them apart. There were people who feel I was not firm enough, but what was I going to do, fire one of them? Mr. Cooke did the firing. Besides, I respected both of them and wanted them to work together for the good of the team. My job was not to knock off one of them, but try to get them together. But there was no way."

They went into Seattle early in February and had a bad game. Bob Rule picked up a lot of points on Wilt, who was peeved with van Breda Kolff's strategy. There is a long corridor there

184

leading to the dressing room. As the Lakers took the long walk back after being beaten, both were raging—Butch about Wilt's lack of hustle, Wilt about Butch's substitutions. As Tom Hawkins remembers it, "Wilt said, to no one in particular, 'That man is the dumbest coach I've ever played for in my life.' Well, I don't know if he knew Butch was right behind him, but Butch just blew up. 'What did you say, you big blank?' he roared. Wilt repeated it to Butch's face. Butch charged him and bumped him —chest to belly, you know. Wilt has a cool temper as far as fights are concerned, but he was ready to go. Baylor and I went in between them and held them apart.

"We got them into the dressing room and I told the guys to keep the door closed and keep out the press. I got some change and I went to a telephone and called Schaus and told him his favorite people were at it again, and Fred had to cool it again. He said he'd meet our plane in LA, and anyone who said anything about it to anyone would be fined five hundred dollars. He met us and he got them together again, but it was always temporary. They got into it all year. I was the player rep and drawn into it from time to time. One time I told them both off and they both jumped on me. That was the only time all year they agreed on anything. The players took sides. They were all on Butch's side."

Wilt swore he would never play for Butch again, while Butch said he'd bench Wilt. Cooke called them in for a conference and it was heated, the owner furious with them, and they backed down. Wilt resented that the players sided against him and he asked for a team meeting without the coach. In the meeting, he charged that Elgin, Jerry, and others seemed more interested in scoring than winning, which just stunned everyone. In turn, others complained that Wilt was embarrassing them by glaring at them openly on court whenever they made a mistake. They reached a sort of armed truce with each side saying they'd try to respect the other, but it was meaningless.

Wilt once said, "People think that players should love their teammates and live as one big, happy family, but it's just not that way. The stars are jealous of each other's salaries. The spear-carriers are jealous of the stars. You've got guys sitting on the bench that want to play, and their whole careers and their lives are on the line, being held back by the man ahead of them. When you're winning, there's not much a player can complain about, so he smolders. When you're losing, everybody's bitching. And everybody always blames everybody but themselves for losing.

"The people out there don't realize we're human and under a lot of pressure. We needle one another to keep our sanity. At the end of a long road trip we're really jumping at each other. The drudgery gets to you. As long as it's verbal, it's all right. When it gets physical, it gets out of hand. The coach has to try to keep things in hand. If the guys are basically compatible they'll make it. But I'm not the only one who doesn't socialize with my teammates a lot. Do you think Jerry and Elg go out together? I've had good friends in basketball like Chet Walker, Nate Thurmond, and Al Attles, but I don't happen to have real close friends on the Lakers."

Wilt had problems with the other players as long as he was with the Lakers. There were times when things were going well and the players thought he wasn't so bad, and then things would go bad and they'd decide he was the worst. When they had their championship year, all seemed sweetness and light on the surface, but dark, bitter feelings were only briefly buried. Other times, others did not try to hide their resentment of Wilt.

No matter how Wilt played, he piled up stats, and there always were reporters around him after the games. Repeatedly other Lakers complained about this over the years. "We do the work and he gets the credit," one muttered, glancing at the crowd in Wilt's corner. West insists, "I had a good relationship with Wilt." But one year when he had a housewarming party at his new home, West failed to invite only one player, Wilt, who has since complained about it.

Wilt later remarked, "West missed more games more seasons than any other player, but he was an 'untouchable' and never

186

criticized for it. . . . Keith Erickson asked for pain-killers every time he cut his toenails. . . . Gail Goodrich is a spoiled brat. I got sick and tired of women telling me how cute he was. Why, because he's small and white? Can't a big black man be cute? . . . Chick Hearn is an exciting announcer, but he has one slight problem, he thinks Jerry West is Jesus Christ. He gave Jerry his nickname, 'Mr. Clutch,' but no one comes through in the clutch all the time, and he failed many times. He's a great guard who did not need Hearn to deify him. Chick is an organization man and he knows who's on the way out and he picks on those players. Anyone who is a student of the game had to know when Happy Hairston would be dropped because Chick started to pick on him. And in Lynn Shackleford he has a weak assistant who is a talent in his own right but is nothing but a yes-man to Chick."

Hearn sighs and says, "I always thought I had a good relationship with Wilt. I liked him and respected his talent. He is an outspoken person and entitled to his opinions. I am an outspoken announcer and I am not afraid to give my opinions on the air. I do not know that I 'deified' Jerry West. He *was* 'Jesus Christ,' if I dare use that term, as far as Laker basketball goes. He was hurt and out a lot, but he played in pain a lot, too. And when he played he was the best all-around player I ever saw. As a guard, he was not as dominating as Wilt or Russell, but he was as smart a player, as inspirational a leader on court, and as consistent in the clutch as any player I ever saw. I am almost sure he won more games in the last minute than any player ever.

"But Baylor was a great and incomparably exciting player, too. And Wilt was as great as any player. I have no complaint with Chamberlain. The players had complaints, but they passed. Baylor and Wilt had disagreements, but they came to an end. It took time, but Wilt got together with the Lakers and we won a title in the end."

Gail Goodrich shrugs and smiles and asks, "What do you want me to say about Wilt? I don't want to say anything against him. I really don't want to say anything." After Happy Hairston came in, he became Wilt's best supporter among the players, and he and Wilt have praised one another, but now even he passes up an opportunity to talk about Wilt. Baylor passes up a chance to talk about Wilt. There it is, that curious intimidation by Wilt which extends beyond the basketball court. He is willing to talk about them, but few of them are willing to discuss him. Some will privately, but not publicly.

The bitterness between Baylor and Chamberlain went on and on. Off court, Elgin was the leader until Wilt came in. It was Elgin who decided when they would eat and where, what movie to see, what card or guessing game to play, how the rookies should be ragged, and then Wilt came in and asked, "Who the hell are you to set the rules, my man?" Baylor told one of his tall stories, Wilt topped it.

One time Baylor was kidding Mel Counts about being slow and about how slow his Oregon State team must have been. Elgin said, "That team must have run like a bunch of turtles with arthritis." And everybody laughed.

Except Wilt. "Are you talking about people again?" he asked.

"I'm not talking about people," Elgin said.

"You always talk about people," Wilt said.

"What do you mean?" Elg asked.

"How do you think people feel when you call them turtles with arthritis?"

"I didn't say they were turtles with arthritis. I said they run like turtles with arthritis."

Wilt sighed, shaking his head. Baylor looked down at the floor. As Frank Deford remembers it, there was only the shifting of suddenly uncomfortable players, the fumbling tying of shoelaces for something to do among the subdued players.

It just went on and on. Wilt would lose his temper about the absence of 7-Ups. Baylor would strut across the room and holler at O'Neill, "Hey, how come there's no grape soda. If I don't get my grape soda, I don't play." Or he'd ask, "Where's

188

my Chamberlain chit? I don't have time to take a shower."

Merv Harris says, "It was basic, between them. Baylor was coming off an injury which had slowed him and he was hanging on, while Wilt was still on top. Like most blacks, Baylor was for Hubert Humphrey. Naturally, Wilt was for Nixon. It was like two old lions circling each other, both wanting to be king of the lair."

Tom Hawkins says, "Elg kept his cool or it would have been worse. But he couldn't stop needling Wilt. Elg was a needler. But Wilt was the only player I ever saw who could get to Elg and knock him off keel. They were always on each other's ability. Of course, they both liked to work inside on court and they got in each other's way, and it carried over off court.

"But Wilt was unpredictable. I remember one time six or seven of us were going to dinner. Baylor was with us. West, too. Wilt said, 'Why not be my guests?' We decided, 'Why not?' And he took us to the Maisonette, one of the most expensive restaurants in Cincinnati and picked up the tab for a tremendous spread. From time to time, he'd do something like that. But, basically, he was a loner."

Mostly, they bickered. Elg would say, "Wilt, you've got a touch like a blacksmith." And Wilt would say, "Count the points, baby." The players chose up sides. Wilt would get one card game going, Elg would get another. Butch would be with Elg, of course. Though the fans knew little of it, even the two LA newspapers picked sides. The players regarded the *Times* as Butch's and Baylor's paper, the *Herald-Examiner* as Wilt's paper.

And they kept saying everything was fine. Wilt told the press, "It takes time to get a team together. It took time in Philadelphia and it will in Los Angeles. We'll do all right. We're not doing bad. Whatever our problems, I don't want to be blamed. My part is always blown out of proportion. I appreciate the pressure on our coach. But I've got problems too. If we lose, I'll be blamed.

"I'm more tolerant than I was, mellowed. Five or six years

ago I would have had it out with van Breda Kolff long before this."

Van Breda Kolff said, "We're trying to work everything out. We're trying. It'll work."

Baylor said, "With Wilt here, I don't have to work as hard. My legs should last longer."

West said, "He should make better players of all of us once we figure out how to use him best."

Wilt had a curious season. He had as many as 66 points and as few as 2. He averaged 20 points and 21 rebounds a game. West averaged almost 26 points, but missed 21 games, mostly with pulled leg muscles. Baylor averaged almost 25 points. The supporting cast—Keith Erickson, John Egan, Bill Hewitt, Hawkins, Counts—was ordinary.

Yet the team won the West with 55 victories and only 27 defeats for a .670 percentage, the most victories and second-best percentage in team history. And it was considered disappointing.

This was the third team that had won more games with him than ever without him, and it was the fourth straight and fifth in his career he had led to a pennant. Atlanta at 48-34 finished eight games back.

Curiously, Wilt's old Philadelphia team had an identical 55-27 record, yet lost the East to a Baltimore team that went 57-25. Boston had fallen to 48-34, finished fourth, and barely squeezed into the playoffs.

The playoffs appeared wide open.

But Boston's old men gathered themselves for one final fling and finished off Philadelphia in five games and New York in six to bounce right back into the finals.

The Lakers had their hands full with San Francisco, which beat them twice before the Lakers bounced back to win four straight, the last by 40 points.

Wilt, who had been held down by Thurmond the first two games, dominated him the final four, and defense destroyed the Warriors.

190

The Lakers then won four of five from Atlanta to advance to the final round once again.

So, old rivals, mixed up, Boston vs. LA, Russell vs. Wilt. What Wilt had done for Philadelphia two years earlier, it was assumed he could do for LA now. The Lakers had the home-court edge. They were favored. Presumably, Boston had gone as far as it could. Celtic time seemed to have run out.

This seemed certain after the first two games before wildly cheering crowds of more than 17,500 fans in the Forum. Wilt and Russell neutralized one another. West and Havlicek dueled. West scored a playoff record 53 points in the first game, while Havlicek had 37. The Lakers won, 120–118.

Havlicek outscored West, 43–41, in the rematch, but Boston was beaten again, 118–112, as Baylor bombed 32, including the Lakers' last 12. Wilt had only 4 points.

But in Boston Garden, the Celtics shot ahead by halftime in the third game by 17 points. The Lakers battled back to tie it in the third period, but lost it in the fourth. Havlicek outscored West, 34–24. West was hampered by a badly bruised hand suffered late in the second game.

West came back with 40 in the fourth game, and the Lakers should not have lost. The rest of the team tallied only 48 points. Still, the Lakers led, 88–87, with two seconds to play. Sam Jones had to shoot. As he jumped, his foot slipped and he lost his balance. He let the ball go and it hit the rim and fell in. "It was an accident," he admitted later, laughing.

The Lakers were not laughing as they went home tied. Wilt was struggling with Russell, who was retiring.

The first of May, the fifth game, Wilt, who had been lethargic, came to life. While West got 39, Wilt outscored Russell, 13–2, and outrebounded him, 31–13. The Lakers won, 117–114.

Back to Boston for the kill. But now West had a pulled hamstring muscle and Wilt had blurred vision from having had a finger stuck in his eye. Shot with pain-killer, West struggled to 26 points. Wilt got 2. The Lakers lost, 99–90, and Boston tied the series.

So it was a seventh game between these two teams for the third time in six finals, and the fourth time in eight playoff meetings between Chamberlain and Russell.

Wilt had won one final, but the Lakers had not. Neither had ever won a seventh-game final, and Boston and Big Bill never had lost one. But the Lakers had the home court.

Confident, Cooke put cases of champagne on ice, hung balloons from the rafters, ready to be released with victory, and brought in the USC band to make the victory march.

But Boston showed poise under pressure. With clutch-shooting Sam Jones and lightly regarded Em Bryant looping in long shots, Boston led through the first half.

The Lakers caught the Celtics at 60–60 in the third quarter, but then suffered a shooting slump, missing 15 shots in five minutes. Boston built back a lead of 15 by the end of the third period. It went to 21 in the fourth period.

The crowd was stunned.

But the Lakers cut the count to 17. Then West, who scored 42 on the night, hit five straight points to reduce the deficit to 12. The fans started to support the home team, screaming.

The Celtics, an old team, were tired and troubled by fouls, and Russell shuffled his players desperately. West twisted his injured leg and started to limp, but continued to come through in the clutch and the Lakers moved within 9.

But time seemed against them. With about five minutes to play, Wilt, who had 18 points and 27 rebounds in the game, came down with a rebound and banged his knee. He said later it hurt like it does when you hit your crazy bone and the limb goes limp. He hobbled to the bench and asked to be replaced. Van Breda Kolff angrily yanked him and sent in Counts.

The Lakers seemed to get new life. West hit two free throws, a jump shot, two more free throws, and Counts hit a basket, and suddenly the Lakers were within 103–100 with more than four minutes left. All of them, including their fans, who had waited so long, were looking for the kill.

O'Neill had sprayed Chamberlain's knee with a pain-killing

salve. Wilt went to van Breda Kolff and said "I'm ready to go back in." Butch said, "No, Mel hasn't hurt us, he's helped us." Counts hit a jumper from the foul line and it was 103–102. All was madness. Wilt signaled toward the court again, then again, but van Breda Kolff first shook his head, then ignored him.

The Celtics were missing. Havlicek missed a free throw and the Celtics had scored only three points in eight minutes. Wilt went to van Breda Kolff again and demanded, "Put me back in." Butch said, "I'm not putting you back in. We don't need you." Wilt took a towel and stormed to the end of the bench and sat down. Counts threw in a long one-hander to put the Lakers in front by one, but the referee called "traveling" on him, nullifying the big basket.

That turned the tide. West missed a shot. He got the ball back, but lost it dribbling off Bryant's knee. Boston got the ball, but Erickson knocked a shot by Havlicek away. By chance it went to Don Nelson. The ex-Laker threw it toward the basket. It bounced off the rim high in the air and came down right through the cords. It was the luckiest of baskets, but it put the Celtics ahead, 105–102, with 1:17 to go.

Counts tried to force a layup, but Russell summoned a last little bit of reserve and blocked it. Erickson tried to pass, but it was stolen. Siegfried was fouled and hit two free throws to make it 107–102. The Lakers and their fans sagged. The teams traded free throws and the Lakers got a last basket at the buzzer, but it was too late, 108–106.

Suddenly, it was all over. The balloons remained in the rafters. The musicians packed up their instruments and departed with the subdued fans in silence. The players' wives went to the press room to wait for their husbands, and some wept. The champagne went warm, unopened, as the Lakers drifted in, defeated by Boston and Russell for the sixth time in eight seasons in a playoff final and the third time in a seventh game.

It was like some Greek tragedy, the blows of life having hit them almost too often to be endured. For Baylor and West, who had been belted by each of these blows, it was deep disappointment. Wilt at least had won one, though it was his seventh playoff defeat by Boston in ten seasons as a professional, and fourth in a seventh game.

Wilt was bitter. He and Butch battled verbally in the dressing room. Butch called Wilt "a quitter," while Wilt called Butch "a liar." They had to be held apart.

Although others thought the Lakers had come closer without Wilt than with him, Wilt said, "By refusing to put me back in the game, he not only humiliated me, he deprived me and my teammates and the Laker fans of an NBA championship."

Later, he called van Breda Kolff, "By far the worst coach I ever had . . . so ignorant of basic human relations that he was an utterly hopeless coach . . . just a rotten coach. . . . Worst of all, he wasn't the kind of man you could respect off the court."

Well, Wilt won to the extent that he remained while Butch went. Muttering bitterly about Wilt, but flatly refusing to say anything out in the open about that blank-blank-blank-blank, hiding behind his silence, a gypsy coach moving from town to town and team to team without a championship to show for his career.

Russell retired that night, as both coach and player, so West, Baylor, and the Lakers never would defeat him. Wilt had, but only once, and in the moment of his last triumph, Russell said Chamberlain should not have left the contest in the clutch, hinting as others did that he was "dodging defeat" and "trying to get out of being blamed."

"Wilt copped out," he said. "Any injury short of a broken leg isn't good enough. When he took himself out of that game . . . well, I wouldn't have put him back in the game either."

Wilt was stunned. "What he said was unforgivable for any professional. He has been my house guest and he's broken bread with me. I'd like to jam a ball down his throat," he snapped angrily.

Well, they had been friends, or had seemed to be. They met each other at airports when their teams came to town, hosted

194

each other. In Boston, Wilt liked to play with Bill's extensive toy train layout.

They said kind things about each other, expressed respect for each other. Wilt remarked how remarkable it was that their off-the-court friendship endured through ten years of bitter battles on the court. It was remarkable, since one of them, Wilt, usually wound up the "loser."

This stopped that night. After a while, Wilt said he was willing to forgive and forget, but Bill showed no interest in it. He became a broadcaster, repeatedly rapped Wilt, and refused to interview him, asking how could he interview someone he wasn't talking to?

Wondering why, Wilt seems confused. He feels betrayed. Bill says, "What's between us, we settled on the court. Look in the record book." Wilt says, "I wouldn't trade my peace of mind for all his world championship rings and playoff checks combined."

Jack Kiser says, "Russell pulled the con job of the century on Chamberlain. He welcomed Wilt into the league. He played father-figure. He flattered him. He told him, man, you're going to better all my records, but you have things to learn and I'm going to teach you because I admire you. He made friends with him.

"He got Wilt to the point where Wilt worried about making Bill look bad. Russell would put his hand over the rim and Wilt would draw the ball back. Phil Jordon used to say, "That dirty son-of-a-bitch, if I did that Wilt would bust my fingers with the ball. Wilt hated to lose, but he liked Bill so much he didn't mind losing to him.

"Wilt could destroy Russell when he was inspired. But he held back just enough to get beat. He tried to win over Russell, but he wasn't driven like he was against guys he disliked. I might point out Russell never said a bad word about Wilt until the night he retired and he hasn't stopped rapping him since.

"Bill is one of the smartest men I ever met, and crafty."

195

One time Wilt was trying hook shots on Russell. They were missing. Russell said, "Why don't you try to kick it in." Wilt broke up. He thought Russ a funny fellow.

George Kiseda says, "There's no doubt Russell used psychology effectively on Chamberlain. He kept saying Wilt was the greatest player ever but just didn't have the team to beat Boston. Wilt wanted to believe it, so he did.

"Russell's teams were better than Chamberlain's teams most of the time, but there were a few times when Wilt's might have won and did not. Russell really may have been a better team player, but Wilt was a much better player. About a third of the time Russell played better, a third Wilt did, and a third Wilt treated Bill like a boy.

"Russell really didn't respect Wilt, but he didn't tell anyone until it was too late for him to be hurt by it."

Tom Hawkins says, "Wilt was more a physical player, Russell more mental. Wilt was superior as a pure player, but Russell complemented other players better. Wilt didn't have as good a team as Russell most of their careers."

Fred Schaus says, "There is absolutely no doubt that Boston was the best team in basketball for ten or twelve years. A lot of us were lucky to come close. The Celtics had a lot of top players and the same coach. Wilt would have won as much with them as Russell did."

Frank McGuire says, "Wilt was superior to Russell. He just played his normal game against Bill. If he'd determined to take him apart, he'd have left him in little pieces."

Bill Sharman adds, "Bill outsmarted Wilt, but he could never do the things Wilt could."

Jerry West says, "Wilt had more ability, but Bill must have been easier to play with. Bill was always there when you needed him. He won the most so I rate him first."

Red Auerbach says, "There can be no comparison. With Russell, we had a team. With Wilt, it was Wilt and four other players. The book shows who won. That's all that counts—the bottom line."

Statistically, Wilt is superior. While both averaged 22 rebounds a game, Wilt averaged 45 minutes and 30 points over 14 seasons, while Bill averaged 42 minutes and 15 points over 13 campaigns.

However, playoffs were something else. Wilt fell off while Bill built up. Again they were equal in rebounds at 24 each. Otherwise, Wilt averaged 47 minutes and 22 points, while Bill averaged 45 and 16.

Season by season, voting prior to the playoffs, the writers seemed more impressed with Wilt. He was voted first All-Star center seven times, Russell three times and only twice while Wilt was in the league. Wilt was voted MVP four times, Russell three times.

Yet, in retrospect, the press seems to favor Russell by a wide margin.

His teams won more, writers and broadcasters say. Russell's teams won eleven league playoff championships in his thirteen seasons, including nine in a row at one stretch. They lost to St. Louis his second season when he was sidelined with an injured foot, and to Philly his eleventh season when he started to coach. His teams also won nine divisional pennants, all in his first nine seasons.

Wilt's teams would wind up winning only two league playoff crowns in his fourteen seasons, though they did win seven divisional pennants, five in one stretch of six seasons in the last part of his career. His teams were not as good as Russell's teams most of this time, even his critics conceded, but they seldom won even when they were better, the critics add. This, the reader can decide for himself.

Russell has said, cackling, "Hey, I used everything I had. Psychology, sure. If I could get the big guy off guard, I was determined to do it. Off the court, I lulled him to sleep. On it, I sacrificed myself the way he wouldn't. I brought out the best in my teammates and he didn't. And I won and he didn't."

West was MVP of the playoffs that last year. "How come, if I didn't bring out the best in him?" Wilt asked angrily.

Earlier, once they were on a plane together. "A little gin rummy, baby?" Russell asked. He knew Wilt was a sucker for card games. "Before we start, there's something you should know," Russell said. "I've got this thing," he said, pulling a card from his wallet. It was a license to carry a gun. "You win the game," Russell said, "and I'm going to shoot you dead." And he broke into that crazy cackle of his. Wilt laughed. The way it ended it wasn't funny. Russell left Wilt for dead, wondering when he had been shot down.

It's gone now and Wilt has no more shots at Big Bill, who coaches Seattle and is making a lot of money doing commercials on television, which make him more famous than ever. "He's fantastic in that telephone commercial he does," Wilt admits wistfully. They are both big black men, and to some, they *all* look alike, of course. "I get a lot of people saying to me, 'I just love you in that television commercial,' Wilt says. "I say, 'Thank you.' "

Advising a rookie, Wilt Chamberlain once said, "If you make it in the pros, you had better save your money and be ready to retire at any time. It can all end like snapping your fingers." It almost ended for Wilt Chamberlain in October of 1969, his second season with the Lakers in Los Angeles.

It started like it might be a successful season. Wilt, West, and Baylor had a year behind them in their efforts to get used to one another. They had come close to taking the title the year before despite problems. Now, with Russell retired, their chances seemed the best they ever had been.

Van Breda Kolff was gone, an irritant removed. Joe Mullaney had been brought in from Providence College to coach. Like all the others, he said, "I think I can handle Chamberlain." Wilt snapped, "Animals are handled, not men." Mullaney accepted it. "Wilt has a point," he said. He apologized. In preseason practice, Wilt said, "He seems fine. He doesn't act like he wants to be boss."

That's all Wilt asked of his coaches. And he really wanted to make it with this coach to prove it had not been his fault that he had not made it with van Breda Kolff. Mullaney was a warm, pleasant person and a low-key, experienced coach, the kind who could cut it with Wilt. They were friendly from the first. Mullaney says, "I was warned no one could coach Wilt, but I'd always gotten along with all my players so I thought I could work it out. After the press conference called to announce me as the new coach, I was aware nine out of ten questions had been about how I would work with Wilt. Nothing about Baylor or West. I didn't call a conference with Wilt or anything like that. I didn't want to make it look like I thought there might be trouble. I just started to coach.

"I talked to him the first time in Cooke's office the day before preseason practice started and we just talked pleasantly. Then practice started. I hadn't been around a pro club since I stopped playing in 1950, but I sensed a strained feeling on the team. There was no closeness among the players that I could see and I supposed this was a carryover from frictions I'd heard about the previous year. I tried to establish togetherness on the team by stressing teamwork without lecturing about it. I'm not a slave-driver. I like my teams relaxed. I don't want them to leave their games on the practice court.

"Fred Schaus had set up a meeting for me with Dr. Robert Kerlan and Dr. Vince Carter. We had lunch together and they told me Wilt had arthritic knees and if I pushed him in practice I ran the risk of reducing his career or losing him. When I saw Wilt didn't work hard in practice, I didn't push him. I accepted it.

"I told Wilt I wanted him to play a low post, and that pleased him. I asked him and other older players about this player or that player that I didn't know, and he liked that. I remember we were thinking about picking up a certain player and Wilt said he didn't think the player could help us.

"I relied on Schaus a lot while I was learning the league, but Schaus relied on Wilt, too.

"I thought we were going to be all right, but then Wilt got hurt."

That was nine games into Wilt's eleventh season, and he had

missed only twelve games as a pro to that point. That was the year Alcindor came into the league, before he became Jabbar, and Wilt had opposed him for the first time. Two weeks later, the Lakers were hosting Phoenix. During the third period, Wilt was dribbling toward the basket when suddenly he collapsed in a pile of pain. No one had hit him and it was awhile before anyone went to his side. He lay cursing softly on the hardwood court under the basket until trainer Frank O'Neill and then Dr. Kerlan, crippled by an arthritic back, got to him to examine him. He was helped to the dressing room, his right leg dangling limply.

A French girl from Long Beach, with whom he had made a date for that night, sagged in her seat, sensing herself shut out.

Jack Kent Cooke rushed into the doctor's room to ask Wilt if it hurt. Wilt lied that it did not. But perspiration beaded on his brow and his eyes were narrowed by the pain. He was rushed to the hospital where Dr. Kerlan diagnosed the injury as a rupture of the entire patella tendon, which was torn away from the kneecap.

"It was unusual, severe, one of the worst I ever saw," he said after one hour and forty minutes of surgery the following day.

"Basketball players jump up and down, pound up and down hard courts. They twist and turn. Their knees are subjected to tremendous strain. The tendons receive little tears. Wilt's may have been stretched in boyhood by his rapid growth, and they have had to carry a lot of weight. The tendon finally gave way, but I'm sure it was not the result of this single incident."

The memory of the previous season's playoff incident flooded in.

The tendon was sewn up, reattached to the kneecap by Drs. Kerlan and Frank Jobe, and the leg encased in a long cast. Cooke asked, "Please tell Wilt I wish it was me instead of him."

"So do I," Wilt laughed.

Jack never blamed Wilt for the defeat of the previous season. "He did all I could have hoped," Cooke had commented. Now most assumed all was lost for this season. Not Cooke.

When the doctors said that Wilt might be as good as new the following season, Cooke said, "Wilt will be back before this season is over. He is more than a normal man. Doctors are of necessity cautious individuals. They prefer to be pessimistic rather than have patients disappointed by lack of progress. I am by nature an optimist."

Wilt wore No. 13. Perhaps thinking of that, Jack predicted Wilt would be back within 13 weeks. Studying a calendar, he decided March 13 would be about right.

That would give him two weeks to prepare for the playoffs.

Told this, Chamberlain agreed. "The man is paying me a lot of money. I would be stealing it if I did not try to get back into action as soon as possible."

Meanwhile, some were predicting Wilt would not return not only that season but ever. "A big man like that has to be through after an injury like that," one player claimed.

When the cast was removed, Wilt had to exercise to loosen the knee and rebuild the strength in his leg. He endured lonely and painful periods of lifting weights with his legs, running, riding a bicycle, took to playing volleyball on the beach.

Trainer Frank O'Neill says, "I've gone through this with many players, and I never knew one to work as hard. He had a weight table delivered to his home so he could work there. He went at it without letup seven days a week."

Wilt said, later, "I wasn't ready to retire. It was wanting to play again that gave me the push I needed." A friend said, "He had always been the master of his own destiny. He wanted to retire on his own terms at his own time. He didn't want it taken out of his hands."

In January, the All-Star Game was held in Wilt's hometown of Philadelphia. His injury denied him an eleventh straight appearance. And he was bothered because he wasn't invited as a guest. "They've done it for others," he said. "I'll be there, but I'll buy my own ticket."

He went and limped into the arena wearing velvet and a huge gold chain, and when the fans saw him they cheered him. "I'll be back," he vowed. "I won't let them forget me. They'll know my name again."

He grumbled about Wes Unseld and Willis Reed having run one-two in the All-Star center and MVP polls the year before. "I was superior statistically and every other way. They just want to take it away from Wilt if they can find someone to give it to. But I'm still best."

The fans' support did inspire him. From the first, he was welcomed in Los Angeles as he had been in no other city. Wanting a championship, they welcomed him with even greater ovations than they gave West and Baylor. Now, fans everywhere wrote him, wishing him well. The injury had done what nothing else in his life had done—made him seem human. And for the first time he found fans supporting him when he could do nothing for them. "I am moved by it," he admitted.

He has confessed it altered him, softened his suspicions of the world, made him feel warmer toward his fellow man.

The Lakers did not do badly without him. Young Rick Roberson was adequate at center with Counts as support. Happy Hairston was obtained in a trade to help on the boards. Baylor averaged 24 points a game, but missed 18 games with injuries. Paired with at best an adequate guard, Dick Garrett, West carried the club. He led the league in scoring at 31 points a game, led the team in assists, led defensively, led the league in steals.

"Without West, we would have been dead," admitted Mullaney. "He had the greatest single season I've ever seen." Many agreed and have not since taken seriously the MVP award which was voted to a black, Willis Reed, by the mostly black players in the league. So goes Crow Jim.

For a while, there was the feeling that the team was better without Wilt—faster, more mobile. But eventually it became clear that life on the court was a lot tougher without him. "We have to work harder, it takes more out of us, and we'll have less left for the playoffs," pointed out West. Baylor said, "We've been getting by, but we could use him."

Dr. Kerlan advised against it, but with Cooke's encouragement, Chamberlain came back with three games to go, and played them, within one day of the timetable that had been set out for him by his owner. Wilt was not sharp, but he did surprisingly well. The fans cheered his return and the players regarded him with new respect. "I can't do it all, but what I can do should help," Wilt observed.

They finished at 46–34, only two games short of Atlanta in the Western Division standings.

The Lakers faced Phoenix in the first round. In the first game, Wilt was wonderful, the Lakers won, and everyone was enthusiastic about his comeback. In the next three games, Wilt was slow and awkward, the Lakers lost, and everyone said he was hurting his team. "You don't expect them to blame anyone else, do you?" Wilt asked.

It never has been written, but Mullaney now reveals, "We had gotten to play a certain way without Wilt. We had not adjusted to him totally, and I wondered if we just didn't have the time to make the transition and maybe would be better without him.

"I considered taking him out before the fifth game, but it was at home and I went with him and we won. But the sixth game in Phoenix figured to be something else, and I went to Wilt the night before the game and told him what I've told you. He said, 'It's not my fault.' I said, 'I know that, but if we get in trouble in the sixth game and I take you out, I want you to know what I'm thinking. I'm not blaming you, but I can't wait until we get blown out.'

"I'm sure he was worried about looking bad the way he had the year before, but I couldn't help that. He said, 'You're the coach.'

"Well we fell far behind and I began to worry I was waiting too long. I was worried about Baylor, too. I had been playing him out of deference to his reputation, but he didn't play defense and no longer had mobility. I tried taking him out and that helped a little. I was about to take Wilt out, too, when we rallied. Wilt played so well and we came on so strong after that I never thought of benching him again."

With a massive effort, this massive man turned it on. He lacked agility, but that never was his strong suit anyway. He rebounded, blocked shots, fed off, scored when needed. West and the rest responded. The Lakers became only the second team in the history of NBA playoffs to come from a three-games-to-one deficit to win a best-of-seven series.

With Wilt a mountain on defense, Laker momentum carried them to a four-straight sweep of Atlanta in the divisional finals. After the first game, Hawk coach Richie Guerin complained the refs protected Laker stars and warned that if this continued, "there's going to be blood on the floor . . . Baylor, West, and Wilt may not be around at the finish." Playing protector for his team, Wilt said, "If they want to try anything funny, I'll be the equalizer." Meekly, the Hawks submitted, as the Lakers set an NBA playoff record of seven straight triumphs.

The Lakers won the third game over Atlanta in overtime after Wilt hit two free throws with thirteen seconds left in regulation time to tie it. The crowd responded as if Wilt had worked a miracle. Afterward, he was asked if he'd ever hit two free throws in the clutch like that, and he said he had many times, but no one believed him. Cooke came in to congratulate him. "I knew you'd make them," he enthused.

"You were the only one," Wilt said softly after the owner left.

After the fourth game, Guerin came in to congratulate the winners. The losing coach leaned over to congratulate Chamberlain, slapping him on his scarred, sore knee. Wilt winced.

Thus they gained the playoff finals once more, but this time against a New York Knick team which had set an NBA record with 18 straight victories during the season, won 60 of 82 games, bounced the Bullets and Jabbar's Bucks from the playoffs, and deservedly were favored. Led by Willis Reed, Dave DeBusschere, Bill Bradley, and Walt Frazier, Red Holzman's team was superb.

The first two games were in New York's new Madison

Square Garden, crammed to its capacity of 19,500 fans. In the opener, Reed outmaneuvered Chamberlain, scored 37 points, helped the Knicks to a 124–112 victory. But Wilt took the battle to Reed in the rematch and West won it with two free throws at the end, 105–103.

In a filled Forum, the third game was a classic. West's jumper put the Lakers in the lead, 99–98, with 38 seconds left. Dick Barnett banged one in to put the Knicks ahead, 100–99, with 18 seconds left. Wilt was fouled and missed one, but came through in the clutch with the second that tied it at 100 with 13 seconds left.

The Knicks came down and when DeBusschere hit to make it 102–100 with three seconds left, the Lakers seemed doomed. Wilt threw the ball to West and started to walk to the dressing room. West dribbled briefly, then from 55 feet fired a one-hander at the basket. The buzzer blew and the ball went through. Pandemonium!

The Knicks stood stunned. Some of the Lakers started to run off, thinking they had won. Old Doc Kerlan hobbled on court waving his cane as though in conquest. But it was only tied and the two teams had to go into overtime. Then came the letdown as the Knicks pulled themselves together to win, 111–108. The Lakers seemed to have spent themselves emotionally and had little left.

In the dressing room, West patiently answered questions about his shot until finally he lost his patience and said, "What does it matter? We lost," and left to hide in the shower room.

The reporters kept asking Wilt, mikes thrust into his face, if he'd ever seen such a shot, and he kept saying he hadn't. All the time his big hands were moving nervously on his scarred knee. Finally, a ballboy brought him a can of 7-Up and he squeezed that.

Left alone for a moment, he leaned back and closed his eyes. Then a writer came up to him and asked him if he'd ever seen anything like West's shot, and Wilt couldn't help himself, he just laughed. Later, Wilt blamed West for the loss, saying he couldn't "buy a basket in overtime."

In the fourth game, Chamberlain outrebounded Reed and the Lakers came back to win in overtime, 121–115.

In the fifth game, the Lakers led by 10 when Reed tore a muscle in an upper thigh and was through for the game. Sub centers failed to contain Chamberlain, and the Lakers went 16 in front. However, Holzman went to quicker forwards DeBusschere and Dave Stallworth on Wilt in the second half, and it worked.

Wilt took only three shots, West only four the entire second half and Baylor was the only Laker to hit from the field in the fourth quarter. Incredibly, the Knicks rallied to win without Reed.

Afterwards, Wilt was ridiculed. But he blamed Mullaney for not getting the other players to pass to him. And he blamed the officials for not calling fouls on his smaller foes, who swarmed all over him: "It was almost criminal-type negligence by the officials. They don't think I can be fouled by a smaller man."

For the Lakers, it was a long flight home. Back in the Forum in the sixth game they slaughtered their Reed-less rivals. Wilt had 45 points and 27 rebounds. But when the reporters got to to him afterward, he was sullen. "It don't matter if Reed plays or not. If my game is going, it goes against anyone."

Standing up, he exploded, "American sports fans are spoiled. They only want to win. They don't realize one team has to lose. They treat losers like animals. They can't just enjoy great games between great teams. They'd rather win a lousy game than lose a great game. They don't realize it's how you play that counts, not whether you won or lost. They can't give credit to a team for getting this far. If it doesn't go all the way it's nothing."

Finding the 7-Ups gone, he stomped about, pouting. He shook his head angrily, and dressed in a brown velvet suit. He said, "So I'm a hero tonight. And tomorrow night? If they boo me when I lose, I don't want their cheers when I win."

207

He waded through the fans outside, pausing to sign autographs, and, like a condemned man going to his execution, limped to the flight for New York and the seventh game.

Another seventh game!

Admitted one Laker, "We don't want to go back there for it. We know we'll lose."

So they lost. The game was delayed until Reed could be brought in dramatically from the dressing room to start. He got a tremendous ovation and it didn't seem to matter that he couldn't play well and didn't last long. The Knicks seemed inspired, the Lakers depressed. Led by Walt Frazier, the Knicks blitzed the Lakers, led by 14 points at the quarter, 27 at the half, and coasted in to win by 14 at the finish.

Wilt later said, "Walt whipped West's ass—as he usually does."

West got 28 points to set a new single-season playoff scoring record of 562. Wilt got 21 points and 24 rebounds, but he did not dominate substitute opposition as expected, and the papers put the blame on him. So did some players. One said, "Without Willis, Wilt should have single-handedly destroyed them. Well, maybe it was his knee."

Wilt said, "My knee was fine. We just lost. I didn't lose, *we* lost. We all lost. I can't let this disrupt my life. There are other things in life. Now I can turn to them for a while. I welcome summer."

So, another splendid summer was spent prior to a new winter of discontent. Wealthy and woeful, his spirit bore scars as well as his knee.

Later, Wilt raged, "It was written that Reed outplayed me. How could that be? Reed grabbed only three rebounds and scored four points. I had 22 rebounds and 21 points, and I think I made about 77 percent of my shots from the floor.

"They wanted to give Willis a medal of honor because he was playing on an injured thigh. I was coming back from a much more serious injury. We should have won that series, and the one the year before with Boston, but don't blame me that we didn't."

It is generally agreed that the last final with Boston and the first one with New York (after Reed was hurt) were two the Lakers should have won. Cooke concedes, "They were deep disappointments."

Schaus says, "I think about them often and they hurt, but I lost finals when I was coaching and I can't condemn other coaches for doing so. Sometimes things just don't seem to work out the way you want them to.

"But in blaming Wilt, people completely forget that he had a weak knee and came back long before any other player I've ever known with anything like that. He had an easy out, but he was dedicated, he subjected himself to suffering, and put his career on the line to rush back. It was as admirable as anything I've seen in sports."

Cooke comments, "I'll always remember the near nobility of the man making good his promise to me to return." Dr. Kerlan says, "It was incredible." Mullaney says, "He showed incomparable courage and gave us everything he had. Without him, we would not have reached a seventh game. He was not at his best, but blaming him for being beaten is to be insensitive to the situation."

Cooke wanted to win, however, and Mullaney had not won and so was under pressure his second season. He had problems with his players. They say he called them by the wrong names at times. They called him "the absent-minded professor." They complain about tough coaches. They complained this coach was too soft.

They went to Schaus and said practices were disorganized. Schaus spoke to Mullaney, who tightened up. But three weeks into the season, Cooke was considering replacing Mullaney with Schaus when in their ninth game the Lakers made a remarkable comeback to beat the Knicks before a frenzied Forum crowd, and that saved his job.

Around Christmas time, Joe and Wilt had a run-in. Wilt had gone to Philadelphia to visit his mother and missed his flight back and a practice session. Mullaney put in some new plays and told the team Wilt wouldn't start the coming game. Jim Brochu remembers, "Everyone except Wilt knew that night that he was going to be benched, and no one wanted to go down to the dressing room. I recall Jerry was in my office and he said, 'God, I don't want to go. The explosion is going to tear the building apart.' "

However, when Wilt walked in, Mullaney just took him aside and told him because team morale demanded it and because he didn't know the new plays, he would be punished for missing a practice by not starting, and Wilt just said, "Fine." But when the team left to take the court, Wilt failed to follow. Furious, he complained to Schaus and started to dress to leave the building. Fred promised to talk to Mullaney, and talked Wilt into rejoining the team. Fred did talk to Joe, and Mullaney did put Chamberlain in the game. Strangely, Wilt says if Joe had started him, then taken him out, it would have been fine. Of course, Chamberlain never minded being taken out.

Mullaney's authority suffered. The team was struggling, and after it was blasted by 34 points by Cincinnati in a nationally televised game in Omaha, Schaus flew in to meet the team in Cleveland. He found Wilt eating a box-full of hot dogs in the dressing room before the game, and he lost his temper. He blamed defeats on a lack of conditioning, concentration, and intensity. He said to Wilt, "You're too busy feeding your face to get ready for a game. That's why we were embarrassed in Omaha." Wilt said, "I scored forty-one points in Omaha." And offered Fred a bite of his hot dog.

It was hopeless.

The team wasn't too bad. Gail Goodrich had been brought back from Phoenix to team with West at guard, and each averaged 17 points. Wilt averaged 30 in the pivot, and everyone played off him. Wilt averaged 18 rebounds and Hairston averaged 10. Hairston averaged 18 points and might have been effective teaming with Baylor up front, but Baylor tore a tendon and was sidelined the entire season. Jim McMillian, a rookie, was rushed in, but took time finding his way. Then West tore up his knee twelve games from the finish. The Lakers were done.

The NBA had been split into four parts. The Lakers put together a 48–34 record to capture the Pacific Division, but by the playoffs were a crippled club. Mullaney's men managed to upset Chicago in the first round, but were no match for Milwaukee in the next round. With a year's experience behind him and with the veteran star Oscar Robertson brought in to support him, Jabbar ripened and the Bucks became the best. Chamberlain was more than a match for Jabbar and led the Lakers to one win, but they were badly beaten in four other games, and blown out in five. The Bucks went on to win the championship.

It was the ninth time one of Wilt's teams had lost a playoff to the team that won the championship, but Chamberlain was cheered for his efforts with a crippled club in this series and given a standing ovation by the enemy fans in Milwaukee when he was taken out at the end of the last game. He recalls this with pride.

Jabbar was the All-Star center and MVP that season, but Wilt at thirty-four was still able to handle Jabbar at twenty-four. Jabbar was more mobile and graceful. The feeling then was he would surpass whatever Wilt had done, but he has not. The Bucks were supposed to start a dynasty, but they did not.

Wilt has said, "Jabbar had so much ability he was bound to become the most devastating force in basketball, but I do not believe his all-around game has developed the way I expected. He does not seem as intense as he might be, is not as intimidating a defender or shot-blocker as he might be, and he is not as aggressive rebounding as he might be. His supposed unselfishness does not show the way it was expected to.

"When I first faced him I didn't do as well as I expected, but Mullaney coached me and gave me some instructions which helped. He pointed out that when you play a player of his size and skill you can only try to take his best shots away from him. You get position on him so he has to take harder shots. You can't stop him, but if you take two or three or four baskets away from him, that may be enough to beat him.

"That made sense to me because I'm a percentage player and that's playing the percentages. I did well against him after that, and I think if you set him up right you can have success in holding him down. No one ever stopped me. There were nights I stopped myself, but no one ever stopped me. The shooter has all the advantages. He knows when he's going to shoot and where.

"The good defensive players like Nate Thurmond and Bill Russell gave me the hardest time because they devoted themselves to defense and worked on me to take my best shots away from me, but they never really stopped me. The good outside shooters like Willis Reed gave me trouble when I was on defense because they got me away from the basket, but that put them away from it, too.

"Jabbar was not the most troublesome center I faced by any means."

Although Wilt said he did not know Jabbar when first he faced him in pro ranks, he had hosted him in his New York apartment and counseled him. He was hurt when Jabbar did not later respond to him as a friend. He has said, "When Jabbar was growing up in New York, he tried to play like me on the playgrounds. Growing up, he wore his hair like mine, grew a goatee like I did. I befriended him. Now he won't talk to me. I don't know why. He has turned on me as Bill Russell did, and I don't know why."

Jealousy, perhaps. Or politics. Or perhaps because Wilt was not prominent in black causes as was the religious Muslim Kareem, who had a different life-style. Whatever, it seems to have wounded Wilt.

After the playoffs in 1971, Mullaney was fired. A New York newspaper headlined, "Wilt Fires Another Coach." Wilt complained, "Cooke fired the man, not me. I liked the man, thought he was a good coach. I never fired a coach in my life, and I'm fed up with the thought that I have."

Mullaney says, "Wilt called me to tell me he was sorry I was fired and that he was for me. I know he was. We had minor run-ins. I like Wilt and we remain friends. I could not possibly complain about his play for me.

"We had the three great players, but I only had them together thirteen games in two seasons. I thought I did well with what I had. But I was fired because Mr. Cooke thought he could get a coach who could do better. I was not fired until he was sure he could get the man he wanted. I was not fired until after the draft, and by then I was not expecting it. I was called in and told there was going to be a change. By the time I got home I had figured out it had to be Bill Sharman.

"It's funny because Bill later was kept hanging the same way. If the man gets who he wants, Bill is out. If not, Bill is brought back and given one more chance.

"Well, you have to win. Not one year, but every year. With Wilt or without Wilt," concluded the coach.

Wilt Chamberlain, the most famous "loser" of the last twenty years in sports, says, "All I ever wanted to be was a winner. Who doesn't? What athlete? You use what you have. You do what you can. Hey, my man, flip a coin, if I call it heads, I hate to see it tails. Hold your cards low, I'll peek. I don't want to cheat, but I don't want to lose. It's never easy to endure defeat, even if you're not blamed for it. But it happens. I can't cry. I've had victories. And defeats. But my life is not a loss."

Entering the 1971–72 season, he signed a two-year contract calling for $430,000 the first season and $450,000 the second season, with the option to purchase two thirds of the original amount offered of Cooke stock—$66,667—which his attorney, Seymour Goldberg, says he exercised and "sold at a fantastic profit" after it "went crazy" and before it came down. Tax shelters written in were written out. Such negotiations are delicate. Compromises often produce odd figures.

Like all owners, Cooke had to keep content competitive people who were as concerned about salary as success. For some, salary was success. One of his superstars wanted more than the other, so amounts never were announced. One got a tax-paid contract so what looked like less to the other superstar really was more.

When later court action revealed to West that Wilt was making more than he was, West became estranged from Cooke. As columnist Melvin Durslag commented, "Any man making a mere $300,000 a year has a right to pout." On the eve of the 1974–75 season, West retired to the country club. He played golf instead of basketball. Cooke contended this was in violation of his contract and refused to pay his salary. West took him to court.

Later, they settled their differences so Cooke could make West the new coach for the 1976–77 season after Bill Sharman had suffered two straight losing seasons and had been kicked upstairs."

An owner's lot today is difficult. The stars have the upper hand. Cooke wanted to win so much he was willing to pay for the privilege.

Bill Sharman was hired in '71. Brilliant, intense, Sharman was the only coach to have won championships in both rebel leagues, the ABL and ABA. He came close to another in the NBA with San Francisco when it lost to Philadelphia with Wilt in 1967. Sharman had a reputation as a coach who could make the most of what he had. Cooke worked hard and went high to land him, and he brought him in as "the best coach in basketball."

The former All-Time All-Pro with the Celtics, Sharman had run-ins with Rick Barry in San Francisco, and was regarded as a tough coach who disciplined his teams to dedication during the season. He says, "I was not worried about Wilt's reputation. When I was with Boston, Eddie Gottlieb introduced him to me back when Wilt was but a boy. I'd known him a long time, liked him, and respected his talent. If he had been a loser, I felt it was because he had not been used properly. I was sure I could work with him and win with him.

"I have my own ideas about basketball, and I think I know how to win. And I was walking into a situation where I felt I

215

had the talent to win, which is not the case most times a new coach takes over a team. I was aware that my stars—Wilt, West, Baylor—were older guys, but because they had been denied championships I felt they must still be hungry. I felt if I could get them to play with intensity, unselfishly, and could pull the supporting talent together, I would win with them.

"One thing I have always believed in is a running game, fast-break basketball. I believe you maintain intensity and concentration better running, apply pressure to your opponents, and get more shots, while taking shots away from your foes. Maybe with my older stars this was an unlikely system to impose on them, but I believed in it and I wanted them to go along with it and give it a good try, at least.

"There was a time when I just told my players what I wanted them to do. This is not an easy thing to do with experienced professionals who have been making big money doing their own things. But I never knew a player who didn't want to win. My record showed that I was a winner and I felt I could convince my players. I went to each of them to talk the possibilities over with them, to tell them how I wanted to work and to ask them how they wanted to work. I showed respect for them.

"I played golf with Jerry, and he was frank about the players and agreeable to a running game in which he would be more a quarterback than a shooter. Of course, I knew West played both ends of the court as well as any guard ever. I met with Baylor and he was willing to try, but he was coming off his second serious injury and was concerned about his ability to fast-break forty-eight minutes a game for eighty-two games. I was concerned, too.

"Wilt was in Europe so I didn't get together with him until practice started. I took him to lunch at the Marina and we discussed different ideas. One hurdle I had to clear right away was that I was the first coach to have practices not only on off-days but on game-days. I do not have intense practices on game-days, but I believe in morning sessions, shooting, passing,

216

loosening up, to get in a groove for the game. Now, everyone does it, but they didn't then.

"Wilt told me that he had trouble unwinding after games and suffered from insomnia, so seldom got to sleep until the wee hours and usually slept late the day of the game. He also said that he had problems with his legs and didn't want to leave his game on the practice court. But he said if I wanted him to try it, he would go along with me until he saw how it went. He did, though he didn't like it, and he complained about it at times. We were winning so he was stuck with it.

"One thing I asked was that if he was going to miss a practice for any reason he call me to tell me so he and I would not be embarrassed if the players or press were not prepared for it. And I must say he missed only four or five practices or shootarounds the two years he played for me, and with maybe one exception called every time and had a valid excuse. He complained, but he cooperated.

"I also told him I wanted to take him out of games from time to time when I thought he was tired or we needed a change. He said he stiffened up when he sat on the bench, but he was getting on in years by then—he was thirty-five when I took over—and he agreed he wouldn't be embarrassed if I rested him for a minute or two at a time here and there.

"As for how he would play, I left a lot of that up to him. He said he always preferred a running game. He said even with his leg problems he was a greater runner than people realized and was happy to go to a fast-break style. As we went along, we worked out what he would do. He was a great rebounder but I wanted him to work on making the outlet pass off the rebound, the fast pass to get the fast break going, and he did.

"I said I was more concerned with rebounding and defense from him than offense. He said he'd done all the scoring he ever had to do and was agreeable to that. I think we both knew he couldn't score as well as he once had except in spurts. There were certain players he could destroy, so we'd have him play the low post and turn into the basket on them, but there were others like Willis Reed, Wes Unseld, Dave Cowens, who could hold him out, so he'd go to the high post and the other players would play off him.

"He didn't have great hands and wasn't a great passer, but he was a smart player and made smart passes and seldom threw the ball away.

"He complemented this team perfectly. He just did everything I wanted him to do and he did a tremendous job. I think Jabbar is a super player, but it was a joke that Jabbar was the MVP that season because Wilt was by far the most valuable player on the best team in the league. If not Wilt, West, who did everything for us Wilt didn't do.

"The one high hurdle I had to clear shortly after the season started was that I could see Elgin could no longer cut it, and we would be a better team with young Jimmy McMillian in there. I hated to do it, but I had to talk to Elg about it. I knew he'd be embarrassed to become a sub. He decided to retire. I'll always feel bad about that.

"However, we then had a perfectly balanced team that fit together like five fingers in a glove. West quarterbacked the club and led defensively. He still shot superbly, especially when we needed it, but Gail Goodrich gave us great outside shooting from the other guard. We had one forward, Hairston, who rebounded, and one, McMillian, who shot. Wilt covered up their defensive shortcomings. He was the glue who held us together, rebounding, defending, ball handling.

"We did not have a great bench, but Pat Riley, Flynn Robinson, and Leroy Ellis contributed in spots. We had five strong starters and were fortunate we did not have any serious injuries."

"The funny thing about my meeting with Wilt was when I reached for my wallet I found I'd forgotten it. It was embarrassing. He had to pick up the tab and the tip. He always said he'd refuse invitations from me from then on.

"I really liked Wilt and I had no more problems with him

218

than with any other player. He seemed to be going out of his way to be cooperative and to contribute to the team.

"There were times when I saw him charm people and times when he was rude to them. He has an overpowering personality and can turn people on or off as he wishes. Personally, my relations with him were always super."

Like an evangelist, Sharman preached perfection. There was a joke running through the team at the start of preseason drills: Told Sharman had reveille at eight, practice at eleven, a meeting at four, and the game at eight, Goodrich said, "I know what's next, we wake up Wilt," and Wilt said, "That's fine, just pick one, any one, and I'll be there." But Wilt was there for everything.

He hated being blamed for the firing of Mullaney, he respected Sharman, and he didn't respect writers who wrote that he and Sharman were bound to have problems. He just determined to show everyone how wrong they were. He went on his best behavior.

The season started with four straight victories on the road. Then West hurt his ankle and was out for five games and the Lakers lost three, including their home opener, and all were worried it was going to be one of those seasons again.

After the seventh game, Baylor sat as though resting up from an ordeal. Sweat shone on his skin. There was the suggestion of a paunch at his waist. Gray curled in his long sideburns. He was struggling and he knew they wanted to bury him.

"I've got no time for gravediggers," he said.

But after the ninth game and his conversation with Sharman, he announced, "It's time to retire." It was sad, one of the greatest careers spent. Now, he never would win a championship. And he shifted through the shadows this season as this team did, ironically starting a record winning streak the night he left.

Wilt took Elg's place as team captain. It was offered to both West and Wilt, but West said, "Let him have it," and Wilt took it. West returned to the regular lineup that night and McMillian moved into it and Baltimore was beaten. The next night, the Warriors. The night after that, the Knicks. Then Chicago, Philly.

In Philly, Jack Kiser of the *Daily News* asked Wilt what he thought of his new coach, and he said he seemed fine, always thinking up something to give them an edge, but that he, Wilt, could live without Bill's game-day shoot-arounds. The *Herald-Examiner* picked up the story and welcomed the Lakers back to LA with headlines that Wilt was complaining about a coach again, but Wilt denied it, and Sharman laughed it off. So he cut it off as an issue.

The team continued to win—Seattle, Portland, Boston. As the winning streak built, enthusiasm built. They passed 10 straight, then 15, then 20, in an overtime thriller with Phoenix to tie the league record. Then they beat Atlanta to set a new mark.

Afterward, Wilt said, "It was just another game. I don't count 'em. Streaks mean nothing to me."

After the reporters left, Wilt went into the shower room where he was heard to let out a sudden, delighted scream of triumph.

Trainer O'Neill says, "He always put the games down. He was always putting people on and telling stories and seemed the most relaxed guy in the world.

"But before big games he sometimes came early into the dressing room and went in my trainer's room and turned off the lights and shut the door and lay down by himself for a while. He said he took naps, but I think he was psyching himself up. He was a very private person who got wound up tight and had to get off by himself to get ready to do what he was expected to do.

"He was always afraid someone would see through him or look inside him."

Capacity crowds roared approval at home, while enemy crowds watched in despair on the road.

The longest listed team record for winning streaks in professional sports was 26 by the baseball Giants in 1916. Three nights before Christmas, the Lakers passed them. Between November 5, 1971, and January 7, 1972, more than two months, the Lakers won 33 straight games in one of the most remarkable sustained efforts in athletic history.

Finally, in Milwaukee, they lost one. They lost four out of six. During this slump, Los Angeles hosted the annual All-Star Game. West and Goodrich started and Wilt played. The West team won and the West Jerry won the MVP award. Three nights later, the Knicks dealt the Lakers their first loss at home in 12 weeks and 18 games. And the next night, the Lakers lost in Phoenix. But then they won 8 straight, lost 1, won 5 out of 6, won 5 more, lost 1, won 8 more, lost 1, and won their last 2.

They were a tremendous team which had a tremendous season of 69 victories and only 13 defeats for a staggering .841 winning percentage, adding those new records to their list.

Bill Bertka, a brilliant basketball mind, who was the Lakers' chief scout at that time and later built the new New Orleans franchise, says, "It probably was as good a team as this sport has had. Other teams may have had better individuals, but none that fit together better. Others have had better depth, but this one didn't need it.

"I'm not sure it was better than Russell's Boston teams of the middle 1960s or Chamberlain's Philadelphia team of the later 1960s because there were fewer teams then and the talent was more concentrated, but this Laker team did surpass the records of those teams. This team did defeat some weak teams during its winning streak, but it was an absolutely amazing streak. It had to go on to win the playoffs to prove itself, but it did that, decisively.

"Sharman handles men beautifully, he prepares a team properly, and he is the best game coach in the business. His strategy, his substitutions, matchups, time-outs, are superb. I was not surprised he had little trouble with Wilt because he can get along with anyone. I was surprised by Wilt. I'd heard about him

221

and I didn't like him without having met him. That's the burden that guy bears. People who don't know him dislike him because of what they've heard of him. Once I got to know him, I liked him.

"Sharman was one of the first coaches to use scouting films in basketball. I knew the old guys didn't want to be bothered. The first time they came in, Wilt made some wisecracks. But I had the films condensed to eight tight minutes. The chairs were set up and the film was ready to roll when they walked in. Eight minutes later, they were free to go. Wilt never complained again. Whenever we had films, he was the first one there. I doubt that he used them that much, but he respected what we were trying to do.

"I came to respect Wilt. I have a TV show in Santa Barbara and he made the drive up there to be on it and was a great guest. Whatever time I spent with him off the court, I enjoyed. And I certainly enjoyed watching him on the court."

Jerry West says, "Our respect for Wilt went up with the way he came back off the injury list. We were a pretty happy family that 1971–72 season, the way we were winning. Wilt was captain and the most important player we had."

In March, Wilt had a party to celebrate the completion of his new house in the Santa Monica Mountains. A $1,500,000 palace, it awed its visitors. A triangular structure of redwood, glass, concrete, and stone, it was encircled with a swimming pool and had a 360-degree view of metropolitan Los Angeles.

West had not invited Wilt to his housewarming, but Wilt invited West to his. The party lasted all night. The next night, the Lakers had to play a game. They played and won by almost 40 points.

That season, Wilt averaged 42 minutes, 14 points, 19 rebounds, 4 assists, and 8 blocked shots a game. Goodrich and West averaged 25 points each, McMillian 18, and Hairston 13. Hairston also averaged 13 rebounds, while West averaged 9 assists. West led the league in assists and Chamberlain led in rebounds. Balanced scoring carried the Lakers to 100 points or more 81 times in their 82 games.

Wilt sat in the dressing room after the final victory of the regular season. His long legs were stretched out and you could see the scar from the operation of almost two years back. He should have but he did not show a lot of age or wear and tear. There was little gray in his hair and beard. His face was not old. His eyes were hard, but he is a hard man.

Someone asked him if, under Sharman, he hadn't become the "new Wilt." Annoyed, he arose so fast sweat flew from his face as he snorted, "New Wilt Chamberlain, shit!" Then he said, "I'm the same man I've always been. And the same player. I changed my style a long time ago. What I'm doin', I been doin' for a long time. Why credit the coach? Who the hell does the work out there?"

He sighed and sat down. He had heard too much praise of Sharman and too little of Chamberlain.

Someone asked him about the playoffs. He sipped from his 7-Up and said, "I suppose I'll play in them."

He played. He was suffering from sore hands, but he played. Dr. Kerlan came up to him before a game and looked at one of his hands, and said, "It's discolored." Chamberlain laughed and said, "Color never bothered me none."

An old fracture had separated in his right hand, but he hadn't wanted to try to play with a cast on the hand or miss any games, so he played with it taped. He also had a fracture in his middle finger where it joined his left hand.

The Lakers got Chicago out of the first round in four straight, but Wilt hit his left hand on a rim and it started to hurt more than his right hand. Hairston had a sore foot, McMillian a bruised thigh, and West a wrenched back, but they all played. Even Sharman suffered from strained vocal chords, his voice a croaking rasp.

On a Sunday afternoon they opened the Western final at home against Milwaukee, and the Bucks blitzed them badly,

93–72. Chamberlain outrebounded Jabbar, 24–18, but was outscored by him, 33–10. West made only 4 of 19 shots.

They were shocked, but Sharman said in his sore voice, "It was just one game. It was just today. Tomorrow's another game."

On Wednesday night, the Lakers had as many points at halftime as they'd had all day Sunday. West missed 20 of 30 shots, but he came through in the clutch with a basket and a pass to Hairston for another which won it by one.

In Milwaukee, Wilt was magnificent and led a Laker rally to win. He took only three shots, but he blocked five by Jabbar and five by others. He dominated Jabbar on defense and off the boards. Goodrich, as he did all season, hit clutch shots. In a frenzied finish, Wilt rebounded, was fouled, and dispassionately sank two from the free-throw line to settle it.

Jack Kiser says, "This was a better game for him than the one in which he scored a hundred. Everyone was ready to quit except him. He just turned it around and saved the season when Milwaukee was set to spoil it."

Milwaukee won the next one, but Wilt took in 26 rebounds to lead LA to a win in the following game.

In Milwaukee, LA won the sixth game to win the series as Wilt grabbed rebounds and made free throws through a rough finish. He had the ball in his hands at the buzzer and he heaved it happily downcourt as the crowd in the old Arena and their Bucks sagged in disappointment.

Later, in the Laker dressing room, Wilt raised his fist and roared, "That's the way to go, big team."

Asked how he had handled Jabbar, he said, "I don't want to talk about it. I don't even want to think about it. I just want to enjoy it."

For a final foe, it was New York, without Reed. A brilliant, balanced team, but without a domineering big man.

As they had against Milwaukee, the Lakers let down and were embarrassed by a bad beating in the first game, 114–92.

As they had against Milwaukee, the Lakers bounced back.

224

As he did all through the playoffs, West shot poorly, but he stole the ball repeatedly on defense and passed off for baskets by others. Wilt took up the slack in the second game, hitting 14 of 18 shots, to pace an easy victory.

A rumor spread that Wilt had suffered and concealed a heart attack. When Wilt walked into the dressing room, West said, "Back from the dead." Wilt growled, "I've got some ideas about some people I'd like to bury."

In New York, after Wilt ordered writer Milt Gross from the dressing room, the Lakers won the third game on Wilt's 26 points and 20 rebounds.

Early in the fourth game he fell and landed on his right hand and, as he has said, "It hurt like hell." After that, every time he took the ball, he winced with pain and shook his hand as if to rid it of its evil spirits. But he played the last part of the game with five fouls and hit two free throws, grabbed a rebound and fed West for a basket that should have won it. However, little Walt Frazier went to Wilt, climbed right up the giant's back, stole a rebound from him and put it in the basket to tie. Still, the Lakers won in overtime.

Flying home, Wilt held his sore hand in his lap, acting crippled. "You'll play," Pat Riley assured him. "Maybe," muttered Wilt. "After all, I'm not human."

On Wilt's return, Dr. Kerlan X-rayed the hand and announced Wilt could not play in the fifth game. He played. It was said to be a sprain. It was a break, but he played. He took a shot of Celestone and treated the aching hand with ice packs and whirlpool baths overnight in his mansion.

When he went to the Forum, he went into O'Neill's room and returned wearing elastic hand-pads over both hands. Sub John Trapp asked, "You gonna' punch the bag?" Wilt said, "I'm gonna' punch your head."

Kerlan came in and threw a basketball at him. Wilt caught it. "You can play," Kerlan said.

He played and blocked 10 shots, scored 24 points, and grabbed 29 rebounds. The Knicks tried everything, but could not contain him, as he passed off to his teammates for baskets in a balanced attack that left the Knicks farther and farther back.

Ten points ahead with 90 seconds to play, Sharman celebrated by pulling West and Wilt, and the cheering fans gave the two veterans a standing ovation. Cooke stood in his box smiling proudly and applauding heartily. West sat down and closed his eyes. He admitted later, "It was an incredible feeling. I couldn't believe we finally had won."

It ended at 114–100, the organist struck up "Happy Days Are Here Again," and the fans poured onto the court to congratulate the champions.

In the crowded dressing room, madness erupted. Baylor stood off to a side, almost forgotten. Asked how he felt, he said, "Glad for the fellows, really." West went to him and shook his hand. Elgin said, "Congratulations."

West said to the reporters, "I don't know what to say. I really don't. I'm happy." He had learned how to handle defeat. Now he had to learn to handle victory. Someone asked him if this made up for all those defeats. "Nothing will ever make up for those," he said.

Wilt stood tall and proud, insisting his hand never hurt him enough to matter. Softly, he said, "I can't think of anything greater. Now me and my fans can walk in peace."

Later, dressing in his silks and velvets, diamonds sparkling, he said softly to a friend, "You know, it's nice we didn't have to go to a seventh game."

He did go back to New York later, broken hand in a cast, to accept a car from *Sport* magazine for being MVP.

The players had a party at La Marina that night. Assistant coach K.C. Jones stood up and sang "More" to cheers. Some stayed up all night. The next night, Cooke and his wife Jeannie threw a party at the Forum. But at this party an argument broke out and the players and writers and representatives of management broke up into little groups and bickered about playoff shares, worth more than $15,000 each. The Players'

226

Association had voted that management should pay the coaches, so the Lakers did not vote their coaches shares. Management had never done so before, and the Laker management did not want to do so now, though eventually it did.

As usual, the great moments one waits for rarely are what you expect them to be.

Wilt was one player willing to be quoted that management was in the wrong. Cooke didn't care for that. Wilt also wanted to renegotiate his contract upward. Cooke didn't care for that.

Wilt says he was working on the second of two option years written into a five-year contract, but court records have revealed he signed two contracts, one for three years and one for two, and was on the last year of the second with an option year to follow.

According to Wilt, Jack said, "Wilt's no longer my friend." According to Jack, "I have always tried to be Wilt's friend."

They hassled through the summer, the championship that had been so long and eagerly awaited all but forgotten.

Wilt toyed with the latest of several offers he received from the ABA, but was advised by his attorney he had to serve out at least the last season on his contract, though he might be able to get out of the option year to follow. Wilt says he signed a one-year contract just before the new season started in 1972, but court records reveal he signed a two-year contract in 1971 for the 1971–72 and 1972–73 seasons.

He did not seem inspired during the season. Yet he played every game, averaging 43 minutes, 18 rebounds, and 13 points. He took only 7 shots a game, a far cry from the 40 of his prime. He took only 586 shots all season. Someone said, "He used to take that many in one game."

He still led the league in shooting percentage for the ninth time and rebounding for the eleventh time after 14 seasons.

Hairston tore up a knee and missed most of the season. West pulled a hamstring muscle and missed a dozen games, which took the team right out of a winning streak. Wilt still led the team to 60 victories and 22 defeats. It was considered disappointing, despite the fact that it was the second-best record in the history of the team, and produced another divisional flag.

The playoffs *were* disappointing. It took the Lakers seven games to get by the Bulls in the first round. Wilt says he cried for Chicago because he thought they deserved to win, and he knew what it felt like to lose when you deserved to win. Then they got by the Warriors with Barry, as Wilt put it, "stinking up the joint."

So they were back in the finals, but there they lost to New York in five games. Willis Reed overcame his ailments to play well, but West was hampered by pulled hamstring muscles in both legs. Later, Wilt said he was tired of hearing how courageous they were. He, he said, had played with a swollen eye, two fingers taped together, a pulled hamstring, and a sore heel.

He played, he said, as well in those playoffs and that season as he ever had.

The coach was, after all, he said, just another coach who coached poorly.

After the last game, Bill Russell, working in television, went to open the door to the Knick dressing room to interview the winners when Wilt came out after having congratulated his conquerors. They saw each other. They were within an arm's length of each other. Then without a word they looked away and went on their ways, coldly, curtly.

Wilt spoke to other reporters, but not that one. "It's just another season," he said.

Well, that was Wilt's last season, as it turned out.

So there it was: 14 years, 1,045 games and 47,859 minutes of regular-season play—31,419 points, 23,924 rebounds, 4,643 assists. And 13 seasons of playoffs—160 games, 7,559 minutes, 3,607 points, 3,913 rebounds, and 673 assists.

Every number a drop of sweat, an effort.

Nine coaches. How many, if any, did he "fire"?

Fourteen years, 7 divisional pennants, all in his last 8 seasons, 10 playoff losses to the champions, 7 to Boston; 4 in the finals,

2 to Boston; 2 titles, 1 from San Francisco, 1 from New York. Quite a few disappointments in these figures. Wilt always found someone to blame for each one.

Bill Bradley says in *Life on the Run,* "If an individual claims superiority in everything then it is impossible to avoid the ultimate responsibility for victory or defeat." Bradley contends Wilt was more interested in promoting himself than in the success of his teams. He says, "I have the impression that Wilt might have been more secure in losing. In defeat . . . he . . . would wonder why the American character insisted on victory."

Bradley believes acceptance of defeat was Wilt's final error. "Wilt's emphasis on individual accomplishments failed to gain him public affection . . . and assured him of losing . . . until he lost often enough to become a symbol for losing, the ultimate insult."

A loser? Maybe. Wilt will recite the list of other famous "losers."

Baylor's teams never won a title. Nor West's, until Wilt came along, and then only one. Bob Pettit's teams won only one. Jabbar's teams just one and Barry's one so far. Robertson's teams none till he got to Jabbar, then only one. These are the all-time all-stars, aside from Russell.

Other sports, too. Bobby Orr's hockey teams won only two titles in ten years, and he's supposed to be the best ever. Johnny Unitas' football teams only two. Jimmy Brown's one. Namath's only one. Fran Tarkenton's none. O.J. Simpson's none. Bob Feller's baseball teams won only one. Henry Aaron's one. Ted Williams' none. The list is lengthy.

Wilt's three teams won more games in the regular season and went farther in the playoffs with him than they did without him. His team in Philadelphia set an all-time record for victories, then his team in Los Angeles topped it and set other records for victories.

The greatest player? Maybe. Maybe not.

Asked what happened when Wilt Chamberlain left the Lakers, Jack Kent Cooke says, "I've forgotten. You can quote me on that. I'm not forgetting for the sake of convenience. I've just forgotten."

There are those who think the mind works in wondrous ways, that it wipes out what is too much to be endured. Having given of himself to the extent he suffered a heart attack, having had his championship shrouded in haggling over shares, Cooke was entitled to forget.

He did not want to pay what Wilt wanted.

In the insanity that had become a bidding war for basketball players, an American Basketball Association team had offered Wilt more money than it could make if every seat in its 3,200-seat arena were filled for every game.

That was all Wilt wanted.

There was a method to the madness of the owner, dentist Leonard Bloom. He wanted his own San Diego arena built in suburban Chula Vista because the proprietor of the existing San Diego Arena, Peter Graham, did not seem to him hospitable.

Bloom believed a charismatic superstar such as Wilt would

provide the promotion to sell this plan to the public which was to vote on it.

It was not the first time the ABA approached Chamberlain. In 1968, when he had decided to depart from Philadelphia and was working on a plan that would land him with the Lakers in Los Angeles, the ABA Stars of that city offered him an alternative.

In July, Wilt met at the Biltmore Hotel in LA with ABA president George Mikan, league official Don Ringsby of the Denver team, and president Jim Kirst and manager Jim Hardy of the Stars. A tentative agreement was reached in which Wilt would be contracted at $1,500,000 for five years.

The league felt the investment would be repaid when it won, with players like Wilt, recognition as a "major league" and forced a merger with the NBA. However, before the contract could be formalized, the Los Angeles *Times* broke the story. Jack Cooke called Irv Kosloff and the agreement between them was finalized.

Cooke called Chamberlain in and satisfied him.

In 1969, a new deal developed in which a new ABA team was to be put in Los Angeles with Elgin Baylor as coach and Jerry West as star. West declined and Wilt was approached. The rub was he did not want to play for Baylor. Nor did he want to coach. It fell through.

By 1973, however, Chamberlain no longer was satisfied with Cooke. When a fantastic offer came along from Bloom and the ABA, Wilt was receptive. They worked it out at $1,920,000 for three years. The ABA agreed to pick up a third of it by waiving $640,000 of the $1 million purchase price Bloom owed for the franchise, provided Wilt stayed two years.

Chances of Chamberlain returning to the Lakers collapsed when Cooke, though recovering from his heart attack, had moved into New York's Waldorf-Astoria while waging what turned out to be a successful fight to keep alive the financially troubled TelePrompTer Corporation, of which he was the major stockholder.

231

"There was no one to talk to," complained Chamberlain. "The Lakers seemed to have lost interest in me. I was not excited about returning to them, but I was willing to talk to them about it. I admit there might have been some chance I'd have gone back if Cooke had been around. He's an eloquent talker and a master of negotiation.

"But I liked Leonard Bloom as a friend. I didn't at first think anything would come of our talks, but he kept coming after me and he got to me. I would like to see the new league succeed. There is no reason the old league should have a monopoly on this sport. It does not do everything right."

The Conquistadors, as the club in San Diego was called, believed Wilt was free to play, having completed his contract with the Lakers. The Lakers contended the option clause in the standard NBA player contract bound Wilt to one year beyond expiration of the pact.

Laker attorney Alan Rothenberg announced, "The Lakers feel a sense of loss. We wish him well. But we will take all necessary attempts to keep him from playing for any other club." This step carried them to court, where the judge ruled in their favor.

Later lawsuits between the Lakers and Wilt remain unresolved.

The Lakers already had dealt to obtain a new center, Elmore Smith, from Buffalo. A promising young player, he proved a bust and later was traded away. The Lakers started to sink in the standings when Wilt left, and hit the bottom when West, too, went.

Chamberlain had been hired as player-coach of the Q's, and he was prepared to coach them for one season while waiting to become eligible to play for them the second season. "It's a challenge," he said. "I like challenges. I've played for a lot of coaches. I think I can be a good coach."

From afar, Elgin Baylor said, "I don't think he can coach. What could he possibly help a player with? He doesn't have the temperament to be a coach. He never had any discipline. He

232

hardly ever came to practice, and when he did, he didn't work. He hardly went to practice at all the last part of last season."

Wilt asked, "Hell, how does he know? He wasn't there."

Wilt, himself, in his book said he didn't have the temperament to be a good coach, but now he thought otherwise. "I expect to use the offense of Bill Sharman, the defense of Joe Mullaney, the tactics of Alex Hannum, and the psychology of Frank McGuire," he said. He did not suggest the gentle touch of a Butch von Breda Kolff, the kindness of a Neil Johnston, the toughness of a Dolph Schayes.

Also in his book, Wilt said a coach could do only so much with a professional team and it was too late to teach experienced players. Now, he said, "A coach can do a job for a club. A coach can't be just a coordinator. He's got to be a teacher, too." Wilt said he would be a "tough coach," who wanted "tough players." He said, "A coach can be too nice a guy."

He didn't have many tough players, and some of them say he was not too nice to them. He got to the regular-season start late, so an assistant, Stan Albeck, really ran the opener, a victory. After two defeats followed, Wilt had a long blackboard session and called a Sunday morning practice for 9 A.M. He failed to show up. Albeck conducted it. Wilt reported his plane had been diverted by bad weather and delayed.

Between games he went home to LA. He was living in the LeGrand Motel in San Diego, which was a far cry from his mansion in Bel Air. But he did not like it when some said Albeck coached the club. Wilt had a volleyball coach with a whistle turn out to conduct one practice session, which embarrassed Albeck. Some said he was on his way out from that moment.

Wilt tried to teach in his first practice sessions. He was enthusiastic. The players seemed enthusiastic. Red Robbins said, "He's more knowledgeable than you'd think, and he can express himself as clearly as any coach I've had." Bo Lamar said, "He's a good dude. You gotta respect him." Wilt said, "There's only one thing I really care about—that they respect me."

He cut commercials on behalf of the Q's. He sat on the bench in his finery, chewing JuJu Fruits and sipping 7-Up, baiting the officials and encouraging his players. And the team did better than expected. But it did not win as many games as it lost. After a while Wilt started to get testy. And the players started to complain.

Wilt told reserve center Otto Moore he was overweight and out of shape. Moore said he was the same weight he'd played at all his career. "Don't give me any of your crap," Wilt snapped. Turning to the trainer, he said, "Get him a plane ticket. He's goin' home."

Wilt said he was proven right when Moore went on waivers and wasn't picked up by any other team. Moore said, "The majority of this team hates to see him come through the door. . . . You could never do anything right."

Red Robbins and Chuck Williams had words with Wilt and were traded. Later, Robbins, one of Wilt's first supporters, said, "I can't speak the truth. I have to live with the people in this league. I'm alive. I'm in Kentucky. And I'm thrilled to death to be out of San Diego."

Williams said, "There just aren't many good things I can say about the guy, so I'd prefer not to say anything. I have some pretty bad memories. Are those the feelings of the other Q's? Absolutely."

Wilt said, "Guys who get traded feel hurt."

Joe Hamelin of the San Diego *Union* wrote, "Nearly half the team has asked to be traded rather than play any longer for Wilt." Wilt said, "Reporters were always snooping around here trying to get the guys to say things."

Chamberlain complained the San Diego media were "negative."

Ans Dilley, the team publicist before resigning, said, "He wouldn't talk to the media. I'd make appointments for him and he wouldn't show up. He made up a three-part form I had to fill out to apply for an interview. I had to send it through Bloom. I sent twenty or so and never got an answer on one.

"He was just impossible. We'd have autograph parties or book-signing sessions and he wouldn't tell me if he'd come, then he wouldn't show, or if he did and there wasn't a good turnout, he'd bitch about it. One bunch of kids started to curse him, the way he treated them.

"We're trying to sell this team and he's being paid big money to help, but he isn't doing a thing."

He did fail to show up for two games in February. Assistant Albeck said, "He's probably out scouting or something." Manager Alex Groza said, "I have no idea. He could be sick. He wasn't feeling well last time I saw him."

Chamberlain's attorney, Sy Goldberg, said, "He'll probably be in New York when the team gets there. If not, he'll see the team in San Diego. He's around. There's no big problem." Fred Furth, another attorney who represents Wilt, said, "I wouldn't worry. Wilt's not apt to stay out of sight too long."

One day, Dr. Bloom announced Wilt was home sick. The next day he said he was out doing some business for him.

When he turned up, Wilt said, "What difference does it make? My mother wasn't concerned. The world has so many problems, but all the press wants to know is what Wilt's doing. It's between Bloom and me. It's not the players' business."

The players were weakening. One player said, "He says things not even Ripley would believe." Another said, "No speeka de Engleesh." Asked about Wilt's strategy, a third asked, "What strategy?" Wilt walked to the bench three minutes before game-time. A player, pointing to the clock, commented, "He just got here." Another said, "I suppose we should consider ourselves lucky he came at all." Another said, "That's luck?"

In one newspaper story he was called the world's tallest dwarf.

At season's end, Wilt exploded. "I'm no saint. But there appears to be a special vendetta to get me. I missed two games. I was on a mission for the owner to try to sell the franchise. I never missed a practice I wanted to make. There were a lot of times that I missed the shoot-around. That's what I pay my assistant for. Maybe I was home asleep, or in Oregon scouting talent. The team did better than expected. Wilt Chamberlain did a respectable job with what he had. My skin is thick. But I'm a sensitive man. I'm outraged."

Mitch Chortkoff said, "He came in with enthusiasm and worked at it, but the team wasn't too good, attendance was terrible, the owner was losing money, and as the situation got worse, Wilt lost interest.

"The team tied for last with a 37–47 record. Wilt pointed with pride to the fact they made the playoffs, but eight of the ten teams did, and the Q's did only with a special playoff. They lost in the first round of the playoffs.

"He might have been a good coach, but the situation was so bad no one will ever know."

Wilt Chamberlain turned out to be the tenth coach Wilt Chamberlain had run through.

He didn't bother to go to Chula Vista to campaign for the arena Bloom had invested so much in getting. "If I have to go there, they can't want it very much," he said.

The proposal lost by only 294 votes.

The Q's quit.

And Wilt quit the Q's.

Reportedly, Bloom lost the $640,000 the league had promised to waive if Wilt stayed two years, but still had to pay Wilt. He lost more than a million dollars on the single season alone.

Wilt neither played nor coached during the 1974–75 season. He did tour with his women's volleyball team. On a visit to Madison Square Garden in New York where his women were to face a Russian team, he went to visit the basketball office.

When the elevator door opened, two workmen struggled to wheel a loaded cart into the corridor. "You look like you need a little help," smiled Wilt. Taking a rope, he pulled the cart free.

"That's an eight-hundred-pound load," one of the workman said in awe.

The Knicks had signed ABA star George McGinnis to a fat contract, but lost him and the money paid him when NBA

236

president Larry O'Brien ruled draft rights to him were held by the 76ers, who subsequently signed him. Wilt talked to Red Holzman of the Knicks about the power player and gate attraction the struggling New Yorkers needed.

"You need a Wilt Chamberlain," Wilt Chamberlain said, though it was not clear if he was serious.

Later, Wilt told a writer, "I think with me the Knicks might beat Boston. I think Red Holzman is the best coach in the NBA. I think he feels he can win with me. I also think he feels that if he loses with me, he'll be blamed. I can understand that.

"I'm not anxious to go back to basketball. My competitive instincts are satisfied by volleyball. I want to become the greatest spiker in volleyball history. I already am, but I'm the only one who knows it. When others know it, I'll be satisfied.

"I don't need the money. Another million won't change my life. I couldn't eat any better steaks, or sleep in a better bed, or go out with any prettier girls. A Japanese magnate just offered me six million dollars for my house and I turned him down.

"I started it, but I think the sums being paid athletes are silly. I remember when I thought fifty thousand was fantastic. Now, when I'm offered millions, I giggle. But I expect to be paid the going rate for my services. If they give me a number they'll put on a contract, I'll give them a quick yes or no."

He played a game in the Catskills for charity and looked surprisingly good for a guy who was thirty-nine and had not played for almost two years. Red Auerbach coached and said, "Wilt could play until he's fifty. He has no fat on him and what he can do, he could do for a long time."

Chick Hearn said, "Wilt can't score anymore." Wilt said, "I can, but Chick can't."

Knick management talked it over. Holzman talked it over with some of his players and they weren't too enthusiastic, but Mike Burke, executive officer of the Garden and the Knicks, was intrigued. He contacted Wilt's attorney, Sy Goldberg, and was told Wilt might be interested.

The story leaked out. Jack Kent Cooke contended that until

Wilt played out the option year of his contract, he was still Laker property, and any team wanting him had to deal with them. He did not say the Lakers wanted him. The Lakers had just dealt for Jabbar and signed him to a five-year $2.5 million contract. Goldberg contended that sitting out the season was sufficient, as had been the case when Rick Barry went from the Warriors of the NBA to Oakland of the ABA.

Commissioner O'Brien ruled that Wilt was free to deal with any team, but that team would have to compensate the Lakers to their satisfaction. Goldberg was furious. He said, "I do not want Jack Kent Cooke to get anything for Wilt because he does not own Wilt." Wilt said, "The thing that bothers me is that Jack baby is getting his way. I think everybody's afraid of him."

The San Diego Sails, successors to the Q's, claimed Wilt was their property and the ABA's. Goldberg discounted this: "We signed with Bloom, and Bloom went bankrupt. The contract is invalid because he still owes us money." Burke discounted this too, and talked to Cooke. Cooke asked for Earl Monroe, a first draft choice, and cash for Wilt. Monroe had just signed a no-cut contract, so Cooke agreed to take Phil Jackson. Burke hedged.

Wilt threatened to report to the Lakers. "I'll sit on the bench and pick up my money," he said. The Lakers said they would send Wilt away if he turned up at preseason drills. Apparently when they were paying a regular center $500,000 a year, they did not want to pay an aging backup man $450,000. On Goldberg's advice, Wilt thought better of his idea and went to Hawaii instead. Burke talked to Goldberg and said he wanted to be sure Wilt wanted to play before he invested a large amount in getting the rights to negotiate with him. Goldberg set up a meeting with Wilt in Los Angeles the third Friday in October.

Burke and manager Eddie Donovan went to the meeting. Wilt didn't. Burke was furious and flew home. "This finishes it," he said. "We've been trying to talk to Wilt, but the only person we've been able to talk to is his attorney. I don't think his attorney can play center."

Wilt returned to say it was a misunderstanding. He said he

238

didn't know he was supposed to be in LA. He said he expected the Knicks to telephone him. Burke said, "I won't call him. He stood me up. Why should I pursue him?" Wilt said, "I didn't come to them in the first place. They asked for my services. Mr. Burke has to give me a number."

On the eve of the NBA season opener, Wilt was called by a New York reporter. He was asked what he wanted. He said, "If you'll send out two fine New York women and a corned beef sandwich, I'll be happy." He also said he considered Cooke the culprit in the case, and he was not going to play a party to any deal from which Jack profited. A reporter said to Goldberg, "Wilt wouldn't blow a big deal on principle?" Goldberg said, "You don't know Wilt."

He and Wilt announced they were suing the NBA and its member teams for denying him the opportunity to earn a living. They did. Burke said, "I think they may have been using us to strengthen their court case, to show Wilt was still wanted. Well, he no longer is." He telephoned Sam Schulman in Seattle to ask about the availability of the reportedly discontented Spencer Haywood. Bill Russell had come out of retirement to coach Seattle, but he had decided Haywood was uncoachable. Schulman sided with Russell and sold Haywood to the Knicks for $1.5 million and a first draft choice.

Seattle did about as well without Haywood as they had with him. They made the playoffs and won the first round, but lost the second round for the second straight season. Haywood helped the Knicks, but he did not turn them around. Their slide continued, they landed in the cellar of their division, and they did not make the playoffs. The Celtics won the division and went on to win the playoffs for the second time in three seasons as a new dynasty dawned in Boston.

The 76ers landed the spectacular George McGinnis, but he was not "the new Wilt," they did not win their division, and they did not even make it out of the first round of the playoffs. Jabbar helped the Lakers—in fact he was voted the league's Most Valuable Player—but he did not turn them around. The

Lakers finished next-to-last in their division and missed the playoffs for the second straight season since Chamberlain left.

During the summer, the NBA allowed four of the ABA teams to buy their way into the established circuit as the rebel league folded. But Wilt had long since left and the San Diego franchise had long since folded.

Life had taken strange turns for some members of the cast of characters in the Wilt Chamberlain story.

The magic the Lakers captured in the 1971-72 season started to disappear during the party the night after the championship game and vanished entirely when Wilt and West left. Baylor, of course, was long gone. Others came and went as management made desperate moves. By the summer of 1976, just four years after the Lakers captured the championship, not one member remained from that title team.

Within a few months, Jack Kent Cooke's mother, his long-time personal aide, and his best friend died. Cooke and his wife both suffered health problems. Meanwhile, Jack continued a six-month search for a successor to Sharman to coach his Lakers. Finally, he settled his financial and legal differences with West and named Jerry to coach the club.

West had visited the Forum only once or twice during his differences with Cooke. He had done little but play golf. He had missed basketball badly, but had refused other offers which would have taken him away from southern California. Tears misted in his eyes as he formally accepted the position he had very much wanted.

Baylor was serving as an assistant to old Laker coach Butch van Breda Kolff in New Orleans.

When West was named Laker coach, Wilt wondered why he wasn't offered the job since he also was suing Cooke and had even better qualifications, having coached, if briefly. Pointedly, he added, "I'd like to know—and it has no racial tinge to it— was Elgin offered the job? I just wondered, since Elg and Jerry both did so much for the Lakers and since Elg has coached at the assistant level . . ."

Elgin had no comment.

Sharman, Newell and Chick Hearn were with West on the podium at the press conference in which the new coach was re-introduced. Hearn had been critical of Sharman and had favored West as the new coach. However, West had voiced criticism of Hearn similar to that of Wilt. Newell now was looking over his shoulder at Sharman, named the assistant GM. Newell quit and Sharman moved into his chair.

Remaining were brilliant men who could give the Lakers strong leadership if their differences could be dissolved.

Sharman had wanted another season coaching the Lakers in an effort to recapture the magic that had slipped away into thin air. He settled for an executive position. A court had ruled that Sharman had violated his contract when he left Salt Lake City of the ABA to join Los Angeles in the NBA. While the case was in appeal, it was not clear whether the substantial settlement awarded the Utah team was to be paid by Sharman or by Cooke. Meanwhile, Bill was not inclined to stray far from Cooke.

Sharman's coaching career entered into a decline as he suffered through more than a year of agony watching his wife die of bone cancer. When it was done, he seemed unable to instantly regain the intensity that had marked his past performances. He lived alone in the Marina, looking for a new life. He had been such a successful coach it was hard to believe his abilities had deteriorated to any lasting extent.

The team lacked depth of talent and balance and all its failures could not be laid at the coach's feet.

Most observers, however, agreed a coaching change was called for in this situation. Resolving to make that change, Cooke nevertheless refused to cast aside Sharman, whom he liked and admired. He went out of his way to keep Bill in his organization. All were seeking to put together the pieces of their splintered lives.

West and Baylor both had been divorced from their wives and had become visitors with their children, living alone, the spotlight cooled.

241

Wilt Chamberlain remained without a wife, also living alone, but used to it, and happy with it.

Wilt said, "I will not marry unless I am prepared to make a complete commitment to one woman. I have come close at times, but I like a variety of women, and I would not want to take one as my wife and then be tempted to be unfaithful to her. There is no rule that says a man must marry."

Merv Harris says, "I have spoken to Wilt about his inability to commit himself to one woman. We drove around Phoenix talking about it one day. He has enormous, self-gratifying appetites in many areas of life, including his relationships with women. Yet, he is family-oriented and likes children. I think he would be happier with a wife and children in his home, but he's not so sure, and it's his life."

Doug Krikorian of the Los Angeles *Herald-Examiner* says, "My wife promised to get Wilt a date one time and he never let her forget it. He was always bugging me, 'When's your wife going to come through for me.' It was funny, as if he couldn't get his own dates. I've seen him turned down and embarrassed at times. Yet I can't believe a player like Wilt ever had trouble getting a woman. No player does. The women are always around. And Wilt is so prominent. And I really like him and feel women must. But he was funny about it."

A surprising number of players and reporters say they never have seen Wilt with a woman. Others say otherwise. There were rumored relationships with actresses Kim Novak and Gina Lollabrigida, which some observed and which Wilt confirmed in his book. He spoke of them in polite terms, but spent a lot of the book discussing other women impolitely, claiming he "copped" this one in the back seat of a car, that one in an airplane rest room inflight, and so forth. Jack Kiser says Wilt let him listen in on an extension phone while rapping intimately with Lollabrigida. Others speak of having observed Wilt's relationship with an actress who did car commercials on television, a couple of singers, and so on.

Harris says, "One thing with Wilt, he always treats his

women with courtesy and consideration." One who dated him says, "He is a gentle man, but a bit unusual." Wilt says, "Most people seem most concerned with whether I am dating black or white women. I date all colors and all kinds. I am not interested in the myth of any 'Super Nigger.' I never invited a woman to watch me play basketball because bringing in girls is a showoff number. If they want to watch me play basketball, let 'em buy a ticket. If they want to be with me, I'll pick up the tab."

He makes light of suspicions he may be gay or bisexual. "I am the heterosexualest heterosexual anyone ever was," he laughs.

He seems able to live as he wants. He says he invested wisely the money he made in basketball, though he has spent freely to live the good life and reportedly took a beating in the stock-market decline.

He has bitter memories of childhood financial frustrations. Once, he and some friends were offered $125 to work at a camp one summer with the understanding that they could play ball and take advantage of the recreation there on the side. When they got there they found they were working sixteen hours a day. Caught riding a horse when he was supposed to be washing dishes, Wilt was fired. Later when Wilt became famous, the owner asked him to come back as "an alumnus" to speak to the kids. Wilt said he would for one day for $1,000. He went, got his money, and told the kids how tough the man had been on him.

He bought race horses and nightclubs. He has owned Small's Paradise in Harlem, which he says was the best investment he ever made, and Basin Street West in Los Angeles. He has owned apartment buildings in New York and Los Angeles. With his first professional salary he paid cash for a $30,000 home for his family in a good section of Philadelphia, and he later moved them into his round-the-pool complex in LA, "The Villa Chamberlain." Football player Dick Bass used to live there and he jumped into the pool with his clothes on when he returned every evening until Wilt's mother finally asked him what in the world he was doing. "I thought you'd never ask," grinned Dick.

Wilt has made many major and minor investments and has had a lot of stocks and bonds, but the one thing he has never publicized are details of his salaries or business investments. He says, "I have done as well as anyone ever did financially in sports," and apparently he has.

He has done several successful television commercials, notably one for Brut. More recently, he is in one, identified in captions as "Wilt Chamberlain, famous tall person," as he moves through a swinging saloon, past admiring ladies, to buy Miller's Lite beer from an eight-foot bartender, who looks down on him and calls him "shorty."

Wilt formed a partnership with veteran film-maker and psychologist Paul Rapp and attorney Richard Rosenthal, and in association with Hal Jepsen presented *Go For It* to youthful movie-goers in the summer of '76. Wilt took credit as executive producer on the documentary, which featured skate-boarding, hot-dog skiing, hand-gliding and other faddish athletic activities around the world.

When he talked of retiring, he said, "I'd like to see the ski resorts at St. Moritz in the winter just once instead of in the summer." Retired now, he can do so. He travels extensively. He has said, "The fjords of Norway fascinate me the most." He has said, "I speak French fluently. I understand German and Italian very well. And some Spanish. And a little Persian. The only way you can really become good at languages is with practical use. I've gone many times to many countries and I have been able to talk to girls. I'd like to speak ten or eleven languages. I studied to learn." He says he does not read as much as he used to, but can read 1,400 words a minute. The average is supposed to be 200.

He says he likes all kinds of music, from the classics to country-and-western, and including jazz and hard rock. He says he likes Beethoven, Schubert, and Wagner among the classicists and has a sound system with thirty-five or forty speakers in his house. He has parties at his house. One frequent guest has been Bill Shoemaker, the jockey. Wilt and Bill are Mutt and Jeff friends. Wilt loves the horses. An impulsive gambler, he says he and Jim Brown once got $225,000 ahead and wound up winning $65,000 in a London casino, breaking the bank and settling for fifty cents on the dollar.

His home is his castle. Everything in it is outsized to suit him. It sits on two acres and has 8,300 square feet of living space. There are a 45-foot-high stone fireplace, a 14-foot chandelier of Venetian glass, and 175 pieces of art. There are a 280-gallon bathtub of gold mosaic tile and a shower with mirrored walls and six showerheads set high so the spray will hit higher than his stomach. There is a 72-square-foot master bed with a mirrored roof, which rolls back at the touch of a button to reveal night skies full of stars.

Asked why he built such a mammoth place, Wilt told Tom Hawkins, "It is a monument to me." He feels he has never received proper tribute and points out he never received nights such as West and Elgin did. He told this reporter, "I wanted this house less for myself than as a home away from home for my friends from all over the world. They will be able to drop in from Paris or Berlin or New York and get a hot meal and a soft bed." He calls it "Ursa Major," which is the Latin equivalent of "The Big Dipper." He says it has the grand sound he feels is fitting.

He also says it is his hideaway. It remains hard for him to go out in the world. The startled looks of those who see him, the old jokes about his height, the persistent pressing in on him, have bothered him and he has shied from public exposure. He remembers once when he was buying a hat in a New York shop and a passerby kept coming back to take another look. Finally, the man walked inside indignantly and said, "Listen, buddy, are you kidding me?" Admitting to one woman he was seven-one, she became indignant and insisted he was at least eight or nine feet tall.

He has had fun with this at times. When he was living on Central Park West he used to take his Great Danes on walks through the park for the fun of frightening strollers, maybe even muggers, who happened on them. But he so terrorized the sedate tenants in his fancy building by allowing his dogs to bound about the lobby that he was evicted. He has always loved dogs, and he considers his dogs his friends; he takes them with him many places and treats them with tender care, spending a fortune merely to feed them.

He is often alone at home with his dogs. Or perhaps whipping up lasagne or pies or cookie specialties for visitors, male or female. He considers himself a superb cook and a gourmet. He dines in the best restaurants, is in contact with people of consequence. Usually, he outshines them. One time he was walking through an airport with actor Chuck Connors, who was disturbed when fans ignored him and went to Wilt for autographs. Wilt recalls being with Richard Nixon shortly before he was elected president when fans ignored Nixon while gathering around Chamberlain.

Wilt was, as were so many others, disappointed in Nixon, and says it started when Nixon named Spiro Agnew his vice-president. Wilt did think that through Nixon he could do good for blacks. He told me, "The thought of having a say in shaping society excited me."

He marched in the front ranks at Martin Luther King's funeral. But he is a moderate, who says, "Everyone has problems. The blacks have problems, but so do poor whites. When the Panthers and Muslims pester me, I send them on their way. No one uses me.

"I believe the best way I can help blacks is by setting a good example and by using my money to run businesses in black areas and give jobs to blacks."

He is bothered by those who are racially extreme. He was angered when he tried to buy and was refused a home in a white section of San Francisco.

He says now he thinks he'll stay out of politics, though he

246

likes LA Mayor Tom Bradley, a black, and California Governor Jerry Brown, a white, and is interested in overpopulation and undertransportation.

He travels fast, himself, in his Bentley, his Maserati, a Cadillac, a Dodge station wagon which holds his dogs. After his senior year in high school he crashed into a telephone pole in the Catskills, and he has been flirting with deadly danger driving at super-speed ever since. A death wish? "Oh, my man, no, I love life too much. I just have to go fast so they can't catch me." As famous as when he was at his peak, he feels pursued. Somehow, for all of his size, he slips through shadows; for all of his height, he keeps a low profile these days.

So, you put all the pluses and minuses down and see how they add up.

As the seasons slipped away, he seemed a disappointing player, but going back over them, he seems to have been better than believed, and did more when it meant more than is assumed. As the years went by, he seemed a hard man, arrogant and demanding, and he has been, but also with soft spots, given to generosities, suffering from pressures. Many hate him, but more than I expected like him.

What does he think he is like? He once said, "I am unusual because everything about me is bigger than the norm." What did he like least about his life? "Never being able to hide behind sunglasses. The balcony of my New York apartment overlooked Central Park and I used to look down on boys strolling with their girls and envy them and wonder what it would be like to be ordinary." On the other hand, what he liked best—"Not being ordinary. Being bigger, making myself better than others, becoming outstanding in many things, some of which had nothing to do with size."

What were his worst faults: "I'm short on patience. I open my mouth too quick. And speak too bluntly." And his strengths: "My individuality. My honesty. My willingness to speak out. I am sorry when I hurt people. I am sensitive to people's feelings. I have more friends than enemies, and I will do anything for my friends." Was he happy? "Yes, I have made a lot of my life. I have done a lot. If I lost everything tomorrow I couldn't complain. But I do not believe I could lose my friends except through death. I have lost family through death. I feel that loss a lot."

I remember Wilt wishing he could play cards with his father just one more time. And Frank McGuire remembers Wilt at Ike Richman's funeral. "Ike died watching Wilt play basketball. At Ike's funeral, Wilt was holding Ike's children on his lap. The Jewish people mourn by sitting *shivah.* Wilt sat with them. He wore a little white skullcap as Jewish people do in religious ceremonies. It looked funny up there on his head, yet there was a majesty about him. I had come up from Carolina for the funeral. Ike's mother and father were very old and very nice. They said, 'You must be cold, Mr. McGuire. You have to have a drink, you know.' And I had a drink and I sat with Wilt while he held those youngsters on his lap. I will never forget it."

Wilt Chamberlain is a complex, contradictory individual. Bill Russell says Wilt seldom smiles because he's lonely. Maybe he is. Wilt, himself, remembers walking alone in London when he came upon some boys who were getting ready to play soccer in a park. He asked if he could get into the game. They said, well, they'd choose sides and see how it came out. He says he could see after a while that he would not be chosen at all, unless last. When he was not chosen, he walked away.

What, he was asked, has hurt him most in life. Being degraded in a profession he dominated? That, he said, but that is not the important thing. He has been, he said, betrayed by people he trusted and respected and cared for. "People," he said. "Just people. People are the only ones who can hurt you."